A SOUTH AMERICAN WAR

A SOUTH AMERICAN WAR

Behind the Scenes in the Fight for the Falklands

Jeremy Brown

Book Guild Publishing
Sussex, England

First published in Great Britain in 2013 by
The Book Guild Ltd
Pavilion View
19 New Road
Brighton, BN1 1UF

Typesetting in Times by
YHT Ltd, London

Printed and bound in Great Britain by
CPI Group (UK) Ltd, Croydon, CR0 4YY

A catalogue record for this book is available from
The British Library.

ISBN 978 1 84624 923 5

To Daphne, my wife, and to Sally Barra,
Veronica Meanwell, Wendy O'Neill and Lucy Crouch

Contents

Foreword
by
Brigadier General Sergio Fernandez (Retired)

Brigadier General Sergio Fernandez had a long and distinguished career in the Argentine Army. He graduated from Military College in 1972, and from Infantry School as a commando in 1976. He was assigned to No 601 Commando Company and fought in the Falklands in 1982. On 21st May, he fired the Blowpipe missile that shot down Flight Lieutenant Jeff Glover's Harrier aircraft. Promoted to Brigadier General in 2004, he served his last appointment in the army as a Corps Commander until retiring in 2009. He is married, has two sons, and is an accomplished water-colourist.

Establishing the truth about the past is rarely an easy task for a historian, even when only 30 years have elapsed since the events took place. Jeremy Brown has, nevertheless, accomplished his task superbly.

This book is a very honest, professional and balanced work, which brings together the diverse recollections and views of many well-qualified contributors. It then provides a clear analysis of events – during a dramatic, fast-moving, and action-packed period – in a light and easily digestible style.

As servicemen fighting for our respective countries, we all did our best in 1982. Today, the war is a distant memory. We can still, however, share our experiences and thoughts, not only to create a better rapport and understanding between our countries, and to contribute to history, but also in order to remember with respect and a sense of shared comradeship, all the men from both nations who fell in combat.

Thank you, Jeremy, for your important contribution, with its particular emphasis on creating a better understanding of how and why the other

South American countries responded to the fast-moving situation; a war between 'one of their own' and another country far away, for which many of those countries, nevertheless, had a great deal of respect and admiration.

Sergio Fernandez
May 2013

Author's Note

I should perhaps explain why, many years after the event, I decided to write this book about the Falklands War. Many have already been written. Why should I believe that my effort might, nevertheless, be of interest?

I was fortunate enough to have served in the British Embassy, Brasilia, as Air Attaché from 1979 to 1982. My three years in Brazil, doing that most interesting and rewarding job, would have been unforgettable anyway, but were even more memorable for two important reasons.

During those years the world started to become aware, and not before time, of what was happening in the Amazon region. We are now only too well aware of the tragedy that continues relentlessly to unfold as the tropical rain-forest is cut, burned and plundered, whilst corruption abounds and politicians mouth platitudes, but do little else.

My job allowed me to travel at least as much as, if not more than, other diplomats in the Embassy. Thanks to friendships formed with officers of the Brazilian Air Force (FAB) I flew the DC3 and the Catalina, FAB's two main work-horses in that vast, inhospitable region, and was able to see for myself what was happening.

The other reason, the single most significant event during that three-year period, was the Falklands War. Many years later I regularly gave talks on both these subjects, which were usually well received. I was then persuaded to put pen to paper on the subject of the war.

My talk on the Falklands War aimed to give an idea of what it can be like working in an Embassy overseas when your own country goes to war 'just down the road', and how it can affect the lives of a few for the duration. However, the scope was not broad enough to translate to a book of any substance. A new slant had to be found; one that had not been done to death by other authors.

It occurred to me that the broader perspective I sought could be provided by a South American approach – how, when, where and why the war impacted on mainland South America – of which 'The View from the

British Embassy' in Brazil would form just a part. I started my research with only a vague idea of what lay ahead and drew up a dream list of people I would like to track down and talk to. Most of them had one thing in common; they had been in South America in 1982 and therefore should have something useful and relevant to contribute.

The list therefore included all the British Ambassadors who had been there at that time, other diplomats who had worked for them, our service attachés, SIS (Secret Intelligence Service) representatives, journalists sent to South America to cover the war, people working on defence-related contracts and as many servicemen and others as possible whose contribution to the war had involved visiting that continent. Many others were swept up for the essential background information. The list seemed endless and hopelessly ambitious.

I thought that perhaps fifty per cent would be impossible to track down so many years after the event, and that many of the remaining fifty per cent might be unreliable or unco-operative. My experience over the next few years proved how wrong I was. I discovered that, with patience, most people can be tracked down. A few had died and clearly time was not on my side. Almost everyone wanted to be helpful.

Researching the book has proved immensely interesting. Any lingering doubts that I may have had regarding whether it was, in fact, a good idea at all, or whether it might be of interest to others, have been dispelled. It has been a hugely rewarding experience.

The use, or over-use, of rank sometimes does not lend itself to easy reading. With a few exceptions therefore its use has been restricted, and then usually only if officers were of Brigadier, Air Commodore or Commodore RN rank and above in 1982. My apologies if this should cause any offence.

For clarity and consistency, the word 'Malvinas' has rarely been used but there is, emphatically, no intention to cause any offence to Argentine or other South American readers, many of whom have been extremely co-operative in the course of my research.

The book reflects the views of a great many willing contributors who, not unnaturally, were not always in complete agreement, but every effort has been made to ensure accuracy. The author apologises if there are, unwittingly, any genuine errors. Finally, it was always made perfectly clear to all those interviewed that any information given might be used.

List of Acronyms

AA – Air Attaché
AAR – air-to-air refuelling
ACAS (Ops) – Assistant Chief of the Air Staff (Operations)
AEW – airborne early warning
AD – air defence
AFB – air force base
AGL – above ground level
AOC – Air Officer Commanding
ASMA – airspace management aid
ATC – air traffic control
AVM – Air Vice-Marshal
BAC – British Aircraft Corporation
BAe – British Aerospace
BFSU – British Forces Support Unit
BRIC – Brazil, Russia, India and China
CA – Controller of Aircraft
CANA – Argentine Naval Air Command
CAS – Chief of the Air Staff
CBFSU – Commander British Forces Support Unit
CINDACTA – Centro Integrado de Defesa Aerea e Controle do Trafego Aereo
CDS – Chief of Defence Staff
COS – Chiefs of Staff
COSI – Chiefs of Staff Informal
COSSEC – Chiefs of Staff Secretariat
CTA – Centro Tecnico Aerospaciale
DA – Defence Attaché
DED – docking and essential defects
D/F – direction finding
DIC – Defence Intelligence Centre

DINA – the Directorate of National Intelligence (Chile)
D/SAS – Director SAS
DZ – dropping zone
ECM – electronic counter measures
ELINT – electronic intelligence
ELN – National Liberation Army
EPL – Ejército Popular de Liberación, a group dedicated to Maoist thinking
ESMA – the Naval Mechanics School
FAA – Federal Aviation Administration
FAB – Brazilian Air Force
FARC – Revolutionary Armed Forces of Colombia
FCO – The Foreign and Commonwealth Office
FDS – field dressing station
FIDF – Falkland Islands Defence Force
GA – ground attack
GEC – General Electrics Company
GCHQ – Government Communications Headquarters
GOU – Grupo de Oficiales Unidos
GPMGs – general-purpose machine guns
GW – guided weapons
HQSTC – Headquarters Strike Command
HE – high explosive
H/F – high frequency
HMA – Her Majesty's Ambassador
HUD – head-up display
IAI – Israel Aerospace Industries
IFF – Identification Friend or Foe
INMARSAT – International Maritime Satellite Communication System
KEP – King Edward Point
LFC – Land Force Commander
MDB – Brazilian Democratic Movement
MEZ – missile engagement zone
MIR – Movimiento Izquierdo Revolucionario
MoD – Ministry of Defence
MRR – maritime radar reconnaissance
MU – maintenance unit
NA – Naval Attaché
NCO – non-commissioned officer
NVG – night vision goggles

OCU – Operational Conversion Unit
PI – photographic interpreter
PLO – Palestine Liberation Organisation
PNG – pilot night goggles/precision nuclear guidance
PLR – probe long range
POW – prisoners of war
PPS – Principal Private Secretary
PR – photographic reconnaissance
PRU – photographic reconnaissance unit
RCDS – Royal College of Defence Studies
RFAs – Royal Fleet Auxiliaries
RHAG – rotary hydraulic arrester gear
RIB – rigid inflatable boat
RIC – reconnaissance/intelligence centre
RM – Royal Marine
RV – rendezvous
SAS – Special Air Service
SBS – Special Boat Squadron
SCOT – satellite communications terminal
SF – Special Forces
SIGINT – signals intelligence
SIS – Secret Intelligence Service
SPAG – Submarine Parachute Assistance Group
SSB – single sideband (radio)
TEZ – total exclusion zone
VHF R/T – VHF radio transmitter

South America

Caracas

Venezuela

Georgetown

• Bogotá

Paramaribo

Colombia

Surinamé

French Guiana

Guyana

Quito

Ecuador

Recife •

Peru

Brazil

• Lima

La Paz

• Brasilia

Bolivia

Rio de Janeiro

Paraguay

Chile

Asunción•

Sao Paulo

Uruguay

Santiago

Buenos

• Montevideo

Aires

Argentina

Mar del Plata

Punta
Arenas

Falkland Islands

Rio Grande

South Georgia

xvi

Falkland Islands

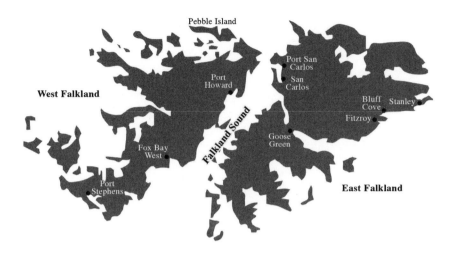

Introduction

The Falkland Islands archipelago consists of over 700 islands with an estimated 15,000 miles of coastline. The largest islands are East Falkland and West Falkland. Stanley, the capital, port and business centre is situated at the eastern end of East Falkland. It also has the world's most southernmost cathedral, Christ Church Cathedral, consecrated in 1892. A commemorative plaque on a wall inside reads:

In Proud and Loving Memory
Of
Flight Lieutenant Donald Eric Turner
RAFVR
Killed in Action in the
Battle of Britain August 8th 1940
At the going down of the sun and in the morning
We will remember them

Although the Falklands were not touched directly by the fighting during that war, over 150 men and women from a meagre population of 1800 left the islands to serve our nation. They served in the armed forces and the merchant navy. They worked in our factories. Some became nurses. Others joined the land army or became involved in civil defence duties. Twenty-four men gave their lives. Two became prisoners of war in Japan.

Throughout that war, many fund-raising activities were organised by those left behind. The Legislative Council of the Falkland Islands succeeded in raising over £72,000 for the war effort, and ten Spitfire aircraft were bought with £50,000 from this contribution. The aircraft flew in action, all bearing the name *Falkland Islands*. The Minister of Aircraft Production, Lord Beaverbrook, personally acknowledged this gift as being '... more than a contribution; it is... a sacrifice... in an hour of crisis... '.

Another hour of crisis arrived when Argentina invaded the islands on

2nd April 1982. Diplomatic relations between Britain and Argentina were broken off, and Argentine troops were in occupation for ten weeks before British troops forced their surrender on 14th June.

These islands are, and have been for a long time, a little bit of Britain far away. Quite simply, not to have responded immediately to help this small, loyal population would have been a crime. The problem was, and still is, that most Argentines have been brought up to firmly believe that the islands are a little bit of Argentina, and not so far away.

So it was that, with little warning, the Task Force sailed south with British troops determined to recover this bit of British territory. Argentina had badly miscalculated if it thought Britain would not respond as it did, and that is indeed what it thought. Both countries had their reasons for claiming to have history on their side to support their ownership of the islands, but the islanders themselves were enthusiastically British.

The inhabitants have been given many labels, but prefer to describe themselves as 'Falkland Islanders'. They do not like being called 'Falklanders', a title that is compared with 'Englanders', as the Germans once called the English! Neither do they like to hear the war they became embroiled in being described merely as a 'conflict'.

They can be forgiven for being perplexed at the way the islands became a political football during the decades following the Second World War, as successive British governments side-stepped the Falklands issue, devised policies aimed at buying time, fudged the question of eventual ownership, and all this with little regard for the feelings of the islanders themselves.

This book aims to present what is essentially a South American perspective, and to describe how, when and why the Falklands War impacted (as it surely did) on the various countries of mainland South America. Each country was forced to take a position when it learned that the Argentine Navy had sailed in April 1982. That position would have taken into account not only its relationship with each of the two belligerents, but also with neighbouring countries. It would also have considered the consequences if Argentina happened to win. Beyond these considerations was the need to preserve South American solidarity. After all, when it was over they would have to continue to coexist, sharing borders, problems and trade. Brazil, for instance, shares a border with every country in South America except for Chile and Ecuador.

Although, quite understandably, some countries felt closer to Argentina than to far-away Britain, we nevertheless had friends, strong trade links and were held in high regard in certain quarters, even with affection.

Those countries that were inclined towards the Argentine position, tended to be cautious in their support.

Many Argentine friends have enthusiastically co-operated during the course of researching this book. None appear to have had much affection for President Galtieri's junta. They all still have, however, that conviction that the islands rightly belong to Argentina, and that one day it could possibly all happen again. Even amongst the members of the junta, there were different degrees of commitment. The Argentine Navy was very much in the fore-front in its determination to invade, led as it was by a rabid anglophobe. Recently-elected President Galtieri was bound by his debt to Admiral Anaya, whose support for his bid for the presidency was conditional upon the invasion taking place – but no one thought it would happen so soon. The Air Force chief was lukewarm about the whole business.

South America is a beautiful continent. It is a curious fact that most of its countries tend not to care very much for their immediate neighbours, but to get along well with the country beyond. Memories of past conflicts or disputes were a constant reminder that another war in the region could inflame passions, reignite old alliances, resurrect dormant aspirations or be used to settle old scores. Much could hang on whether Argentina was defeated in a Falklands war. If not, then suitably emboldened, she might decide to pursue another dream, such as retaking the disputed islands in the Beagle Channel. Chile had particular reason to be concerned if Argentina was successful.

So, in different ways, and to a greater or lesser extent, the other countries of South America became players, even if unwilling ones, in our limited war. It was, mercifully, a limited war because neither adversary was hell-bent on the complete destruction of the other. The objective was simple, limited and clearly understood – the possession, or repossession, of territory remote from either belligerent. It was also bound to be limited in time for both sides would soon exhaust whatever resources they had available to commit.

Finally, whilst one's enemy is usually well-understood, one also has to be aware of the other players who may wish to become involved in odd, irritating ways, e.g. offering support for that enemy. What did we really know at the time, for instance, of the roles played by Israel and South Africa? Was there a French presence in Argentina contrary to promises made at the time? If so, did it matter? Was Libya involved? If so, how?

I apologise if I have occasionally strayed away from South America. Inevitably, it became necessary to include mention of London, Ascension Island, South Georgia and... the Falkland Islands.

Part One
Argentina Goes To War

Argentina

Argentina Invades the Falklands

From Spanish Domination to the 1980s

Spanish influence (and later domination) in what we know as Argentina today, was a slower process than in other South American countries to the north and west. Argentina crucially lacked the precious gold and silver that attracted the *conquistadors* elsewhere.

Some of those who arrived to colonise it came from Chile and Peru, and for a while it was part of the Viceroyalty of Peru and administered from Lima. In 1776 the Spanish Crown established the new independent Viceroyalty of La Plata, with Buenos Aires as its capital.

In 1810, a significant year in the nation's history, the government of Spain fell. This led to the formation of several independent states, including the United Provinces of Rio de la Plata. Full independence was declared in 1816. The final defeat of the Spanish occurred eight years later. Much of the rest of the century was marred by endless fighting, either with neighbouring countries or with the indigenous Indians, who were virtually decimated.

Between 1853 and 1861, the United Provinces evolved and became Argentina. It gained its constitution in 1853, and Buenos Aires was recognised as the federal seat of government.

Initially Argentina prospered and grew. There was plenty of foreign investment, agriculture was modernised and successful, and Europeans from many different countries went to settle there. During the early part of the twentieth century, Argentina was considered to be one of the richest countries in the world, with an economy that was growing faster than the USA or Germany. Later, it declined to become a country with rampant inflation and a huge external debt problem. The reasons for this decline are many and complex, and have much to do with frequent military coups, mismanagement and corruption.

Those events in Argentina's history that were relevant to the attitudes

3

still prevailing in 1982, and to the style of leadership in the country at that time, occurred from about 1930 onwards. It was in that year that a coup resulted in years of military rule, the leaders of which tended towards fascism.

During the early part of the Second World War, whilst the government had sympathy for the allies, the armed forces – ever fearful of the spread of communism – leaned towards the Axis nations. Peron and some of his army colleagues visited Germany in 1943 and were impressed with what they saw. The civilian population on the whole favoured the adopted policy of neutrality.

In June 1943, power was seized by a military junta, all members of a secret alliance which called itself the *Grupo de Oficiales Unidos* (GOU), one of whom was Juan Peron. In every way, the GOU was modelled on Nazi ideology. On 27th March 1945, and only when it became clear that Germany was heading for defeat, Argentina finally declared war on Germany and Japan, becoming the fifty-third nation to be officially at war at the time. It happened to be the day that Germany fired the last V2 rockets of the war from their one remaining launching site, near The Hague.

Peron was elected President in 1946 and the stage was set for those who henceforth became known as the Peronistas. Their policies were a curious mix of left-wing and right-wing, and Peron was noted for his use of thugs to help enforce them. Although he was re-elected in 1951, his attacks on the Roman Catholic Church, coupled with the dire state of the economy, turned army and navy units against him; the navy was known to have been the most anti-Peron of the three services. He was finally toppled in a coup in 1955. His first term as president will be remembered for the economic mismanagement; the ill-treatment, torture and imprisonment of those who opposed his government; for corruption and for the appointment of ministers and officials on the basis of loyalty rather than quality or suitability for the job. It will also be remembered for his second wife, the popular and charismatic Maria Eva Duarte Peron (Evita) who died in July 1952, aged thirty-three years.

An Argentine schoolgirl herself at the time of the Falklands war, now living in Britain, Cristina Bishop learned from her grandmother what life was like during Peron's presidency. She said:

My grandmother was a state schoolteacher and the breadwinner of the family. Everyone had to pretend they were enjoying the Peron era. It was advisable to keep a few books about him and the Peronist party in the house, and the odd picture or photograph of him on the wall. She would not have dared to voice any opposition, or criticise him in any way. The price would have been the loss of her job. Meanwhile the wealth of a (at that time) rich nation was being squandered.

Captain Julio Felix Cano was a B747 pilot with Argentina's national airline, Aerolineas Argentinas, in the late 1980s. He recounted the fascinating story of his involvement in the attempted coup of June 1955. He said:

> I was a navy pilot at the time, a *Teniente de Fragata*, and was involved in the first, abortive attempt to oust Peron in June 1955. I took off with some of my colleagues on 16th June from the navy's shore base, Punta Indio, and we bombed Peron's official residence (known as Casa Rosada because of its pink colour) in Buenos Aires. We were informed on the return flight, on the aircraft's radio, that the coup attempt had failed and that it would be dangerous for us to land in Argentina.

> We diverted to Montevideo in Uruguay. We didn't have to stay there for very long because Peron was finally toppled three months later, in September 1955. The earlier (June) coup attempt was unsuccessful essentially because the three services failed to get their act together and jointly plan the coup as a co-ordinated effort.

The same reluctance to plan and operate together was a criticism levelled against the navy many years later – in the context of Falklands – by the Argentine Air Attaché in Brazil. It seems that little had been learned during the intervening years.

Peron went into exile in Spain until 1973, when he returned to Argentina to be re-elected with sixty-two per cent of the popular vote. He died nine months later, and was succeeded by his wife Isabel, although she was never elected to the position. She fell victim to another military coup in 1976, which was precipitated by an army anxious to deal swiftly and firmly (i.e. brutally) with the ever-growing wave of terrorism that was sweeping the country. As always in Argentina, the dire state of the economy was also a factor. The next Peronista to become President of Argentina was Carlos Menem in 1989. Those dark years during the 1970s are often described as the 'dirty war' years.

The Rev. Terry Brighton worked in Argentina throughout the 1970s as an agricultural missionary. He remembered the coup in 1976 that ended Isabel's reign as president and brought in President Videla. He said:

Suddenly the army were everywhere. Even the local elected mayor in the small town where I worked was replaced by an army man.

It was the end of democracy (again); petrol became hard to get, and travelling became difficult too because there were roadblocks and identity checks everywhere. The army were ruthlessly searching for the Montoneros and were very nervous of bombs.

The Montoneros naturally grew in numbers and became stronger – a sort of equal and opposite reaction – and the situation became progressively worse. Many families experienced the loss of relatives and friends, many of whom had joined the ranks of the 'desaparecidos' (disappeared). Others knew people personally who had been abused or tortured, which routinely happened if someone was just vaguely suspected. Proof was not necessary. The country was based on corruption and brutality, which progressively worsened. People knew about ESMA – the Naval Mechanics School – but few dared to talk about it.

Howard Pearce was at the British Embassy, Buenos Aires in the mid-1970s and, later from 2002 to 2006, served as Governor of the Falkland Islands. (He achieved the distinction of becoming the first governor to be married in the Falklands, in Stanley's Christ Church Cathedral.) He recalled that during President Isabel's brief term of office, tension and terrorism were increasing and spreading, mainly attributable to the Montoneros, who were right-wing Peronists, and the left-wing Revolutionary Army of the People (ERP). The military coup of March 1976 was inevitable, following which the 'dirty war' swiftly gained momentum. He said:

Argentina became increasingly aggressive and assertive at that time. The government concentrated on its internal war and paid little attention to domestic issues, the economic problems and so on. The Embassy found it very difficult to know what was going on. Information seeped out sporadically over time. It was an extraordinary period.

But all this was also being further complicated by the Falklands issue which was becoming a growing irritant. We were co-operating well with Argentina then and trying to build on that co-operation. There was therefore pressure on the Foreign Office to find a compromise solution. The Falklands have been, over the years, a diversion to be used when necessary by successive Argentine governments to generate support or to divert attention away from other – thornier – problems.

Dudley Ankerson held a diplomatic post in the British Embassy in Buenos Aires from 1978 to 1981, i.e. during the latter part of the 'dirty war' years. He recalled that there had been a move afoot to retake the Falklands just before he arrived in Argentina. The Head of the Navy, Admiral Massera, had been pressing President Videla to act. The President's response, which took into account his desire to have the prevailing US arms embargo lifted, was to ask the Admiral to prepare a detailed plan for such an invasion. The task was delegated to (then Captain) Jorge Anaya – a rabid anglophobe – but later put quietly to one side. Duncan Ankerson said:

> We were all well aware at that time of the Argentine Government's four principal objectives: to crush terrorism; address the question of the ailing economy; resolve the 'injustice' of the Beagle Channel situation and, at the appropriate time, retake the Falklands. These objectives were defined in the early 1970s and were known as 'The Process'. However, as far as both President Videla and his successor, President Viola, were concerned, although retaking the Falklands was certainly an important objective, it was also one to be dealt with preferably by negotiation. Admiral Massera saw things differently, whilst the army and the air force were perfectly content to concentrate on what they perceived as being the higher priorities at the time; stamping out left-wing guerrilla movements and neutralising political dissent.

President Videla's period in office – which embraced most of the 'dirty war' years – will be especially remembered for the disappearance of thousands of Argentines whose only crime was to have been suspected of holding left-wing views. It was an ugly, but nevertheless important, period of Argentina's history. Although it preceded the Viola and Galtieri presidencies, it gives us a better understanding of those we fought against

7

in 1982, especially the members of the military junta, who were all on the ascendancy during the 1970s.

During the brief and unspectacular Viola presidency, the man who was destined to succeed him, General Leopoldo Galtieri, spent much of it preparing himself for when he would move Viola aside and take over himself. As Head of the Army, he was automatically the likely candidate. This was painlessly achieved in a bloodless coup in December 1981 on the pretext of Viola's ailing health.

The 'Dirty War' Years

Any discussion about the 'dirty war' of the 1970s would be incomplete without mention of ESMA located outside Buenos Aires. Some reference to that loathsome establishment – set up and run by the Argentine Navy and masquerading as a bona fide training school – is unavoidable, simply because one or two officers who 'worked' at ESMA and helped to give it its reputation, had significant roles in 1982. One naval officer – also a trained commando and intelligence officer – who achieved particular notoriety was Alfredo Astiz.

Astiz would have attracted little attention in Argentina, and none outside the country, but for his sadistic nature and the obvious pleasure he took in inflicting pain on others. It was for these attributes that he was tolerated by his superiors and rewarded with a succession of (what were probably regarded at that time) attractive appointments. Astiz's career in the 1970s – and up to the time he surrendered to the British in South Georgia in April 1982 – paints an interesting picture of the Argentine Navy and its priorities during that period.

Julian Mitchell, the British Naval Attaché in Buenos Aires, said: 'At an early stage in Astiz's career, when he was the captain of a submarine, he inadvertently went aground in it.' Those who follow the fortunes of the Royal Navy will know that that should have been enough to terminate any promising career. Astiz, it seems, went from strength to strength.

Admiral Emilio Massera, appointed Head of the Argentine Navy in 1973, was dedicated to creating a much stronger navy – both militarily and politically – and it was during his time in charge that it played a particularly active role during the 'dirty war'. ESMA became notorious as an interrogation and torture centre, and was at its most brutal throughout the last half of the decade. By the time the Falklands War started, prisoners were still being held there, but atrocities were less common.

Admiral Massera, as a member of the ruling junta, was too senior to be closely involved with ESMA himself, but he knew what was going on there and the part it played in the war against opponents of the government. As all young officers were expected to become willing participants in this 'work', those who sought a future in their service would not have objected. Astiz excelled himself.

Captain (later Rear Admiral) Ruben Jacinto Chamorro was appointed ESMA's Director, and he and his staff were responsible for the torture and cold-blooded murder of thousands of prisoners. It has been estimated that about ninety per cent of those taken to ESMA lost their lives. A favourite method of disposing of people was to throw them out of an aircraft over the Atlantic. Chamorro liked to become personally involved in his work, and according to a well-placed diplomat in the British Embassy in Buenos Aires, he married one of his prisoners.

Dudley Ankerson recalled that the Embassy was divided into two schools of thought at that time; those whose priority was to win commercial contracts – and who would not therefore have wanted to 'rock the boat' by reporting human rights breaches – and those who felt strongly that they should be reported and publicised. The Anglo-Argentine community knew about ESMA and what went on there, and the majority were concerned about the abuses. They thought the Embassy should be doing more about it – after all it was the role of an Embassy to report as accurately as possible – but otherwise, for their own good, were largely in denial about ESMA.

Jimmy Burns was later the *Financial Times* correspondent in Argentina, and he recalled being invited to a dinner party in the early 1980s at the home of Colonel Stephen Love, the British Defence Attaché. He said:

> Together with other guests present, there were representatives of the three Argentine services, and they started loudly competing with each other, boasting about their own service's heroism and achievements during the 'dirty war' years. Suddenly the Spanish Air Attaché's wife shouted out: '... and well done too! I've always said that's what we should have done with ETA; shoot the b****y lot of them.' It was all rather embarrassing.

Eventually a point was reached when it was decided to move the by-now infamous Astiz somewhere else, and to allow things to cool down a bit. He was attracting too much attention and elements of the media were bravely exposing him for what he was. His boss, Ruben Chamorro, left

ESMA in 1979 with the rank of Rear Admiral to be Defence and Naval Attaché at the Argentine Embassy in South Africa. He promptly requested that Astiz should join him as his Assistant Naval Attaché. Astiz had already just left ESMA – also in 1979, but just before Chamorro – to take up an appointment in Paris. As he was obliged to depart hastily from Paris anyway, he went to join his old boss in South Africa instead.

Colonel John de Candole was the British Defence Attaché in Pretoria from early 1980 until the end of 1982. He recalled that Admiral Chamorro had arrived in the country just before him and that it was unusual to appoint such a high-ranking officer as a Defence Attaché. He thought it must have been either a reward for services rendered, or an attempt to sideline him and get him out of the way to somewhere not too important. However, it is highly likely that he was specifically sent to South Africa to enlist its support in every way possible, and especially in respect of supplying defence equipment. Although no one in Argentina was talking openly about invading the Falklands then, the plan for 'recovering' lost Argentine territory in the South Atlantic, which had been produced a few years earlier by (the then) Captain Anaya for Admiral Massera, was soon to be updated.

Whilst Astiz was in South Africa, his reputation was widely known, and the word inevitably spread about his previous working relationship with Chamorro at ESMA. John de Candole said: 'He was young, unmarried and very charming. He was also extremely popular with the ladies, very personable and spoke excellent English. But everyone knew of his reputation.'

After less than a year in South Africa, Astiz was again forced – by media exposure of his previous misdemeanours – to move on. However, his superiors in the navy still held him in sufficiently high regard to give him another good appointment (or, being all tarred with the same brush, perhaps they were simply fearful that a witch-hunt might lead from him to them).

Astiz was selected to lead the operation to capture South Georgia. The thinking behind his selection would undoubtedly have been that this would improve his tarnished image, help cleanse the reputation of the armed forces generally following the 'dirty war' years, and hopefully too, put to rest some of the (accurate) rumours still circulating around.

When Rear Admiral Chamorro's tour of duty in South Africa ended, after the Falklands War, he was disinclined to leave South Africa and return to Argentina, and promptly disappeared. Doubtless he was mindful of ESMA's nefarious activities and the part he personally played. He also had acquired a South African girlfriend who might not have wanted to leave her country, and a wife in Argentina who might not have wanted him back. He was eventually tracked down by the Argentine authorities, however, and forced to return.

Seizure of South Georgia

The island of South Georgia, although said to have been first sighted in 1675 by a London merchant, Anthony de la Roche (and therefore named Roche Island on some early maps), was sighted again by Captain James Cook a hundred years later. Cook, though initially dubious as to the value of the island to the British Crown, claimed it, and named it 'The Isle of Georgia' in honour of King George III. Its importance initially was as a base for sealers, and later for whalers, until whaling ended in the 1960s.

An Argentine company was granted a lease to process whales at Grytviken in South Georgia, in 1906, but Argentina is believed to have made its first serious claim to South Georgia in 1927. This was followed by another claim in 1948. History does not seem to record, however, whether anyone ever took these claims very seriously.

An Argentine scrap-metal merchant, Constantine Davidoff, formally applied early in March 1982 – to the British Embassy in Buenos Aires – for permission to clear the long-defunct whaling station at Leith. It had already been the subject of negotiations, a contract had been signed, and a survey had been carried out. For some time prior to March, the Argentine Navy had been pulling the strings and had evolved a plan to use Davidoff's mission to establish its own presence on South Georgia.

On 19th March, Davidoff and his workforce arrived at Leith in the navy transport ship, *Bahia Buen Suceso*, and occupied the abandoned whaling station there. They were accompanied by Alfredo Astiz and his naval party. They hoisted the Argentine flag, failed to present themselves at Grytviken – as was required of them – and started work. Davidoff was undoubtedly, if not exactly operating under duress, taking instructions from the accompanying naval party who were posing as members of his workforce.

Robert Headland, biologist, archivist and historian – also known for his work as Curator of the Scott Polar Research Institute in Cambridge – was employed from time to time by the British Antarctic Survey Team. By chance, on the day that Davidoff and his fellow Argentines landed at

11

Leith, he and his three colleagues also arrived there, overland, and almost literally stumbled upon the Argentine party. He said:

Not only did we have an excellent view of the proceedings, but I had a hand-held VHF radio and my knowledge of Spanish enabled me to listen to the Argentines' transmissions. I recall that the *Bahia Buen Suceso* was anchored offshore. We were able to use our Albatross launch, which was tied up nearby, to relay the information to our base at King Edward Point (KEP) twenty-five kilometres away.

News of the Argentines' landing was then quickly passed on to Governor Rex Hunt on the Falkland Islands, and thence to London.

Although the Argentines lowered their flag when instructed to do so, they made no attempt to obtain the necessary authorisation to proceed with their work, and declined to leave the island. The audacity of the Argentine party could not be allowed to go unchallenged and, somewhat to the surprise of the Argentine Government – which clearly had not anticipated such a slick British response – the Prime Minister did not hesitate. On 20th March, she and the Foreign Secretary, Lord Carrington, ordered the immediate despatch of HMS *Endurance* (which was at the Falklands and about to return to the UK) down to South Georgia. On board was Lieutenant Keith Mills RM with twenty-two Royal Marines under his command, made up of his own detachment on HMS *Endurance*, and bolstered by others from the Falklands garrison. HMS *Endurance* arrived at Grytviken a few days later with instructions to await further orders.

Meanwhile, although the British Government had responded quickly to the developing situation in South Georgia, there was considerable concern that the situation might get out of hand. The Argentine Foreign Minister, Costa Mendez, received a message from Lord Carrington urging Argentina to evacuate its personnel as soon as possible, and indicating that, if the Argentine Government complied, it would then be unnecessary for Britain to use its Royal Marines to force the issue.

Ambassador Anthony Williams' relief on reading the message in Buenos Aires, however, was short-lived. Costa Mendez may have been regarded by the British as being a moderate, and someone who would probably have preferred to avoid a confrontation, but the military junta had already decided that the Argentine party on South Georgia should 'receive more protection'. The navy supply ship, *Bahia Paraiso*, was ordered to proceed south as quickly as possible to disembark another party of marines.

On 24th March, HMS *Endurance* arrived at Grytviken with Keith Mills and his Royal Marines. Two Argentine Navy corvettes, the *Granville* and the *Drummond*, were also ordered to be prepared for any eventuality, and moved closer to South Georgia. The temperature was rising. A few days of diplomacy then ensued during which Keith Mills received a succession of confusing instructions. During this period, Argentina's military junta decided to invade the Falkland Islands and fixed the date, Galtieri's Chiefs of Staff having all confirmed that they were ready to go.

On 3rd April, Keith Mills and his Royal Marines fought a short and heroic engagement at Grytviken against a superior Argentine force. They were hugely outnumbered, but managed to inflict considerable damage and casualties before finally surrendering. Nigel Peters, who suffered a badly damaged arm, was the only British casualty. (See also Part Three, The Repatriation of Prisoners of War).

The Lead-up to War

Galtieri's preparations for taking over the presidency during 1981 had included several visits to the USA, where he saw the Secretary of State and other senior officials and was also, on one occasion, received by the President himself. A tall, good-looking man of military bearing, Galtieri was well received and impressed those Americans whose concern had been to contain communism and left-wing elements. The volatile nature of South American politics was certainly of particular concern at that time.

Notwithstanding these contacts in the USA, Galtieri never received the clear, unambiguous statement he sought from the Americans spelling out which country they would support in the event of Argentina invading the Falklands.

Although most decent, educated Argentines had no desire to go to war over the Falklands, and would have preferred to see the issue dealt with peacefully, the declining economic situation, coupled with the increasingly ugly mood in the streets, forced the junta to act sooner than it would have liked.

The Head of the Argentine Navy, Admiral Jorge Anaya, is credited with having persuaded General Galtieri to bring forward the invasion of the Falklands (which the President had already agreed to in principle, as the price for getting Anaya's backing for his bid for the presidency). It had been planned for later in the year, but now it could not wait. The government desperately needed a diversion, and Anaya convinced his junta colleagues that, by seizing the Falklands, they could restore their flagging popularity and prevent their almost inevitable downfall, and probably also a return to civilian rule. From all accounts a desperate Galtieri was easily persuaded. However, he must have known that, unless Britain did not respond at all in the event of an Argentine invasion, either winning a war against Britain or obtaining an unambiguous agreement to transfer sovereignty of the islands, would be essential to his survival as president.

Miguel Mora, an Argentine who moved to England after the Falklands War, said:

The vast majority of the Argentine population would have preferred a peaceful solution to the Falklands situation – and very few wanted a war – but 150 years of talking had produced nothing in the way of an acceptable solution. There was mounting frustration over the issue, and a feeling that Britain was always just playing for time, with no real intention of coming up with a meaningful solution agreeable to both countries.

By March 1982 the already fraught economic situation had turned really sour. There were strikes and mass demonstrations in the streets; the population had lost confidence in the government and any vestige of respect for it had evaporated away as well. People were angry with a government that could not pay its workers. They could not understand how such a large, beautiful country, with its considerable natural resources, was always bankrupt.

Cristina Bishop recalled:

A desperate government had to address this explosive situation and offer some good news and hope to the people. Throughout March 1982, the population was rallied – manipulated really – by means of radio, TV broadcasts and a poster campaign. Teachers at the state schools were also told to 'educate' the children. The message was the same everywhere, however it was conveyed. The government was reminding the population that the time had come to boot the British imperialists off Argentine soil. The state of the economy provided the perfect opportunity. Although many middle-class Argentines had strong reservations, most were swept along by the mood in the country.

Many Argentines felt that it was this nationwide frustration over the islands that enabled the junta to manipulate so easily the anger felt over the economic situation, redirecting it instead towards the British and to supporting a military effort to win back the islands. At the very least, many may have hoped, Argentina could dust down its plans, threaten Britain, and make all the right noises. Perhaps, by bringing their armed forces to a high state of readiness to convince Britain it was serious, it just might bring about that elusive solution to the Falklands problem without actually having to go to war. If this did not work, then perhaps an invasion later in the year – which would have been preferable anyway – might be necessary.

Unfortunately the cooler heads, those that were happy to threaten rather than rush to war, were never likely to prevail. The economic situation was too dire and could not be put easily to one side. In any case, the Argentine Navy was not in the mood to wait.

Many of the Argentines who so swiftly turned their attention from the economy to supporting an invasion, did so only because they too, like the government, never imagined that Britain would respond, and thought the country might soon be able to celebrate a long-awaited victory that would restore some national pride. Others simply thought the new mood would help to keep the young firebrands off the streets.

Sadly, the junta sent many of these same young firebrands to the Falklands with little or no proper training and with equally little idea of what to expect. Because of the economic situation, the government tried to go to war on the cheap. The troops had poor equipment and spent much of the time cold and hungry. Perhaps those islanders who took some pity on these men, and offered the occasional bowl of hot soup or a warm dry garment, can be forgiven for these humanitarian acts. The Falklands War was an expensive diversion for Argentina and one it could ill afford. It merely served to further aggravate the prevailing economic situation.

Towards the end of March, the British Embassy in Buenos Aires was reporting that civil unrest on the streets of the city was intensifying each day. It was around this time, said Julian Mitchell, Naval Attaché, that the Embassy started shredding paper, just in case... On 31st March, intelligence indicated that an invasion was planned for the morning of Friday

2nd April and that Argentine naval units, which had ostensibly been on a routine training exercise, were now giving the appearance of assembling for an invasion. (That same evening, the First Sea Lord, in the absence of the Chief of Defence Staff [CDS] who was in New Zealand, assured the British Prime Minister that a task force could be ready to sail within a few days).

On 2nd April, around mid-day, the first indications were received in London that the Falkland Islands had been invaded. Argentina had not envisaged a British military response and had not planned for such an eventuality. It had also believed that the USA, even if it did not actively support Argentina's position, would remain neutral. The military junta certainly had not calculated that the British Government might just feel that there was an important principle at stake here; a duty to defend British territory and protect British citizens against armed aggression that could not be allowed to succeed.

The invasion was based upon false assumptions, but even so the lack of proper detailed planning – to cover every eventuality – was quite extraordinary. The complacency of the military junta was also evident in its decision to send an invasion force largely composed of inexperienced conscripts. US Air Force General John Taylor was quoted in April 1982 as saying that roughly half the Argentine forces on the Falklands had had only between one and two months of military service.

The view of our military attachés in Argentina at that time was that there was little or no communication between most Argentine officers and the men they commanded, and hence little in the way of mutual respect. This lack of communication, and adequate briefings, meant that many of the Argentine soldiers thought at first they were being sent to fight the Chileans. In fact, the junta held back many of its more experienced soldiers, fearing that Chile might decide to take advantage of Argentina's preoccupation with the British and attack from the rear. As we later learned, Chile never had any intention of doing any such thing.

Public Reaction to the Invasion in Argentina

The Anglo-Argentine community in Argentina, most of whom were of British descent, numbered approximately 100,000 in April 1982. Many thousands more British citizens were there for a variety of other reasons. British firms, for instance, including many in the defence sector, had teams or representatives in the country on visits or on contract.

In the early days of the war, newspapers warned that the junta 'was preparing to take measures to control the residents of the enemy country and its allies and sympathisers'. Following these warnings, the Foreign Office, in messages broadcast repeatedly by the BBC World Service, urged all British nationals to leave Argentina as soon as possible.

Daniel Eugenio and his wife Vicky, both Argentines by birth, now live in England. Until the late 1980s, they lived in Buenos Aires, where he was a senior manager with the national airline, Aerolineas Argentinas. Daniel said:

> In fact, the government didn't take any measures against the British community and there were very few incidents, although a small bomb placed in the doorway of the English clock tower (Torre de los Ingleses) in Buenos Aires blew the door down. The building, designed by British architect Ambrose Poynter, and a gift from the British community, was inaugurated in May 1916. It was renamed in 1982 and became Torre Monumental. On 25th May, Argentina's National Day, the Plaza Britannia in Buenos Aires (near the clock tower) was renamed Plaza Fuerza Aerea (Air Force Place).

Some firms, e.g. Shell, temporarily shifted their operations to Uruguay for the duration. There were also concerns about the allegiance of staff. Douglas Webster, Controller of Shell Venezuela SA, said: 'Our workforce in Argentina included a large number of Anglo-Argentines, and they were all forced to consider where their allegiance lay. Were they predominantly British or Argentine? The vast majority said Argentine.'

Benedict Williams was the son of the late Sir Anthony Williams, our Ambassador in Buenos Aires in 1982. He said: 'The Anglo-Argentines weren't threatened and many were behind the idea of the invasion, especially the younger generation, who were almost wholly Argentine in their views. They were products of an education system that taught them the Falklands belonged to Argentina and they didn't doubt it.' Others have also confirmed that many families were divided in their views, causing considerable tensions and even in some cases, family break-up. Invariably the younger generation would be pro-Argentine whilst the parents would have some sympathy for the British position.

Benedict Williams' mother, Lady Williams, agreed that many of the older Anglo-Argentines were most unhappy about the prospect, or possibility, of a war and were much more sympathetic to the British position than the younger generation. She added that although everyone was

17

bilingual, the young preferred to speak in Spanish. They could also look forward to a spell of military service in Argentina.

Lady Williams also had one or two interesting comments to make about the Argentine Navy. She said it was widely perceived as being an effective upholder of law and order in the country. It was a very privileged class, and sons often followed their father into a career in the navy. In their final exams (before passing-out of the Naval College) there was always a question relating to the Falkland Islands and how to deal with them, i.e. how to occupy them.

On 13th April, three British journalists (Simon Winchester, Ian Mather and Tony Prime) were arrested on trumped-up charges of spying and briefly imprisoned in Tierra del Fuego for reporting on Argentina's military build-up. Life was frustrating for the 500-plus foreign journalists in Buenos Aires during the war. They had military 'minders', were fed misinformation, and could not get to where the war was being fought. Also, use of the word 'Falklands' was forbidden during the regular afternoon briefings they received.

David Joy, who arrived at the British Embassy in January just before the war to take up the position of Head of Chancery, received one of the (not uncommon) threatening phone calls made at the time. He still has a recording of the call, which informed him that he 'would face the consequences next time he stepped out of the British Residence', where he was being temporarily accommodated.

Life was not much easier for the Argentine journalists. The junta detailed a group of them to witness the invasion of the Falklands, and the arrival of Argentina's new but short-lived Governor, General Mario Menendez. Shortly afterwards, most of them had to return to the mainland, leaving just three who were not actually allowed to witness any fighting. They later said only ten per cent of their carefully-scrutinised material was ever used. Jimmy Burns, the *Financial Times* correspondent, said:

The Argentine press, however, joined enthusiastically in the distortion of the truth from the beginning. The past, the economic problems and the bad old days, were temporarily forgotten. Most Argentines were completely taken in, and so for them the shock of defeat, when it came, was even greater. Some of the more astute turned to the BBC World Service for an accurate account of what was going on.

However, whilst the World Service in English was unaffected, broadcasts in Spanish were jammed from time to time from May 1982 onwards. It took the form of a fast and continuous dialling tone. It was reported at the time that some of Argentina's neighbours were similarly affected.

Jimmy Burns said that throughout the war, Argentina's successes were exaggerated and British successes played down, distorted or simply ignored. But in times of war are not most nations, to a degree, guilty of acting this way, if only in the interests of maintaining morale?

The Recollections of Three Argentine Officers

Many of Argentina's officers, especially from the army and navy, who rose to high rank during the 'dirty war' of the 1970s, had acquired – indeed earned – unsavoury reputations. The members of the military junta (with the exception of the Head of the Air Force) in 1982 when its forces invaded the Falkland Islands were amongst the last of these military hard-liners. A new generation of young men, dedicated to their profession and service, were already rising through the ranks when Argentina went to war.

Two officers who subsequently reached the rank of general, who were untainted by the events of the 1970s, and one other who had already reached that rank, were amongst those that held views refreshingly at odds with their predecessors and the junta. Their feelings for the British were more of respect than of hatred. They understood why Britain had responded the way it did. Unlike their leaders, they would have expected it. They probably realised that the junta had miscalculated even before the Task Force arrived in the South Atlantic.

General Martin Balza was one of those officers who acknowledged and understood the errors made by the military during the 'dirty war' years. He was a lieutenant colonel serving with his regiment in 1982 when he first learned of the invasion of the Falklands. He said later that he knew Britain would respond. He felt that the junta's decision to invade had been a mistake anyway; that you could not go to war on an island without first having control over the sea and the skies, or you would be heading for inevitable defeat. Nevertheless, like all good professional soldiers, he just got on with it when, a few days later, he was ordered to the islands. Privately, though, he thought it was a hopeless mission.

His saddest comments, however, were about the reception that Argentina's soldiers received from the junta and other senior officers on their return to the mainland. They were not permitted a warm welcome from their loved ones as they were perceived as having disgraced the nation. Initially, they were locked up in their barracks and forbidden to contact their families. Officers were also forbidden to discuss the war.

The General had a good relationship with elements in Britain during the years following the war, and a decade later became the Head of the Argentine Army.

A few weeks prior to the invasion, General Mario Menendez was informed of the junta's intention to invade and advised that, if all went according to plan, he would become the Governor of the islands. He was sworn to secrecy.

He arrived in Stanley on 7th April, and for him and his colleagues the first few weeks after the invasion were rather unreal. There was no fighting yet; just waiting. As the new Governor, he was adamant throughout the occupation that the islanders and their property should be respected by the Argentine forces.

General Menendez clearly appreciated that, once the decision had been taken by the British Government to send a task force, Argentina would be up against it. He was apparently quite shocked when he learned of Britain's decision and was quoted as having said that Argentina's only hope of averting a disaster was to somehow cause sufficient damage to the task force to create a climate for negotiations.

Argentina, however, soon became seriously short of essential supplies, especially food and ammunition. Meanwhile the junta in Buenos Aires appeared to be waiting for a miracle. They certainly did not seem to appreciate the severity of the situation as perceived by General Menendez, or the problems being experienced at the frontline. If they did, they appeared either powerless, or unwilling, to do anything about it. The conscripts, the General said, were simply not up to the job.

It was rumoured that, towards the end, the General informed Galtieri how bad things were, and even volunteered to take responsibility for the inevitable defeat. He surrendered the Argentine forces on 14th June after apparently failing to persuade Galtieri that all was lost (and was temporarily replaced by Maj. Gen. Jeremy Moore). The junta had wanted to fight on but Menendez felt that further loss of life was quite pointless. He was later to express the view that there should never be another war over the Falklands. It should be sorted out round a table, he said. The following year he was arrested and briefly held under house arrest.

Brigadier General Sergio Fernandez was a young lieutenant in 1982 and saw active service in the Falklands with his company. He has been a willing contributor, and gives a clear, graphic account of events as witnessed from his perspective as a platoon leader in the following chapter, A General Remembers. He happens also to be the man that destroyed Flight Lieutenant Jeff Glover's Harrier aircraft with a Blowpipe missile on 21st May. Jeff subsequently became the only Royal Air Force POW during the Falklands War after he (miraculously) survived the ordeal.

A General Remembers

The following is Brigadier General Sergio Fernandez's account of his company's involvement in the Falklands War. His story actually starts three years before the war. Minor changes only, for the sake of clarity, have been made (although he speaks and writes excellent English). He said:

One day in April 1979 I was told to attend a meeting at the Army General Headquarters in Buenos Aires. I was a young twenty-eight-year-old first lieutenant then, assigned to the Infantry School in Campo de Mayo, near Buenos Aires. Together with some senior officers, I was introduced to a visiting British Royal Artillery Major, who told us about a Blowpipe missile course we could have. Argentina had bought the system the previous year and developed its own short course for a few aimers. He described the system and the way the British Army used it tactically. It was a very useful starting point for me, as it was planned that I would be one of the future instructors, to provide aimers for the Argentine Army.

In November, the instructors' course finally started at the Infantry School. The instructor sent by Short Brothers and Co (the manufacturer) was Mr John Reddick. He was an outstanding teacher, who also became a good friend. He had developed a complete five-week course for us, which ended in mid-December. He spoke clear English that was easy to follow, and which allowed us to skip the translation. Two officers and two NCOs were trained as aimers, and also as instructors. We learned all about the system, theoretically and practically, and also used the firing simulator.

During the next two years, I developed and managed three aimers' courses, training officers and NCOs at the Infantry School. At the end of the last one, in 1981, we fired live missiles for the first time. It was a real challenge, due to the cost of the test, the difficulty of finding a

22

good firing area near Buenos Aires, and the uncertainty attached to actually firing missiles at last; no longer just in the simulator.

Finally, the day arrived and we were ready to start live firing, in front of a crowd in a field in Magdalena, close to the shore of the Rio de la Plata. We fired towards the river in a forbidden navigation area, having created a large balloon target, which was anchored in the river 3 kilometres from the shore and floated 100 meters above the water. I fired the first and fourth Blowpipe missiles. Another officer fired the second missile and an NCO, the third. We came very close to the target, but the most important thing was that we had experienced the whole process. We now had strong confidence in the system and in ourselves.

In March 1982, the South Georgia crisis suddenly escalated and within a few days we faced a British decision to expel Argentine civilians by force. The Argentine Government decided, on 26th March, to recover the Malvinas/Falkland Islands, also by force. Then the war started. The 601 Commando Company was created (it hadn't existed previously) four days after the 2nd April landings. It was formed with fourteen officers (including the CO, Major Mario Castagnetto) and fifty NCOs.

I was assigned as a Platoon Leader. I was still a first lieutenant and expecting promotion in December 1982. I already had four years commando training experience, and was an instructor. I had been an Argentine Army Commando since December 1976, and also a Peruvian Commando since December 1978. The company was deployed to Puerto Argentino (Port Stanley) on 27th April and we immediately started operating. Search and destroy missions were the usual tasks in those early days.

After the first Vulcan raid, we continued operating in the same way – ambushes, patrols, observation posts – all to try and find infiltrated enemy patrols and neutralise them. Around the 6th or 7th May we were provided with the Blowpipe units belonging to the 10th Mechanised Infantry Brigade. The brigade had lost its aimers and was on the islands with Blowpipe missiles, but without the personnel trained to use them.

So 601 Commando Company with its three aimers, Captain Frecha, myself and Sergeant Martinez, was gifted with three Blowpipe units.

At the beginning, some high-ranking officers tried employing our Blowpipes to protect the helicopter assembly area beside Mount Kent, but this proved to be impossible with so few units. The company's plans were to deploy the Blowpipes on each mission, to protect our deployment and our few helicopters and, additionally, to have a mobile and unexpected anti-aircraft ambush capability against British helicopters and Harriers.

Our first Blowpipe-supported mission was in the San Carlos Settlement and Port San Carlos area, on 13th May. It was a search and destroy task employing the whole company, with an additional scouting objective, to prepare for the future deployment to that area of an infantry reinforced company on 16th May.

We stayed there until 16th May, having deployed by helicopter, but remained on the ground because the helicopters were told to return. We found nothing, in spite of good intelligence information. On 14th May the SAS raided Pebble Island and the next morning we were sent there by helicopter to search for any remaining British forces. We found only destroyed aircraft and enemy equipment, but no evidence of enemy personnel. Instead of British ground forces at Pebble, we encountered a pair of Harriers flying at low level, probably returning from a raid at Fox Bay. Sergeant Martinez fired the first Blowpipe of the war against an enemy aircraft, but without success.

On 19th May the 601 Company HQ, and First and Second platoons, including the Blowpipe unit, were ordered to go by air to Port Howard to carry out a scouting task north of the settlement. That day a dense fog almost prevented us crossing the San Carlos Sound, but still delayed our movement to Port Howard by twenty-four hours. We had to leapfrog in our helicopters several hundred metres, staying for hours in the middle of nowhere, until we located the area – when the fog allowed us – in the last daylight of 20th May. After briefly searching the area, our helicopters were ordered by Army Aviation HQ, Puerto Argentino (Port Stanley), to return to the capital.

Port Howard was, in those days, the defensive position of the 5th Infantry Regiment (battalion size). It had, in order to reinforce it, two Engineer Platoons from No 3 Engineer Company, a field medical team and a civil affairs team from the Brigade HQ, totalling over 850 men altogether. The islanders remained in the settlement, performing their normal tasks in the middle of a war that hadn't really affected the area up to that time.

On 21st May it was a lovely morning in the islands, sunny and rather windy. We expected the helicopters to continue the task over the area north of Port Howard. We knew that they would move after daylight from Puerto Argentino. We assumed they would reach the settlement between 0900 and 1000 hours in the morning.

During the previous night the guards had heard noises, including guns firing to the north. Nobody was sure if they had come from San Carlos or Pebble Island. Nobody knew that the landings in San Carlos had started.

The General paused at this point to reflect carefully on the events of 21st May, the day he personally fired the Blowpipe missile that successfully destroyed Flight Lieutenant Jeff Glover's Harrier aircraft. Later, he continued:

Early on 21st May, 601 Commando Company started to get ready to continue its search and destroy task to the north of Port Howard. We were waiting for our helicopters from Puerto Argentino, to move us. The Blowpipe team, three aimers and six providers, deployed close to the 5th Infantry Regiment Command Post and took up positions to protect the helicopter landing zones. It was about 0800 hours (local time) and first light.

At 0815 hours, we could hear the low noise of helicopter engines getting closer from San Carlos Sound. After a few minutes, it became clear that there was only one helicopter, and it was certainly not a Huey; nor did it sound like an Agusta or a Puma. The time that the unseen helicopter spent flying over the water before reaching our position was also an ominous sign.

Finally, it appeared flying through the narrow entrance to Port Howard Bay. The helicopter could clearly be seen. It was a Lynx, and, of course, not one of ours (Argentina had two Lynx helicopters with the Type 42 Destroyers, *Hercules* and *Santisima Trinidad*, but they were far from the area at that time). We gave the warning, and Captain Frecha ordered the team to open fire if the target came within range. The Lynx entered the narrows from San Carlos Sound at low altitude and then headed south. After about ten minutes it headed north again and left the area through the narrows. It was always outside our effective range (the narrows were four kilometres from our positions, and our effective range was three kilometres). It was good training for all of us; aiming at the target, sharing information and evaluating its movements and intentions. After that near encounter, 601 Company waited again for our helicopters. Meanwhile, the 5th Infantry Regiment CP (Control Post) radioed the news about the intruder.

At 0955 hours we felt that combat was shortly going to start. The noise of a jet aircraft was growing louder from the south. We ran again to our positions. We could see clearly, through the aiming lens, the unmistakeable shape of that black bird, a Harrier. It was approaching us at very low altitude – almost the same as our own – and rapidly growing in size. It was only seconds away. The order to fire was shouted again. I kept the Harrier in sight, waiting for it to come into range. As soon as the distance was right, I fired. Almost simultaneously, Captain Frecha did the same. Suddenly the aircraft abruptly changed direction and moved sharply, first to its right and then immediately to its left, resulting in both missiles failing to hit the target, exploding instead on the rocks close to the narrows. In spite of the failure due to the Harrier's extraordinary manoeuvrability, we were confident of our capabilities. Most importantly, we had fired calmly. It had been a good shot. The experience had been valuable, and the frustration (i.e. of not hitting the Harrier), was replaced by self-confidence and determination.

The Harrier continued crossing over Port Howard to the north and, after circling Mount Maria to the west, disappeared out of sight. Only sporadic small arms and machine gun fire followed its trajectory. The aircraft had not fired its 30mm Aden gun, and had not fired its rockets or discharged any bombs on us. Without seeing the Harrier, its sound could be heard going south and decreasing. We thought that the pilot had seen our missiles and had successfully manoeuvred to avoid contact. We recharged the missiles and were ready again.

The jet sound never quite disappeared, and started to increase again from the south. A second Harrier then approached. For three years, until we read about the incident from British sources, and discovered that Wing Commander Peter Squire had aborted his take-off from

Hermes, we had assumed there had been two Harriers. That second opportunity had to be well used by us, so I decided to hold my fire until the very last minute. At the shortest possible range, and with increased accuracy, the pilot would have less time to see the missile and avoid it again.

The Harrier started to fill the whole Blowpipe fire unit lens, then moved a little to its right. At that moment, I fired. After a short flying time of only a few seconds there was a big explosion, and black smoke around the target. The Harrier was, at that moment, approximately eight hundred metres from my position. After the explosion, I lowered the unit to look directly towards the aircraft, to see what had happened.

Small arms and machine gun fire had started all around us, following the smoking aircraft that ended its flight rolling upside-down and then exploding in a big yellow and red fireball, with dense black smoke, hitting the ground more than two kilometres from our position. The pilot and his orange and white parachute floated down and into the sea.

Everybody was exultant. Such success on the first day of combat was amazing. So far the 5th Infantry Regiment had not had any direct contact with British forces. However, 601 Company had been under naval gunfire, had been close to anti-aircraft fire, air combat and air bombardment, and Sergeant Martinez had also fired a Blowpipe missile. Not a great amount of experience, but we were beginning to feel like veterans already. I had fired my two missiles, and so had Captain Frecha. His second missile had failed, and hit the ground a hundred metres from his position, narrowly avoiding a house during its erratic flight.

The pilot might or might not be alive, or he could be injured. Either way, he had to be found and, of course, taken prisoner. I ordered my two officers, First Lieutenants Fernando Garcia Pinasco and Marcelo Anadon, to go and find him, and they started running immediately. Simultaneously, Medical Captain Pablo Llanos took one of our motorcycles and preceded us in the race. It was a long way and we all arrived exhausted.

We saw a small white wooden boat with two men on board about two hundred metres from the shore. They were struggling to lift the pilot from the icy waters. We were relieved to see that he was alive. We were happy to have shot down the aircraft, but we were even happier to know that the pilot had survived. The job of destroying an enemy Harrier had been done, but the pilot's life was a gift that made the action almost perfect for us.

The two young NCOs were finding it very difficult to raise the pilot from the water, because of the wet parachute, the rubber liferaft, and other equipment. Also, he had been injured by the ejection and his left arm was useless.

Meanwhile, we waited on the shore, recovering from the long run. The pilot had been in the water for a long time, but was finally lifted into the boat. It approached the beach and struck the rocks. Captain Llanos and an NCO jumped on board to help. With a knife, the two commandos punctured the liferaft that was an obstacle to attending the injured man on board. He had a bloody upper lip and pain in his left arm, but was ready to disembark. We went to the boat to help him, and a couple of metres of wading through the icy water were enough for us to appreciate what the pilot had suffered whilst he was in it. We saw him trying to erase the numbers written on his (right leg) briefing board, but not before we could copy them. Lieutenant Anadon gave his camera to a soldier who was beside us and we helped the pilot to reach the shore.

We told him; 'Don't worry, you are with friends!' We searched for a gun to avoid any dangerous reaction, but found nothing. Captain Llanos then started the motorcycle, and we helped the pilot to mount. He was freezing so I put my coat over his shoulders to warm him a little. Then the race began, with two of us running beside the motorcycle to help the pilot keep his balance, whilst moving across the rough ground until we reached the Aid Station (at the Social Club, Port Howard) a couple of kilometres away. We then helped the medics to undress the patient, searching very carefully for any useful information. We found his identification card, flight manual and the flight order.

After that, we returned to inform the others. We then learned about the landings at San Carlos. We didn't have any time to rest or eat because the area was being overflown by enemy and friendly aircraft. Two Harriers heading south passed very low, allowing us to see the pilots' heads, and attracting small arms fire. Some Mirages flew north, and one at least was shot down.

Major Castagnetto ordered me to take charge of Martinez's Blow-pipe, as we prepared to face a new incoming Harrier raid from the north, but I didn't have time to reach Martinez's position. The first Harrier was less than a kilometre away. I knelt on the ground, aimed and fired. Simultaneously, there was a loud explosion behind me. It was Martinez firing his Blowpipe, which exploded just beside the aircraft and close to the port wing tip, less than six hundred metres from us. He was successful, thanks to the proximity fuse, and the Harrier probably suffered light damage but, contrary to some rumours, it was not brought down.

At around that time, the Argentine Air Force was attacking HMS *Ardent* near Port Howard, and loud noises could be heard from San Carlos Sound. With all the pilot's equipment (parachute, liferaft and radio beacon), we tried to attract enemy aircraft or helicopters and to organise an ambush. I was once again in my role as a Blowpipe aimer, armed with Martinez's last missile. My platoon was deployed to the crash area with two Instalaza anti-tank rocket launchers, and a sniper protecting an approach from the north. The 5th Infantry Regiment remained in its original positions covering the west side.

At the end of the evening a Sea King appeared, repeating the Lynx movements to the south. Then, we assumed, it had received the beacon signal, because it headed north. Slowly and steadily it continued at low altitude towards the killing zone. It appeared to be a perfect target, increasing in size, at low speed, and with no chance of avoiding enemy contact.

The enormous Sea King entered within effective Blowpipe range. The plan was to allow it to reach the closest point to the 5th Infantry Regiment (the killing zone's centre), and then fire the missile. If it failed, the concentrated fire of all the machine guns and small arms should bring it down.

The helicopter was about a kilometre away from my position, and about five hundred metres from the nearest (southern) A Company/5th Infantry Regiment positions, when suddenly a burst of machine gun fire from those positions was heard. The Sea King manoeuvred abruptly to its right. I reacted and fired. The Blowpipe's noise even surprised me and my ears suffered the effect. The helicopter moved immediately towards the hills to escape the automatic fire. It looked

29

as if it would crash against the rocks, but the pilot succeeded in evading them and just flew over the crest of the hills. Meanwhile, my missile harmlessly struck the rocks. I shouldn't have fired. Having lost the initiative and being surprised by the unexpected and premature machine-gun fire, there was bound to be the risk of a bad shot. The anxiety to catch the target was paramount. I have hated that unknown gunner ever since.

Without any more Blowpipe missiles, we ended as an anti-aircraft ambush team – at least for a while. The feelings that day were a mixture of happiness, frustration, anxiety and determination. We had fought well and had succeeded in shooting down one Harrier aircraft.

We also had the flight order, with information about the mission, the force composition (two Harriers), pilots' names, the departure aircraft carrier (*Hermes*), and some British intelligence information with an appreciation of the area. All the information we collected was radioed to HQ.

It had been a hard day physically. Much adrenaline had flowed and much ammunition had been used. Many people had witnessed new sights, sensations and experiences. Real war had appeared with the power of a raging storm.

At the end of the day, we learned that the British forces had disembarked at San Carlos (but nothing yet about the force's size or deployment) and that contact with the Combat Team had been lost and nobody knew its situation. We also learned about the fate of HMS *Ardent* and that two Gazelles had been lost, in addition to 'our' Harrier. We knew also the high price our Air Force and Naval Air Corps had paid, having witnessed it ourselves.

With darkness approaching, I was ordered to go to the Aid Station to protect the RAF prisoner. Major Castagnetto was thinking not only that the British might attempt a rescue, but that perhaps a local civilian might try to help the pilot escape. I moved my platoon – after recovering my men from the far side of the unsuccessful ambush – to the Social Club. Jeff Glover was resting when we entered. After a while Captain Pablo Llanos joined us, and he and I visited him together. We exchanged only a few words because he was under the effect of analgesics to reduce the pain. We spent the night resting in another room, with guards outside the building.

The next day an air force Bell 212 helicopter on a search and rescue mission arrived. The crew requested guidance to locate some pilots who had ejected, and Lieutenant Fernando Garcia Pinasco was sent to help them. Meanwhile, Major Castagnetto ordered me to prepare the prisoner to fly with him and Captain Llanos to Puerto Argentino. After a short flight the Bell came back. Two Argentine pilots had been recovered. We escorted Jeff Glover from the Aid Station to the helicopter, and only then did I tell him that I had been the Blowpipe missile aimer, which Captain Llanos confirmed. Jeff expressed his congratulations and we shook hands. We helped him into the Bell helicopter and saluted him.

The Argentine pilot was anxious to get airborne as soon as possible owing to the red alerts and the usual shortage of fuel and so, without waiting for Major Castagnetto, the Bell departed without delay. The Major reached the helipad a few minutes later, and was a little upset that the helicopter had left, but there was no denying the air force's urgency. The San Carlos area was not a quiet place for an Argentine helicopter at that time.

After that, Captain Llanos escorted Jeff Glover to Puerto Argentino, with a one-night stopover at Goose Green on the way. Finally, Glover was sent to the mainland, and 601 Commando Company lost contact with its prisoner. We only learned after the war that he had been held in some place far away until he was finally released in Montevideo. Those of us who had had contact with Jeff had a great respect for him. He had done his best in a difficult situation, when he was shot down and after he was taken prisoner. He demonstrated integrity and professionalism. Captain Pablo Llanos told me later that Jeff had also offered his blood, if necessary, to a wounded Argentine soldier who was in a serious condition at the Aid Station. That gesture speaks for itself.

The men of 601 remained in Port Howard on 22nd May, but the next day helicopters were sent to pick us up, to return us to Puerto Argentino. The HQ needed commandos to gather information on the landing areas. As soon as our three SA 330 Pumas and the A109 Agusta crossed San Carlos Sound, they were attacked by Harriers, and all but one Puma were destroyed. The crews all survived, even though one helicopter had a fire on board.

Hugh Bicheno, who held a diplomatic appointment in the British Embassy, Buenos Aires prior to the Falklands War, recalled this particular episode. He said:

.... The Assault Sections of Commando 601 were... needed to scout the beachhead and an attempt to extricate them came to grief on 23rd May when two Pumas and a Hirundo gunship were destroyed by Harriers at Shag Cove. The surviving Puma recovered the First Assault Section the next day.

Sergio continued:

On 24th May, at 0400 hours local time, part of 601 Commando Company was moved in a single Puma to Puerto Argentino. I remained in Port Howard as the senior officer of a 601 detachment that included four officers and sixteen NCOs. We waited for a flight that never arrived.

The same day, as daylight appeared, I went to the 5th Infantry Regiment CP to co-ordinate operations. Suddenly, a single Harrier at low altitude attacked C Company positions, leaving four dead and five wounded, including soldiers and NCOs. We thought at the time that it might have been a revenge attack as Jeff Glover had been shot down in the same area.

The war continued and our small detachment performed all kinds of tasks including observation posts, pilot rescue (we already had experience of that, having recovered Lieutenant Perona, a Mirage III pilot, at Pebble Island) and combat operations.

On 8th June, one of my 4-man patrols had a close escape near Mount Rosalie, when HMS *Plymouth* was attacked by Mirages off San Carlos Waters. It had been providing a British party ashore which was circling my men, with supporting naval gunfire. On 10th June another 4-man patrol fought against SAS Captain John Hamilton and his signaller, 10km northeast of Port Howard. Captain Hamilton was killed and Roy Fonseka was taken prisoner. Curiously, both British POWs were captured at Port Howard, and both resulted from actions involving 601 Commando Company.

For us, it all ended on 15th June. We returned to mainland Argentina, as prisoners, on 19th June on board the Canberra. We went home on 20th June, and on the next day started to rebuild 601 Commando Company. We had no time to waste. Even today you can still see the same spirit within the unit.

Today, Sergio Fernandez is a Brigadier General (Retired) SF (Special Forces), having spent his final years in the army as the 2nd Corps Commander, and also head of the Parachute Regiment. He has discussed the war without any hesitation whenever further thoughts, comments or information were required. He has expressed his gratitude for being allowed to contribute and made it quite clear that he hopes there will never again be a war between our two countries. 'Only by being completely frank and withholding nothing,' he said, 'can we repay all those who so pointlessly lost their lives in 1982. War is not the answer, and never will be, to solving the differences between our two nations.' He deeply regrets the loss of life, and the injuries sustained by both Argentine and British forces. His absolute sincerity, when he described how pleased he was to learn that Jeff Glover had not perished as a result of his action in firing that Blowpipe missile, was genuinely moving.

A British Airman's Thoughts

It is interesting, many years later, to compare Sergio's account with Jeff Glover's recollections (see also Part Three, The Repatriation of Prisoners of War). Jeff recalled that when his aircraft was hit, and including the ejection, time had passed in a flash. There had been no time for thought and he had had no idea what had struck the aircraft. He thought there had been a third man in the boat, a civilian, when he was rescued from the water. This seems unlikely and Jeff would have been very confused at that point.

He had, in any case, blacked out during the ejection having been subjected to intense acceleration forces. He had 'come to' in the water, but found that because of his injuries he could not swim or help himself in any way. He discovered later that his injuries included a broken left arm, shoulder and collarbone, and severe bruising. He acknowledged that he owed his life to the prompt reaction of the Argentines who rescued him.

Jeff thought that Sergio Fernandez's (later) estimate that he had been in the water for 'thirty minutes or more' sounded improbable, given what we know of likely survival times in sea temperatures such as he experienced. He would also have been in shock, traumatised and apart from his serious injuries, was heavily burdened by the weight of his protective flying clothing, safety equipment and parachute.

He recalled that Captain Llanos had been involved in the rescue, but had not been in the boat. He also said that he had been well looked-after by the Argentine orderlies and Captain Llanos in the Social Club (that had been converted temporarily into a makeshift hospital). He had been the only British casualty there and 'some of the Argentine wounded had not seemed best pleased to see (him) getting good treatment as well'!

To this day, a mutual respect still persists between the two professionals; an Argentine general on the one hand, and a Royal Air Force flight lieutenant on the other. To a great extent, it is based upon the knowledge that the one, having successfully destroyed the aircraft, had no desire to see the pilot perish, whilst the other, having so nearly lost his life, nevertheless wanted to give his blood to save the life of an enemy soldier. Whatever the rhetoric of the politicians, nothing can take that away.

Britain Responds

The View from the Falkland Islands

An English navigator, John Davis, is usually credited with having been the man who in 1592 discovered the Falkland Islands. There were then various sightings by other passing navigators who declined to actually land on the islands, until John Strong finally did, a hundred years after John Davis passed by.

A little over 200 years ago, the British and the French both claimed the Falklands at the same time, each apparently unaware of the other's claim. This was further complicated by France then selling its claim to Spain. After a minor spat in 1770 between a small British force on the Falklands and a much stronger Spanish force offshore, the British surrendered and sailed for England.

Spain's occupation of the Islas Malvinas – as they called the Falklands – continued under a succession of Spanish governors, until the war on the South American mainland resulted in the British occupation of Buenos Aires in 1806. The then (Spanish) Governor of the Malvinas (which, for clarity, will be referred to only as the Falklands hereon), upon hearing of this turn of events, hurriedly abandoned the islands, and they became a peaceful, untroubled refuge for whalers and others for the next fourteen years. During this period, Spain maintained its claim to sovereignty.

From 1820 the United Provinces of Rio de la Plata – which preceded what we know today as Argentina – claimed the Falklands as part of the proceeds when Spain's empire in South America disintegrated, and installed a governor in 1828. The British returned to the Falklands in 1833 and have had a presence there ever since, losing control of the islands for just two months in 1982.

Since those days in the early nineteenth century, the United Provinces, and later Argentina, have never been in any doubt as to their entitlement to the ownership of the islands. The claim is partly based upon proximity, though this principle was conveniently ignored by Argentina when the case for the ownership of the island of Martin Garcia, in Rio de la Plata, was argued with Uruguay in 1973.

More importantly, their claim is also based upon the belief that when Spain – which had legitimately acquired the Falklands from the French – eventually abandoned South America, Argentina automatically gained the islands as part of the Spanish inheritance. It initially installed its own governors and did its best to administer the islands, until Britain returned in 1833.

Britain's strongest claim must surely be that the population of the islands, predominantly of British descent, wished (and still wishes) to remain British. Article 73 of the UN Charter recognises the rights of the population to self-determination under such circumstances. The Article says: 'Members of the UN which have or assume responsibilities for the administration of territories whose peoples have not yet attained a full measure of self-government recognise the principle that the interests of the inhabitants of those territories are paramount, and (in developing self-government)... take due account of the political aspirations of the peoples' etc.

The islanders have always felt very strongly about this principle. They were vehemently critical of the British Government when it vacillated over the future of the islands and dared to consider any long-term plan for the islands that was anything other than wholly British. Nicholas Ridley's highly controversial idea to transfer sovereignty to Argentina with a long-term leaseback to Britain, was not only savaged in the House of Commons in December 1980, but was received with equal lack of enthusiasm by the islanders.

Also in 1980, Rex Hunt was appointed Governor of the Falkland Islands and High Commissioner of the British Antarctic Territory. He was sent to the Falklands to win the confidence of the islanders at a time when rumours were rife that they had become deeply suspicious of the Foreign Office and its proposals for their future. Rex Hunt believed they were right to be suspicious, and that a deal might be cut that would not have been acceptable to them.

Back in the mid-1970s, the Foreign Office's Latin-American Department had seriously considered a policy that would have placed the Falkland Islanders in a position whereby they would have had little choice but to accept Argentine sovereignty 'voluntarily'. Such thoughts on Britain's part, albeit a few years earlier, might have encouraged Argentina to feel that the British Government might indeed be a soft touch and given rise to thoughts of aggression.

The local elections to the Falkland Islands Legislative Council in October 1981 reflected a further hardening of the islanders' attitudes against negotiations on the question of sovereignty. Meanwhile, a poll taken at around that time suggested that a majority of the British population thought the Falklands were somewhere off the north of Scotland. In contrast, every Argentine child is taught – from a very early age – that the islands belong to Argentina and knows exactly where they are.

HMS *Endurance*

The original *Endurance* was a three-masted barquentine built to take tourists on polar cruises to hunt polar bears. Financial problems resulted in the Danish owner selling her to Sir Ernest Shackleton, who named her *Endurance* and set off for the Antarctic in her on the 1914 Trans-Antarctic Expedition. She was within 200 miles of her destination, Vahsel Bay, on 15th January 1915 when the prevailing conditions made it impossible to continue. After drifting for months, trapped in the ice that took her remorselessly along in the Weddell Sea, the hull could no longer endure the pressure of the ice, and conceded defeat on 27th October 1915. The crushed hull finally sank on 21st November.

The HMS *Endurance* that was part of the Task Group in South Georgia in 1982 was an old Baltic Trader. She had been built in Denmark and launched in 1956. Purchased by the Royal Navy in 1967, she served as the British Antarctic ice patrol vessel until 1989, when she was finally decommissioned after striking an iceberg. She had been earmarked for decommissioning in 1982, but the Falklands War had intervened and she was reprieved to enjoy another seven years of active service.

There was more to *Endurance* than the name and role suggested in 1982. She was Britain's 'eyes and ears' in the South Atlantic. She may have been old and vulnerable, but she carried the electronics that enabled her to gather vital signals intelligence (SIGINT), and was manned accordingly. Spanish-speaking operators, working shifts, ensured that a continuous listening watch was maintained 24 hours a day to intercept Argentine communications. Information was passed to the Government Communications Headquarters (GCHQ) and then disseminated as appropriate.

Although she only had 2 × 20 mm Oerlikon guns (and did not carry chaff; originally called 'Window'), she did have 2 Wasp helicopters on board, which carried the AS12 missile. One of these missiles was used to great effect by Tony Ellerbeck, one of the ship's Wasp helicopter pilots, when it helped to disable the Argentine submarine, *Santa Fe*, on 25th April.

Following the MoD decision to decommission HMS *Endurance* – as part of the 1981 Defence Review – she paid some farewell visits early in 1982 to old haunts and friends in the Argentine Navy. In January, at Ushuaia far to the south in Tierra del Fuego, Captain Nick Barker and members of his crew noticed that the atmosphere was uncharacteristically frosty.

Later, *Endurance* called in at Mar del Plata, the Argentine Navy's submarine base. Julian Mitchell, the Naval Attaché (NA), recalled that it was a courtesy call en route back from Ushuaia. Another excuse for the visit had been the arrival there of the participants in the Whitbread Round the World Yacht Race. It had been a happy, relaxed occasion – expected to be the ship's last – and the Argentines had been friendly and welcoming, more so than at Ushuaia. Nevertheless, Nick Barker and members of his crew detected an unusual atmosphere there as well.

David McCallion, a Royal Marine on *Endurance*, said they were wined and dined exceptionally well at Mar del Plata. He said he could not help wondering after the war if some of the marines and recruits they had met during that visit had been amongst those they had fought, or killed, shortly afterwards.

Peter Leach, a Royal Marine sergeant-major on *Endurance*, said the visit to Mar del Plata had been of about three weeks duration. He said: 'Apart from the socialising, there had been plenty of contact with the Argentines and we even trained with them at times, visiting their marine camp. Some of the time was spent painting and working on the ship.'

Captain Nick Barker could not shake off his misgivings, however, and duly reported them to the British Embassy in Buenos Aires. As it happened, he was not a popular man with the Ambassador and other diplomats at the Embassy. His relationship with the Argentine secretary of the Ambassador's wife was considered to be inappropriate for a man of his rank – especially with regard to the sensitive nature of his particular command – and his behaviour in her company upset the Embassy staff and the Anglo-Argentine community generally. Many thought it highly unlikely that the Argentine Government would not have appreciated the value of her key position in the Embassy and used it to their advantage. The NA, at the Ambassador's behest, was obliged to inform his superiors of the potential security risk.

Nevertheless, the Ambassador's view of Nick Barker's misgivings –

which were reported to the Embassy following the latter's visits to Ushuaia and Mar del Plata – would not have been influenced by personal considerations. The Embassy's view generally was that he had over-reacted and that there was little cause for concern. His misgivings were not taken very seriously.

The Embassy's view also prevailed after the 19th March, the day that the Argentine navy transport, *Bahia Buen Suceso*, offloaded the scrap-metal merchant Davidoff and his men at Leith together with their naval 'escort'. The Ambassador's view was that patience and diplomacy were more likely to solve the problem.

Nick Barker, meanwhile, found that the Governor of the Falkland Islands, Rex Hunt, had more sympathy for his concerns. Previously, there had been some suggestion that these concerns might have been little more than part of his continuing effort to save his ship from being scrapped. Few would have denied, though, that withdrawing *Endurance* from service would have sent the wrong signals to the Argentine junta, and would have been interpreted as further evidence of the British Government's disinterest in the South Atlantic. As it turned out, Nick Barker's prayers seem to have been answered. When the British Government learned of the Argentine landing on South Georgia and the raising of their national flag – provocative actions that could not be ignored – HMS *Endurance* was quickly despatched to South Georgia with Lt Keith Mills and his party of Royal Marines on board.

The situation then appeared to cool for a few days; the Argentine flag was lowered and the size of the garrison reduced. A week later it worsened again as intelligence was received indicating that several Argentine warships were also now on the way to South Georgia.

Lord Carrington

Good, reliable intelligence on Argentina and its intentions was hard to come by before the war. At that time the threat that really mattered was that posed by the Warsaw Pact. Argentina had a low priority, and the number of desk officers assigned to the whole of Central and South America in the Foreign Office was minimal. The British service attachés in Buenos Aires also found it difficult to obtain reliable information, and what was reported in the Argentine press was only what the junta wanted the population to believe. Mrs Thatcher later said in her memoirs that there had been no intelligence to suggest an Argentine attack on the

Falklands '... until almost the last moment' and on 2nd April, around mid-day, the first indications were received in London that the Falklands had been invaded. Once the war was under way the situation improved; other ways were found to acquire the intelligence, and the USA also co-operated significantly with us in this area.

The Foreign Secretary, Lord Carrington, in the absence of any hard intelligence (e.g. naval movements) that might have confirmed an Argentine invasion was under way, or even imminent, had set off for Israel on 30th March 1982 on an official visit. His mission was to address a completely different matter. The Israelis were rather upset, he said, regarding the position taken by the British Government during ongoing negotiations with the Palestinian Liberation Organisation (PLO). We had apparently appeared hostile towards Israel's position and Lord Carrington felt he should visit Israel to 'straighten things out'.

Patrick (later Sir Patrick) Moberly was British Ambassador in Tel Aviv in 1982. Many years later he recalled:

> Usually British Foreign Secretaries received a rather abrasive welcome in Israel, and were given a bit of a hard time. This was because the British were perceived as being a bit soft on the Arabs. However, Lord Carrington – in his usual way – charmed them during his visit, following which relations temporarily improved. Importantly, Argentina was not discussed during the visit. It was not on the agenda. The talks were only about the PLO and Britain's position. I was present throughout all the discussions.

Sir Clive Whitmore, the Prime Minister's Principal Private Secretary – a position he had held since Mrs Thatcher took office in 1979 – said that earlier the same week they had been alerted to the possibility that 'things could go wrong' (i.e. regarding the Falklands). He had accompanied the Prime Minister and the Foreign Secretary to a United Nations Community Meeting in Brussels. On the return flight – only just before the latter set off again for Israel – there had been talk of developing trouble in the South Atlantic.

Nevertheless, it was felt safe for Lord Carrington to continue with his planned visit to Tel Aviv. Sir Clive recalled that he had advised the PM: '... to despatch a submarine to the South Atlantic. This would send a message to Argentina that they should not assume Britain would not respond if provoked.'

Although supposedly the submarine plan was secret, it was leaked (it had to be, to be effective) and the press picked it up. The Argentine Embassy would have taken note and transmitted the message to Argentina. As it happened, Argentina invaded the Falklands on 2nd April as Lord Carrington was flying back to the UK on his VC10 aircraft; unfortunate timing indeed for the Foreign Secretary.

Pat Tebby was one of the two ground engineers on board Lord Carrington's VC10 aircraft when he visited Brazil in July 1980 (see Part Four). He also happened to be on the aircraft that took Lord Carrington to Israel on 30th March 1982. He said: 'On the return flight on 2nd April, I well remember the Foreign Secretary learning – via the aircraft's HF radio – that Argentina had invaded the Falklands. He was not a happy man.'

Lord Carrington's subsequent noble request that he should be allowed to resign was most unwelcome within the government. Sir Clive commented: 'It had to be allowed since the situation we found ourselves in was as the result of a failure of foreign policy, not defence policy. It also reflected the fact that the government had not successfully grasped the Falklands issue over the years.'

Lord Carrington's resignation put John Nott in an invidious position. He felt that he too should resign, and accordingly wrote to the Prime Minister. However, she generously refused to accept it, saying that under no circumstances 'was this your responsibility'.

Facing the Invasion

During the last week of March 1982, the Argentine Navy staged a joint exercise with the Uruguayan Navy, the decision having been taken in principle by the junta on 26th March – and confirmed on 31st March – that an invasion of the Falklands would take place on 2nd April.

The exercise was designed as a smoke-screen to cover troop and ship movements. It had the desired effect of making Whitehall believe there was no immediate or serious intention of invading the Falklands. Then, GCHQ picked up a message from Admiral Anaya ordering two ships to withdraw from the exercise and head south to join a larger task force that was heading in the direction of the Falklands. London was alerted.

Meanwhile, the Argentine Ambassador in London, and members of his staff, were apparently being kept in the dark about the planned invasion. Perhaps there were fears in Buenos Aires that some might have become a bit pro-British in their thinking. The wife of Jeremy Thorp, Head of

Chancery in the British Embassy in Lima, Peru, was in London and due to have dinner with a senior Argentine diplomat when, at the last minute, he suddenly had to pull out, saying: 'Apparently we have some kind of crisis on our hands!' The Ambassador was away in Italy and not in the picture at all.

The world learned of the Argentine invasion of the Falkland Islands on 2nd April 1982. On 3rd April, the House of Commons was informed, during an emergency session, that Britain would send a task force to liberate the islands.

Gerald Cheek was the Director of Civil Aviation on the Falkland Islands. He was also a member of the Falkland Islands Defence Force (FIDF), from which he finally retired in 1996 with the rank of captain.

Recalling the events of 1st and 2nd April 1982, he said that the first he heard of an impending invasion was when Government House rang him at Stanley airport on the afternoon of the 1st April, requesting his presence at the Governor's office. When he arrived, the heads of the other government departments were already there. The Governor, Rex Hunt, informed everyone that he had received a signal from the Foreign Office in London advising him that an Argentine task force was at sea and that an invasion of the Falklands at dawn next day was likely. He had been told to 'make his dispositions accordingly.'

Everyone then discussed the actions they should take. Gerald agreed to block the runway at Stanley Airport to try and prevent any Argentine aircraft landing. Although this was done with a number of vehicles, the Argentines quickly cleared them off with their amphibious personnel carriers after they arrived the next morning. The Governor asked to have the Islander aircraft flown up to the racecourse so it could carry out a flight at first light the next morning, to see if any enemy ships were around. This was done, but the flight never took place as the Argentines landed before dawn. Decisions taken by the other departments included keeping the schools closed, keeping the hospital fully staffed in case of injuries to the defending troops (Royal Marines and FIDF) and keeping the radio station on-air throughout the night (it normally closed down at 2200 hours). The Governor said he would make a radio announcement advising everyone to stay indoors and not get involved in any fighting. He would also announce that all active members of the FIDF should report to the drill hall at 1930 hours that evening.

When they arrived at the drill hall, around thirty-five men altogether, the Commanding Officer outlined the tasks to be carried out. These included guarding important government facilities such as the radio transmitting station, the power station and the broadcasting studio. Gerald and a few others were instructed to guard the aircraft on the racecourse and, if any Argentine helicopters attempted to land, they were to shoot them down. Their weapons consisted of rifles and machine guns. The riflemen were issued with 100 rounds of ammunition, and the machine gunners with 500 rounds. They were instructed to report back to the headquarters at the drill hall every hour by telephone.

At about 0630 hours the next morning, they heard one or two bursts of gunfire, and what sounded like a grenade exploding in the vicinity of the Royal Marine's barracks. The barracks were empty as all the marines were deployed elsewhere. They realised that the Argentines had landed. A little later, an Argentine C130 Hercules aircraft landed at Stanley Airport. Prior to this, the CO had informed them that the Governor had said that members of the FIDF were not to confront the Argentine troops, but should surrender to them instead. At around 0830 hours, further bursts of gunfire were heard from the Government House area. This went on for about 40 minutes or so and then died down. They learned later that this was Royal Marines fighting the Argentines. Fortunately, no Royal Marines were killed or injured, although the Argentines later admitted that some of their troops had been killed.

At 0930 hours, a number of Argentine troops approached from the racecourse. Gerald and his colleagues surrendered to them and were marched back to the drill hall. On the way, they passed Government House where the Royal Marines were being held on the lawn; a sad sight indeed. Upon reaching the Drill Hall, they were told they could return to their homes and should then take off their uniforms as the defence force was now disbanded. Their weapons had been taken from them when they surrendered.

Recapture of South Georgia (Operation Paraquat)

Immediately after Keith Mills' surrender at Grytviken on 3rd April, planning was under way for recapturing South Georgia. On 7th April, Major Guy Sheridan RM was briefed by Lieutenant Colonel Nick Vaux RM that he had been selected to command the force of RMs that would carry out this task. It was confirmed later in the day by Major General Jeremy Moore and was subject only to approval being given by the War Cabinet.

For the War Cabinet, however, the issue of how Britain should respond to the situation in South Georgia was less straightforward. The recapture of the Falklands was the primary objective and some felt that it would probably be followed automatically by an Argentine surrender in South Georgia. Was the venture necessary at all? Was it, in any case, too risky? There would be a danger from submarines. In the end, the War Cabinet decided to proceed. Britain badly needed a success.

On 10th April, a Task Group, which included HMS *Antrim*, HMS *Plymouth* and the Royal Fleet Auxiliary (RFA) *Tidespring* (HMS *Brilliant* joined the group on 24th April) sailed south from Ascension Island under cover of darkness. It rendezvoused with HMS *Endurance* on 14th April and arrived off South Georgia at first light on 21st April, ready to land reconnaissance parties. Formed specifically for the task of recapturing South Georgia, the Task Group, under the command of Captain Brian Young on HMS *Antrim*, answered directly to Northwood rather than to Rear Admiral Woodward on his flagship HMS *Hermes*.

Unfortunately for all concerned, there was an early disaster. In adverse weather conditions, an unsuccessful SAS attempt to reconnoitre – prior to the Royal Marines assault on the island – resulted in the loss of two Wessex helicopters on the Fortuna Glacier. The British Antarctic Survey team had previously advised the SAS not to use their chosen landing site on the glacier.

Colonel John Peacock (retired) had been working in the MoD at the time. He said:

> I recall being approached to give advice about the choice of landing site in South Georgia. Someone had remembered that, back in the 1960s, I had spent four months down there with a combined services expedition. I felt that a landing on the Fortuna Glacier was quite possible, and said so. This view was relayed to those concerned. It accorded more with the SAS view that nothing is impossible if you are sufficiently determined.

A decade later, Guy Sheridan was approached by John Peacock (at a function they were both attending) who said: 'I have an apology to make to you. In 1982... I had no idea it was you in command of the land forces for the operation. Had I known, I would have told them (the SAS) to talk to you... as you had all the experience and advice that they would need.' Guy Sheridan had been critical of the SAS's 'press on' attitude on that occasion.

The loss of the two helicopters was unwelcome news for the War

Cabinet. Fortunately, there was better news to come. A third helicopter, a Wessex III from HMS *Antrim*, successfully found and recovered all those from the two crashed helicopters. Heavily over-loaded, the pilot took the Wessex, with everyone on board, back to HMS *Antrim*.

Three days later, the Wessex attacked and damaged the Argentine submarine *Santa Fe*. It was supported by other helicopters from *Brilliant*, *Plymouth* and *Endurance*. Unable to dive, the submarine limped back to King Edward Point (KEP). It was decided to take advantage of the confusion caused by this incident to put an assault force ashore without further delay, supported by naval gunfire. The engagement was successful and the Argentine force surrendered at KEP to Major Guy Sheridan. He recalled:

It was dark by the time I took the surrender at KEP on 25th April and I had neither the time nor the inclination to set up a posed photograph, with the challenges my force had to deal with that night and the next day. Removal of all weapons from their Argentine owners was a more important manifestation of surrender to me than a signature.

A home-produced surrender document was drafted on board HMS *Antrim*. The next day Guy Sheridan went ashore with it and obtained the all-important signatures of Capitan de Corbeta Luis Carlos Lagos, the overall Commander of Argentine Land Forces in South Georgia (i.e. including Alfredo Astiz and his force at Leith), and Capitan de Corbeta Horacio Bicain, the Commanding Officer of the *Santa Fe*. The document was then signed by Captain Brian Young and Guy Sheridan.

Vice Admiral Sir Anthony Dymock was a commander serving on HMS *Antrim* at the time. He recalled:

On 25th April, we went into Grytviken and, after planting enough 4.5 inch shells to make them want to surrender, the white flag was raised. The increased pressure had the desired effect. They were called (over the VHF R/T) to come out onto the jetty. At first they declined to do so, but then complied.

I was asked by Brian Young to draft and send the surrender signal, which went, in the first instance, to the Commander-in-Chief at Northwood. The wording: 'Be pleased to inform Her Majesty that the White Ensign flies alongside the Union Flag at Grytviken, South

Georgia. God Save The Queen' was regarded by Sandy Woodward as being rather pretentious, and he was a bit stuffy about it, but we knew that the Prime Minister had been upset by the loss of the two helicopters and needed some good news. The surrender signal was crafted accordingly. It was sent via SCOT (the Satellite Communications Terminal).

As the Prime Minister was informing the House of Commons that Argentine forces on South Georgia had surrendered, the military junta in Argentina was telling its people that Britain had achieved only an 'apparent initial victory' and '... our forces are continuing to fight... with an unbreakable spirit... ' etc. Unfortunately, in those early days many Argentines still believed what they were being told. They grew wiser later on.

Meanwhile, HMS *Plymouth* and HMS *Endurance* had been detached to secure Leith, where other Argentine forces were located under the command of Alfredo Astiz.

Astiz's time in South Georgia proved to be another inglorious chapter in his chequered career. He surrendered his detachment in Leith – to Brian Young's RN Task Group – without much of a fight, on 26th April which (Admiral Anaya said when he faced a military tribunal some years later) had surprised even his own superior officers; but not before Astiz had tried, with the aid of a white flag, to lure British troops over mines he had laid. Astiz was not a man to play by the rules and controversy followed him everywhere. His surrender in South Georgia was no exception.

Notwithstanding the Argentine surrender at KEP which had included all Argentine forces on South Georgia, a second surrender-signing ceremony involving Alfredo Astiz took place on board HMS *Plymouth*. Captain David Pentreath said:

Astiz was brought on board and taken to the ward room where he was invited to sit down. The ceremony, witnessed also by the captain of *Endurance*, did not take long and Astiz was on board for only about ten minutes. A 'home-grown' document had been prepared for him to sign. Specially-prepared surrender documents are not the sort of thing that RN ships routinely carry.

A version had also been prepared in Spanish – *Endurance* carried an interpreter who spoke Spanish – and Astiz was asked to sign it. He studied it and added: 'Due to the superior forces of the enemy, I surrender myself to the invading British Forces.'

He was told to delete the word 'invading', which he did. After the brief ceremony, during which David Pentreath was able to photograph the moment of signing, he was flown to *Endurance* where, it had been decided, an attempt would be made to try and gain some useful intelligence from him.

The photograph was duly despatched to Rosyth, ostensibly for use by the editor of the dockyard newspaper. 'However,' David Pentreath said later, 'he chose to send it by wire to Naval Public Relations who promptly sent it round the world.' There seems little doubt that Brian Young and Guy Sheridan, through no fault of their own, missed a trick by not being able to capture the important moment of surrender at KEP on film.

Tony Ellerbeck was the Flight Commander of the Wasp Helicopter Flight on *Endurance*. He had questioned Horacio Bicain, captain of the Argentine submarine, *Santa Fe*, only the previous day, when he had placed a special emphasis on trying to establish which route the submarine had taken down to South Georgia. He was therefore asked to carry out a tactical questioning session with Astiz, as an 'interrogation' as such was forbidden. He said:

I talked to Astiz for about an hour in my cabin. We were alone but a marine was standing outside, readily available if necessary. I had a tape recorder running all the time too, just in case.

Astiz seemed fairly relaxed. He thought his government was likely to fall, and became angry at the suggestion that Argentina might lose the war. His main concern was that communists might move in. He was arrogant, self-assured, and spoke good English. He mentioned his time in South Africa with Rear Admiral Chamorro and, briefly, ESMA as well but only to describe it as an engineering school (Tony said later that he had known nothing then about Astiz's previous history). After the discussion he was flown to HMS *Antrim*.

On 2nd May, HMS *Antrim* and *Tidespring* left South Georgia and headed north to Ascension Island. *Tidespring* carried 151 Argentine POWs, 39 Argentine civilians – including the scrap-metal workers – 2 members of the British Antarctic Survey Team and 2 female ornithologists. HMS

Antrim carried Astiz, who was kept under guard in Brian Young's day cabin, and a few POWs.

When they were approximately 240 miles south of Ascension Island, a Red Cross team, headed by Andre Tschiffel, was flown down by Chinook helicopter to the approaching ships, to inspect the conditions under which the prisoners were being held. They reported favourably.

Roger Warden was the Commanding Officer of No 845 Naval Air Squadron – flying Wessex helicopters – and was based at Ascension Island. He recalled:

> The task was then to transfer 190 Argentine POWs from *Tidespring* to a chartered Dutch Martinair DC9 aircraft on Ascension Island. This was achieved flying numerous sorties in 2 Wessex 5s and a Sea King Mk 3 helicopter. I remember one young Argentine POW telling me that he was supposed to be going up to Oxford University in October. He was concerned to know if I thought the University would still take him. They were all successfully transferred to the island. Astiz was held initially on *Antrim*, before being transferred to HMS *Antelope*.

On the island, the POWs were taken to a building for interrogation in a coach with blacked-out windows (all of this took place at night for security reasons). Group Captain Jeremy Price, the Senior RAF Officer, said: 'It was essential that none of the POWs should be allowed to see what was on Ascension Island. I also lined up every vehicle I could muster, with lights blazing at them, as an added precaution. The prisoners were then interviewed by members of the International Red Cross Team before boarding the waiting DC9 aircraft to return to Argentina.'

Astiz was brought ashore separately by Wessex helicopter. He was kept apart from his compatriots and was only on the island for a couple of hours. During this time a telephone call was received from London (the Prime Minister was believed to have been present when the call was made), explicitly ordering that Astiz was *not* to be returned to Argentina with his compatriots, but returned to the UK instead. This was duly explained to the senior Argentine Officer, Horacio Bicain, before he left for Argentina.

Roger Warden recalled being the pilot of the Wessex helicopter that then took Astiz back from the island to the waiting ship. He said: 'Astiz sat with an armed Royal Marine guard standing above and behind him;

one who had fresh memories of having been a prisoner of his only a few days before. Astiz looked distinctly uneasy during that brief flight!'

While Astiz was being held off Ascension Island, he was apparently not an easy prisoner. The French authorities wished to get their hands on him, to question him about the disappearance and deaths of two French nuns (for which a French court later convicted him and gave him a life sentence, in absentia, in 1990). The Swedish Government also wanted to talk to him about a young Swedish woman who had disappeared, and was believed to have been amongst those thrown to their deaths from an aircraft over the Atlantic.

During these negotiations, the Foreign Office was obliged to keep Astiz, and he was returned to Britain on the *British Avon*, pending a decision on his future. The government was in something of a predicament. Not only was Britain not formally at war when Astiz was captured, but his alleged offences had been committed in Argentina, and not against British subjects.

Argentina also reminded Britain that British POWs in Argentina had been well treated, and that the treatment of any others captured could be influenced by the way Astiz was handled (Flight Lieutenant Jeff Glover was captured later, on 21st May, and three British journalists held by the Argentine authorities also became pawns in the game to get Astiz released).

The French and Swedish Governments were therefore irritated to learn of the British Government's decision to repatriate Astiz, and they were never given the opportunity to question him. He was held for a while in Colchester Military Prison and finally returned to Argentina on 14th July.

Ascension Island

A high priority for the British Government had been to identify – and confirm the availability of – a staging point to provide the means by which Britain's armed forces could respond to the Argentine invasion. A small number of possibilities were briefly considered – including Chile and Brazil – but our Ambassadors in these countries were quick to point out that support for Britain would not be forthcoming for such a venture. Ascension Island was soon identified as being the suitable and logical solution to the problem; however, its availability had to be confirmed.

The small volcanic island was discovered by a Portuguese sailor in 1501, but remained uninhabited until 1815, when a British force claimed it for King George III and established a small garrison of Royal Marines on it. A century later it became a Dependency of St Helena with a small Administration appointed by Britain.

The airfield was developed during the Second World War, and used as a staging point by American troops en route to Africa and the Middle East theatre. The USA also based aircraft on the island during the war (from 1942), from which German ships, including submarines, were attacked.

In 1982, the island hosted a NASA tracking station, BBC, and, Cable and Wireless relay stations, and the airfield that was maintained and operated by a handful of Pan American Airways staff. It is conveniently located approximately halfway between the UK and the Falkland Islands and about 1,000 miles from the African coast. The population of Ascension Island at that time was approximately 1,000, including St Helenians, British families, and Americans who were mostly unaccompanied. Throughout the brief war they were all loyal and supportive, and played no part. Sir John Nott said later:

> Although the island belonged to Britain, we had entered into an agreement with the State Department which effectively placed the airfield totally under American control. If we were to be able to send our Task Force down to the South Atlantic, and then be able to support it, we had to have unrestricted use of the airfield. When the first ships of the Task Force left Britain, we were still not absolutely certain that the Americans would be co-operative.

Fortuitously, the MoD and the Pentagon already enjoyed a sound, close relationship, and US Defence Secretary Casper Weinberger was thoroughly co-operative throughout the war. The Argentine Government at one point asked the US Government: 'Why are you letting the British use Ascension Island?' They were told that it was a British island that the USA had been granted permission to use.

Casper Weinberger once expressed the view that the Argentine junta probably looked at the map and concluded that any British response (i.e. to an Argentine invasion) would be impossible in view of the distance involved. What many Americans admired so much about Prime Minister Margaret Thatcher was that she simply ignored the map, and the possibility of defeat did not seem to occur to her. Mr Weinberger probably did not know that on 14th May 1982 – at the Scottish Tory Conference – the Prime Minister said: 'It is exciting to have a real crisis on your hands when you have spent half your political life dealing with humdrum issues like the environment!' He would have liked that.

Cecilia James was a teacher at the school on the island. Her pupils were mainly St Helenian children, some British children and one American child. She recalled that prior to Easter Monday there had been no hint of what was to come. She said: 'A number of us were enjoying a beach party on Easter Monday at English Bay when a truck suddenly arrived. An official spoke privately to Don Coffey, the Base Manager. He rushed off in a hurry, and nothing was the same thereafter!'

She had been one of only three single females accommodated in a 'singles' accommodation block in Georgetown. When the forces arrived *en masse*, there was suddenly a desperate need for accommodation, especially for Royal Navy personnel. All the spare rooms were quickly filled; mainly by officers.

The Americans flew in flat-pack accommodation – otherwise known as Concertina City – which was quick and easy to construct. There was tented accommodation for the others. For the duration of the war, the island's residents had to keep away from the base; no one was allowed to make or receive telephone calls to or from the UK.

Initially, Group Captain Michael Tinley, a maritime airman, was sent to Ascension Island as the Senior RAF Officer to help get things set up. He recalled that during those early days, everyone who worked behind a desk in the UK suddenly thought of a reason why a visit to Ascension Island was necessary. There simply was not the accommodation, so he did his best to put a stop to it. One day the Chaplain-in-Chief turned up on an aircraft and was put straight back on it.

Michael Tinley's other main concern was support for the Nimrod, a complicated aircraft and difficult to keep serviceable. It also required highly-specialised ground crew to keep it in the air. One day, Captain Bob McQueen – the Commander, British Forces Support Unit (CBFSU) – without consulting him, cancelled a telex requesting additional technical support. 'It was quickly sorted out,' he said, 'and after that there were few differences of opinion.'

As more and more aircraft flew in, the parking problem became more acute. At times, gaps of only eighteen inches between wing tips or helicopter blades had to be accepted. Great care was necessary when it came to moving or taxiing aircraft. At one point during the war, the airfield – known as Wideawake Airfield – briefly became the busiest in the world.

Bob McQueen had responsibility for the efficient operation of all the facilities, and also for security. There was no neat, straightforward chain of command. The services were all thrown together and had to make it work; for most of the time it was not a problem. He said: 'Admiral Fieldhouse initially wanted me to act as a sort of military governor, but I persuaded him that that would not be necessary. The population of the island would have been uneasy about it, and would have felt it was rather a heavy approach.'

He was concerned about the security of the island, and discussed this with Lt Col Bill Brydon, the Senior US Officer, and Group Captain Jeremy Price (who took over from Michael Tinley). Although he felt that any Argentine action against Ascension Island was unlikely – as it could have been perceived as being anti-USA, which could have upped the stakes considerably – he obviously could not take any chances. The possibility of Argentine Special Forces being either parachuted in, dropped offshore with inflatable rafts, or despatched from a submarine, were all considered.

A plan was put together which involved regular searches of the island by helicopter, searches of the wooded area by marines, dispersing ships offshore at night, and other measures. The anchorages closer to the island were cleared completely. As the number of men, aircraft and equipment on the island increased, so it became an increasingly attractive target. Jeremy Price added:

An RAF Regiment Wing arrived on 6th May for ground defence duties. There was some concern that Argentina might try and drop a bomb of sorts, possibly even from a C130 aircraft. It wouldn't have needed a very big bomb to cause considerable chaos, given the concentration of effort on the ground.

A mobile air defence radar was installed on Green Mountain and started operating on 9th May. Three GR3 Harriers were brought in to counter any possible threat. They were later replaced by four F4 Phantom aircraft.

Another fear expressed was that there might be a 'Cockleshell Hero' type of assault. We knew that Argentina had been working with the Italians to develop a mini-submarine. The water or aircraft fuel supplies, or the aircraft themselves, would have made tempting targets. A Nimrod aircraft was used from time to time to patrol the area around the island.

I saw my role as being largely supportive. Whilst I worked with Bob McQueen on general island matters, I acted quite independently in respect of air-related matters. I dealt directly with Northwood, negotiating what could be handled, or achieved, on any given day. The frequency and scale of operations required by Northwood always had to take island constraints into consideration.

Roger Warden's squadron of twenty-six Wessex helicopters was spread between Ascension Island, the Falklands, South Georgia, and even, at one point, the *Atlantic Conveyor*. He said:

We took the possibility of an Argentine attack of some sort very seriously, however improbable it might have seemed. In addition to the Nimrod searches, Wessex helicopters flew round the island looking for Argentine Special Forces.

We had a delicate balance to strike as well. Obviously some of the islanders had worked out that an attack was a possibility, even if they weren't unduly concerned about it. Surveillance was therefore kept intentionally low-key to avoid causing any panic, but at a level that ensured the job was done effectively.

A couple of times, Argentine merchant ships were spotted in the area, but they passed harmlessly on their way. A Soviet intelligence-gathering vessel also appeared and remained not far from Ascension Island for the duration of the war. There were no instances, however, of any disruptive activity on the part of the Argentines throughout the war.

The need for huge quantities of aviation fuel was evident from the start, and was one of the biggest headaches during the early days of operation. Pan Am had some bowsers (fuel tankers), but not nearly enough. Heavy Lift Aviation brought out some more in Belfast and Antanov aircraft. US tankers tied up to a buoy approximately half a mile offshore, and the aviation fuel was piped ashore via a flexible hose to the onshore bulk fuel installation. Tankers were busy most of the time. It was only aviation fuel because the RN ships refuelled from Royal Fleet Auxiliaries (RFAs).

Another potential problem that Jeremy Price mentioned – but thankfully the RAF's good fortune held out – concerned the use of the single runway by multi-aircraft formations. There was only one access to the runway 14 end from the aircraft parking area. If use of runway 32 had

53

been necessary to launch large formations, it would have presented an almost impossible situation, with many aircraft having to backtrack down the runway itself. Amazingly, the wind direction favoured the use of runway 14 throughout the war. That was particularly fortunate for the Vulcan Black Buck missions when they took off, accompanied by a large number of supporting Victor tanker aircraft.

It was generally understood that US Lt Col Bill Brydon had the job of reporting what he saw, and what caused him any concern, back to the Pentagon. On the whole though he left Bob McQueen and Jeremy Price to their own devices. It was his understanding, however, that Ascension Island would be used only for missions of a supportive nature, and not for launching missions of a directly offensive nature. When he learned of the nature of the Vulcan Black Buck missions, he reported this back to the Pentagon. This is discussed further in Part Four, A Vulcan Arrives.

Ascension Island not only provided the means by which Britain was able to support operations in the South Atlantic throughout the Falklands War, but it was developed further after the war to support Britain's continued presence in the Falklands by means of the 'airbridge'.

The Supporting Organisation and Chain of Command

Whilst confirmation of the availability of Ascension Island was being addressed, the organisation necessary to direct the war was swiftly being put in place.

John Nott felt there was no meaningful role for a Defence Secretary during the war as it was effectively transferred to the Prime Minister for the duration. At the same time, Chief of Defence Staff (CDS) Admiral Sir Terence Lewin wanted a short and effective chain of command. This was established, direct from the War Cabinet, through him, to the Task Force Commander, Admiral Sir John Fieldhouse at Northwood, from where the war would be directed. Each day, CDS consulted with the heads of the three services – his colleagues on the Chiefs of Staff (COS) Committee – and, on the basis of their daily inputs, decided what should be presented to the War Cabinet.

Captain Peter (later Admiral Sir Peter) Abbott RN and Group Captain (later Air Commodore) Joe Hardstaff together manned CDS's office round the clock. Sir Peter said: 'Joe and I rotated each day, one preparing the daily briefing that CDS would give at the Cabinet Office and the other accompanying CDS to assist as necessary.' Joe Hardstaff recalled:

I was always very impressed by the Prime Minister's decisiveness, but less impressed by one or two of the others (whom he declined to name). On one particular day the briefing was given, unusually, in the MoD and specifically covered the landing at San Carlos. Once the plan was approved and the decision taken, the Prime Minister had no doubts or second thoughts. She had complete confidence in the Armed Forces to carry out the plan. The briefings were normally held daily at around 0930 hours, and afterwards CDS would then brief the individual Chiefs of Staff, who would communicate as necessary with Northwood.

At the weekends, when the Prime Minister was based at Chequers, she would often attend the evening briefings for the Commander-in-Chief at Northwood. What impressed everyone present was her enormous enthusiasm and support for what everyone was doing, and also the care she took not to interfere with the military decisions being taken, although Sir John Fieldhouse always carefully explained the rationale for the decisions he took.

Sir Bernard Ingham, the Prime Minister's Press Secretary, said he did not attend the War Cabinet meetings, but 'during the war there was, inevitably, an almost total concentration on it, and therefore much other government business was not attended to at all. There was an enormous backlog of business at the end of the war.' He added that the Prime Minister had an excellent relationship with all the Service Chiefs, and 'Cecil Parkinson was present at War Cabinet meetings as a peace-maker who could always be relied upon to support the Prime Minister's point of view.'

Amongst the many diverse, but nevertheless associated, subjects that had to be discussed was the question of arms sales to South America. Sales prospects always had to be carefully considered and a view taken on whether British arms might find their way to Argentina. A balance had to be struck between not wanting to renege on contracts, and taking any action that might prove to be against Britain's interests. The normal solution was to employ a mix of vacillation and indecision. In the case of the potential sale of torpedoes to Brazil, talks were suspended completely until after the war.

At the MoD, the Chiefs of Staff met regularly and were supported by a large secretariat (COSSEC). There were two levels of meetings: the full Chiefs' Meetings, which occurred approximately ninety times during the war (normally once a week in peacetime), and the Chiefs of Staff

Informal (COSI) Meetings, if matters of a much more sensitive nature had to be discussed. Whilst the full Chiefs' Meetings were attended by CDS, the heads of the three services and supporting teams – totalling about thirty individuals – the COSI Meetings were limited to the four chiefs and one or two others only. Occasionally a meeting would be attended by the Prime Minister or Defence Secretary John Nott. 'As security was paramount, some of the most sensitive issues (e.g. the Vulcan Black Buck missions) were not even raised at the full Chiefs' Meetings. There were too many eyes and ears present,' said Marcus Wills, who attended as one of the Assistant Secretaries (ASEC3).

The chain of command continued down from Northwood to Ascension Island, and thence to Rear Admiral Woodward, Commander of the Carrier Battle Group, and the Royal Marines' Major General Moore on the battlefield. Decisions affecting the Royal Air Force were communicated through Admiral Fieldhouse's Air Deputy, Air Marshal Sir John Curtiss. The Air Marshal said: 'I became a completely independent Air Commander alongside the Admiral, and had total control of all our air assets. The MoD, however, retained logistical control, so getting things quickly was sometimes a problem, and was outside my control.' The Admiral and the Air Marshal had an excellent working relationship, which became a close friendship as well; an ideal situation. 'The Air Marshal,' a member of his staff said, 'didn't ask; he said what he wanted and that's what would happen. Everyone was always very clear, therefore, as to his requirements.'

Northwood had instant secure telephone communication with Ascension Island. ASMA (Airspace Management Aid) was also an essential part of the communications and briefing set-up. It was used for post-flight debriefs, and for relaying tasking instructions from Northwood direct to the Ascension Island Operations Room.

Other headquarters and formations acted in supportive roles including, in the RAF's case, Headquarters Strike Command (HQSTC). Regular daily briefings, and intense pressure from above, were the order of the day. Andrew Roberts was Group Captain Operations at HQSTC. He said:

We operated strictly in a supporting role, supplying the aircraft, weapons systems, etc, to all the air elements, and also arranging the air-dropping of other items of logistic support to the Task Force. We were involved in the preparation of the Black Buck (Vulcan) missions, co-operated closely with Boscombe Down in order to get vital aircraft modifications carried out in short order, and sent

Harrier aircraft out to theatre to replace losses. We sent someone daily to attend the Northwood briefings. Long shifts were spent mainly in front of a computer and we had the facility latterly to maintain an open computer line to Stanley. Until satellite communications were established, we kept in voice contact using single sideband (SSB) radio.

Tony Andrews, Command Mechanical Engineer at HQSTC, recalled that there was continuous, intense pressure from above to get things done immediately, especially where the Vulcan effort was concerned. He said: 'British firms such as British Aerospace responded magnificently and there was never any talk of money or bills. There was a complete understanding that it would all be sorted out later.'

Reaction in Belize

The Argentine invasion was to cause concern in many countries – not just those in South America – and for a variety of different reasons. One of the more unlikely places where the news was greeted with consternation, and some rapid thinking, was Belize.

An RAF Flight equipped with six Harrier aircraft was based in Belize at the time. When it was learned that a Task Force would be heading south, and would include two carriers and RAF Harriers, it became clear that the developing situation could affect the Belize Flight in either of two ways.

If the RAF should lose any Harriers in the South Atlantic, replacement aircraft might be summoned from Belize. Just in case, therefore, the crews considered this possibility and aircraft were prepared accordingly (e.g. by fitting ferry [fuel] tanks to some aircraft).

The other concern was that Argentina, thinking ahead, might conclude that replacement aircraft could be flown down from Belize, and decide to carry out some act of sabotage against the aircraft in case they were called upon. In fact, this may have occurred as one of the pilots on the Flight at that time confirmed many years later that a couple of Argentine 'agents', almost certainly intent upon committing such an act, were apprehended (probably by British Special Forces) as they crossed the Guatemalan border.

The point, not lost on many at the time, was that Argentina and Guatemala shared a common enemy, Britain, which was equipped with the Harrier.

Argentina's Allies

A nation does not go to war without first being quite clear who it is going to fight, and why. That is a statement of the obvious. It is sometimes less clear, however, but important to know nevertheless, which nations would prefer your enemy to succeed, especially those likely to render assistance. There are a variety of reasons why another nation might become involved – whilst perhaps having no desire to take up arms themselves – ranging from a feeling of outright hostility to nursing a grudge, or being, quite simply, driven by the prospect of commercial gain.

A few countries – other than those in South America that offered, or gave, moral or material support to Argentina (discussed in Part Five) – fell into one or other of these categories. They included Libya, South Africa and Israel.

Early on in the war, there were also fears that the Soviet Union and Cuba might try to interest Argentina in buying arms from them. There were strong rumours that Argentina had had talks with both countries.

The Soviet Union, in an unlikely scenario, was going through a phase of improved relations with Argentina, due in part to the withdrawal of the USA from the 1980 Moscow Olympics. The US boycott announced by President Jimmy Carter on 21st March 1980 was one of a number of measures taken by the USA as a protest against Soviet aggression in Afghanistan. It also instituted a commercial embargo on certain exports to the Soviet Union. This, in turn, led to Argentina supplying more grain to the Soviet Union to make up the shortfall from the USA for a period that embraced 1980–82.

Cuba was reported as having offered to supply Argentina with Russian-built aircraft, complete with Cuban pilots to fly them. However, little more was heard on the subject of arms sales, or any other kind of offer, from either the Soviet Union or Cuba.

The British Government obviously could not afford to ignore these rumours. It took the view, however, that a right-wing military junta such as Argentina's would be reluctant to become involved with, or beholden to, a communist regime. It countered therefore by emphasising that its strategy was simply to remove the Argentine troops from the Falklands with minimum loss of life, and that it had no desire to humiliate Argentina in any way.

Libya became involved when it was asked by Captain Carlos Corti (an Argentine naval officer who ran an office in Paris specifically for the purpose of acquiring Exocet missiles) if it would act on Argentina's behalf to try and persuade Iraq to sell some of its Exocet missiles. The Iraqis were not interested, but Libya, recognising an opportunity, offered to supply arms to Argentina instead.

Several flights, carrying a range of weapons, were planned but in the end only two took place. They routed via Recife in Brazil, and are discussed in more detail in Part Four ('Carlos'). Clearance was given for the flights to transit Moroccan airspace, which upset the British Government at the time.

France

Another country that certainly gave a measure of support to Argentina, but in many other ways and at the highest levels was strongly supportive of Britain, was France. Unfortunately, the message did not percolate down to everyone who should have been aware of the President's position.

Allegedly, one of the first overseas telephone calls of support that Prime Minister Margaret Thatcher received after the Argentine invasion came from President Mitterrand. The President was a well-read, cultured socialist, and he had no desire to see right-wing South American dictators succeed in such land-grabbing adventures. He therefore declared his support for Britain and imposed an immediate embargo on the sale or supply of arms to Argentina, including all forms of technical support and expertise. An Aerospatiale team, all set to travel to Argentina to 'marry' the electronics of the Super Etendard aircraft and Exocet missile systems, was prevented from leaving France.

Much has been made of the fact that a French team was in Argentina and remained there throughout the war, and this did happen. This team had been in the country since November 1981 and was never recalled to France. It assisted Argentina's technicians in carrying out some of the essential compatibility work on the aircraft. It was located for much of the time at the Río Grande air base and would not, in all probability, have lived to see another day if Operation Mikado had not been cancelled (see 'Operation Mikado – the Royal Air Force Prepares'). It is equally likely that President Mitterrand was never made aware of their presence in Argentina. Later, when asked why they had remained in Argentina, the leader of the nine-man Marcel Dassault team admitted that they had stayed in Argentina 'because they had never received orders to leave'.

Although it may be of little comfort to some, the perceived wisdom is that the French team's allegiance was first and foremost, if not entirely, to their weapon system, and to ensuring that their product worked satisfactorily, rather than to Argentina's cause. Having said that, perhaps we could have done without the comment made by a certain senior Marcel Dassault official on learning of the successful attack on HMS *Sheffield*. He was reported as having said: 'This is a wonderful victory for French electronic know-how.' Depending on your point of view, it probably was.

Peter Rowe was in Argentina just prior to the war, working for Racal on a contract. He said: 'My team and I were aware of the presence of the French team. On our return to the UK we were approached by the Foreign Office for information about the situation in Argentina. The debrief included a discussion of what we knew of the French team, so London was aware of its presence quite early on.' This feedback from British technicians, and others returning from Argentina after the outbreak of hostilities, contributed greatly to our understanding of the situation and mood in Argentina, and of what was actually going on during those early days.

Little was known at the beginning of the war about Argentina's military hardware, capabilities, likely tactics or training methods. In short order, efforts were made to acquire this information from those nations who had supplied and trained Argentina's military personnel.

The Chief of the Defence Staff wrote to his opposite numbers in France and the USA, seeking information. Willie Rae (later Air Vice-Marshal) was one of CDS's personal briefing officers in 1982. He recalled that one of his first tasks at the outset of the war was to draft a personal letter from CDS to the French CDS who, Willie Rae said, was 'immensely helpful'.

Prime Minister Thatcher also maintained an excellent personal relationship with France's President Mitterrand. He was co-operative throughout, when other allies hesitated or applied considerable pressures on the British Government. His decision to freeze the contract with Argentina, for the balance of the Super Etendard aircraft and Exocet missiles, was taken immediately and without hesitation. This caused immediate concern to those Argentines who had already appreciated what a formidable weapon system they were buying, and particularly to those who had favoured delaying the invasion of the Falklands until after all the aircraft and missiles had been delivered. One effect of the freezing of the contract was that one of the five aircraft that had already been delivered had to be 'cannibalised' to provide spare parts for the others. Only four aircraft were therefore available to fly missions against the Task Force.

The Argentine naval pilots had already been to France, and had carried out a basic conversion to the aircraft type. From November 1981, and as the aircraft were delivered by the French, the pilots returned to Argentina. They did little more flying during the next four months. Then, Squadron Commander Jorge Colombo suddenly received orders to get his aircraft and pilots operational as quickly as possible. This required them to be totally familiar with both aircraft and missile systems. It was a tall order, and greatly to the pilots' credit that it was achieved (albeit with a little French assistance).

Sir Clive Whitmore, the Prime Minister's Principal Private Secretary (PPS), said: 'At the highest levels, the French had a genuine desire to co-operate, although we had our suspicions that this feeling was not shared by everyone, especially at the lower levels.'

Bernard Ingham, the Prime Minister's Press Secretary, said: 'President Mitterrand was utterly sincere in his desire to be helpful. He would have assumed that Aerospatiale would have withdrawn any other technicians that might have been in Argentina, but was probably never informed they were down there.'

Sir John Nott recalled:

The War Cabinet had its suspicions that, in spite of assurances from the French – and President Mitterrand in particular – some French technicians had remained in Argentina throughout the conflict, and were almost certainly at Río Grande where the Super Etendards were based. We took the view that they were just concerned to see that their product performed well, regardless of who was operating it. President Mitterrand's brother, who was the Chairman of Aero-spatiale at the time, was probably also leaning on him not to enforce the embargo too enthusiastically.

Admiral Sandy Woodward later expressed the view that: 'There was always considerable concern that Argentina might acquire more Exocet missiles. French assurances that they would not supply further missiles whilst hostilities lasted were a great comfort. However, we were always concerned that there were other, less reliable sources.'

President Mitterrand's promise to the Prime Minister ensured that France gave Britain, at an early stage of the war, details of all France's military sales to Argentina, any modifications that had been carried out, performance details of French-built aircraft, aircraft serviceability rates, spares consumption and all the technical information we needed on the Exocet missile. Britain was also given information regarding the proficiency of the Argentine pilots, who only a few months before the war had completed their Super Etendard training course in France. Most importantly, France passed on details of all the other countries that had purchased Exocet missiles.

French assistance came in other ways as well. RAF aircraft en route to Ascension Island came to depend heavily on Dakar, Senegal, for refuelling, overnight stop-overs and routine servicing. David Bennett was an RAF officer with the Operations and Ground Support Unit, which was based at Dakar to support transiting RAF aircraft. The unit included a team of servicing engineers. He said:

I made several visits there, usually of about six weeks duration, including during the war. Dakar, with its huge underground fuel tanks, could support the enormous fuel requirements of transiting RAF aircraft. It was also a welcome diversion in the event of technical or other problems. The French were very helpful in persuading and ensuring that the Senegalese Government supported us.

The RAF took over the Air Afrique office. Banjul, in the Gambia, had been considered as an alternative, but it would not have been able to handle the throughput of aircraft (sometimes up to five aircraft a day), as all its fuel had to come in by road.

Thursdays were usually quite exciting. The weekly Aeroflot aircraft passing through Dakar carried Argentine passengers, and they knew exactly why the RAF aircraft were there. There was always plenty of 'eye-balling' and often they had to be discouraged from approaching too close.

On another occasion (discussed in Part Five), when Britain learned that a French ship had departed from St Nazaire with Exocet missiles on board, ostensibly for Peru (but, we suspected, for onward transmission to Argentina), the French Government stepped in and ordered the ship to return to France. Britain had been prepared to mount a Special Forces operation against the ship in the event that it had proceeded on its way.

The French also responded quickly and positively to an MoD request that they provide Mirage and Super Etendard 'opposition' for air combat training for RAF pilots destined for the Falklands. David Brook (later Air Vice-Marshal) was on CDS's staff and recalled, as had Willie Rae, that CDS had good relations with his French opposite number. He said: 'This certainly facilitated, not only the flow of technical information we needed on the products they had sold to Argentina (e.g. the aircraft and the missiles), but ensured that the air-to-air combat training programme was set up with little delay.'

It had originally been planned that RAF Harrier aircraft should operate in the air defence (AD) role during the Falklands war, although their normal role in the UK was ground attack (GA). It was therefore decided that some air combat training was needed before the pilots headed south. If this could be against the types of aircraft they would encounter in actual combat, all the better.

The dialogue with the French resulted in six RAF Harrier pilots going to RAF Coningsby in Lincolnshire on 22nd April for air combat training with French Mirage and Super Etendard aircraft. Several sorties were flown and it was generally agreed that those flown against the Super Etendard 'opposition' were of particularly good value. The pre-flight and post-flight briefings were carried out (with an interpreter present) at Coningsby. The missions were shrouded in secrecy at the time for political reasons.

Tim Gedge was an RN pilot at the time. He said:

RN pilots were specifically prohibited by the MoD from participating in these practice air combat missions, for reasons that were never made clear. Two RN pilots did fly in the rear cockpit of the two-seat Harrier on some missions but they were strictly prohibited from flying the aircraft. A suggestion that an RN Sea Harrier squadron should liaise directly with the French Super Etendard squadron before embarking was also refused by the MoD.

Nobody is suggesting that for the majority of the French, and for French companies anxious to sell their products, it was not 'business as usual' during the Falklands war. After all, it was not their war. Our Naval Attaché in South Africa, for example, reported that France – as well as Germany – was actively sidestepping the South African arms embargo.

He said: 'At the time, some countries that were sanctions-busting were working with Armscor (Arms Corporation) via the Israelis (who were everywhere).' The French also operated through Romania, selling spares for South Africa's Canberra and Puma aircraft. France, like Israel, had a reputation for aggressively trying to sell defence equipment and was noted for the way it seized any opportunities the marketplace offered.

Although President Mitterrand remained a staunch ally for the duration of the war, many others within the French Government and Socialist Party were not so persuaded. Some felt that Britain was engaged in an old-fashioned colonial war that hardly merited French support. Many French newspapers were critical of France's support; some were openly hostile. Worries were expressed within the French Government, and more widely, about the impact that France's support for Britain could have on its relations with other South American countries.

President Mitterrand was obliged to make it clear that his nation's support was for the duration of the war and no longer. After the war, France resumed honouring its contractual obligations to supply Argentina with the balance of the Super Etendard aircraft and Exocet missiles. It could hardly be blamed for that, although it was said that Prime Minister Thatcher was not best pleased.

Finally, it has been suggested that there was Argentine concern, early in the war, that the (Exocet) missiles' software codes may have been tampered with. It is not totally implausible that this could have occurred following the Prime Minister's discussion with President Mitterrand, when she asked for his support. There would certainly not have been any reason back in November 1981 (when the missiles were delivered to Argentina) for the French to supply missiles that might not perform on the day. On the contrary, France took a fierce pride in its products, and would have wanted the missiles to be successful if used. The Falklands War was not on the horizon at that time. A possible explanation, if it is true, is that a member of the Aerospatiale team in Argentina did the tampering, probably on instructions from above. The story goes on that the Argentines became suspicious, and used a disaffected Aerospatiale engineer to smuggle the correct codes out of France, which, allegedly were taken by an Argentine airline pilot to Buenos Aires, via Brazil. It is certainly the sort of thing that could have happened; whether it did is another matter.

On balance, apart from the continued presence of the Aerospatiale team in Argentina and the assistance it gave, France was generally supportive of the British Government throughout the Falklands War.

Israel and South Africa

Israel and South Africa were not on our list of best friends and allies in 1982. Both gave assistance to Argentina, and they were also known to have co-operated closely together.

Our Ambassador in Tel Aviv in 1982 was Patrick (later Sir Patrick) Moberly. He thought that whilst Israel was generally ambivalent towards Britain, nevertheless many Israelis would not have been averse to seeing Britain get a bloody nose in the Falklands War. He had also been our Ambassador in South Africa a little while before he went to Israel. He said:

> Both South Africa and Israel were beleaguered nations at that time. South Africa was suffering the sanctions regime, and Israel was regarded with a jaundiced eye by many nations, so in a sense both felt under threat to a degree, and lacked friends in the world. It was not too surprising therefore that they felt the need to co-operate in various areas (he diplomatically resisted the temptation to be more specific about the 'various areas') against British interests.

He could not, however, personally recall any lack of courtesy during the war, instances of abuse, or even a suggestion of a preference for either Britain or Argentina being expressed.

A few years earlier, during the 1970s, Argentina had indulged in a massive spending spree on arms, fuelled by a belief that some time soon the moment might be right either to act on the Falklands, or to challenge Chile militarily over the disputed Beagle Channel islands. Israel was just one of a number of nations to benefit from this spree, having sold coastal patrol boats, ammunition and Dagger fighter aircraft to Argentina.

Israel had already been a supplier of arms and other military equipment to Argentina before the Falklands War, but so had many other nations, including Britain. The representatives of a number of British defence companies were in Argentina when it invaded the Falklands.

Robin Sleight and his team from Marconi Avionics Limited were in Argentina at this time. They were involved in fitting new 'head-up displays' and a mission computer to the Argentine Air Force's fleet of thirty-plus Dagger aircraft. Marconi was the prime contractor, and Israel Aircraft Industries (IAI) acted as airframe consultant and sub-contractor. Elta, a division of IAI, was involved as well. At the beginning of the war, the British team had to pull out and return to the UK. The Israelis, Robin said, remained in Argentina and took over the running of the programme as prime contractor, thus supporting Argentina against our interests. Robin added that, in fact, in the timescale of the war, it would not have been possible to complete the work on many of the aircraft, and they would have been well short of completing the programme. This subject is covered in more detail in Part Four.

Later on, rumours of Israeli assistance to Argentina during the war came in thick and fast. Their Embassy in London, and government sources in Israel, were constantly forced to issue denials, and reject suggestions of co-operation with Argentina.

After the war ended, ammunition found by British troops in the Mount Harriet area included thousands of rounds of 9mm dum-dum bullets. They cause terrible tearing wounds when they expand on impact and, as a result, have long been banned by international law. Although actually made in Germany, they would have been useable in the Israeli-supplied Uzi sub-machine guns and automatic pistols, and the finger of suspicion pointed towards Israel. There were more denials.

Later, reports suggested that, whilst some Israeli leaders, or senior politicians, may have been ambivalent, Prime Minister Menachem Begin's personal hatred of Britain had much to do with the fact that Israel sent equipment to Argentina during the war, and some of it via Peru with the approval of the Peruvian Government. If this did occur, then the British Ambassador, the Defence Attaché, and other diplomats in Peru at the time, were unaware of it, and the British Embassy there did not have its own SIS representative.

Others simply took the view that Israel had a good relationship with Argentina, and the motive behind supplying equipment was straightforward commercial gain. Paradoxically, this would have been in spite of Argentina's pro-Nazi past, and the fact that many Nazi criminals found sanctuary in the country after the Second World War.

Both Israel and South Africa were regarded by many as pariah states at the time, and pariah states look for friends wherever they can find them. Few would have been surprised to learn that either country had been supplying arms to Argentina during the Falklands War.

Every attaché consulted who had been in one of the South American countries in 1982, had gained a similar impression of the Israeli military attaché who was serving there at the time. He was perceived as dedicated, humourless and with little or no time for the social niceties of the job. He was thoroughly Mossad-trained in the art of intelligence gathering, but was equally driven by his country's obsession with being commercially successful in South America. Everyone agreed that Israel had calculated that helping Argentina in any way possible would be a useful stepping-stone to further successes elsewhere on the continent.

Independent correspondent, author and Middle East expert Robert Fisk, said:

> Israel had a long track record of selling arms to many countries and, although probably mainly commercially-driven, would have been utterly unscrupulous if an opportunity presented itself anywhere in South America. It also had no scruples about buying equipment, modifying it, and selling it on to third parties.

> They were not worried who bought their equipment. Hamas ended up with Israeli-made sniper rifles. China bought tank equipment, with newly-installed enhanced sighting technology that had originated in the USA. The Israelis often did not even bother to remove all the Hebrew writing engraved here and there. They also co-operated with the South Africans in supplying captured Syrian tanks to Christian Phalangists in the Lebanon.

Whilst we were focussed on our war in the South Atlantic, the Palestine Liberation Organisation was continuing to strengthen its presence in Lebanon. Mounting Israeli anxiety gave way to military action in June 1982. Some say that the attempted assassination in London of the Israeli Ambassador, Shlomo Argov, on 4th June by Abu Nidal's organisation was one of the triggers for Israel's decision finally to act decisively in the Lebanon. General Sharon persuaded the Christian Phalangists to help with Israel's dirty work, and terrible atrocities were committed against innocent Arabs and their families during the weeks that followed. Sharon was supposedly backed by Menachem Begin, and other members of the Israeli Government were sometimes not informed of the measures taken. Robert Fisk continued:

> If Israel assesses any country as being in its interest to help, it will do so, vigorously and without hesitation. In my view, 1967 was the turning point for Israel, when it changed from being a good, slick professional outfit, to the rough, ill-disciplined mob it is today. There have also been, over the years, many Russians serving in the Israeli armed forces. They are equally unscrupulous, have the same

lack of respect for such niceties as end-user certificates, and can only have helped the process of declining standards.

Israel's co-operation with South Africa also goes back a long way. Robert recalled that they worked together to develop Israel's nuclear weapons programme, and he remembered President Vorster's State Visit to Israel to 'smooth such collaborative projects along'. France also gave some assistance, mainly in the early days, although General de Gaulle was known to have been uneasy about it. He had wanted Israel to go public and declare its intentions. As we know now, Israel never had any intention of being 'up front' about its plans. The world had to make do with rumours until 1986, when Mordechai Vanunu, the former Israeli nuclear technician, went public and paid a high price for it. He was imprisoned for many years, followed by many more years of tough restrictions.

John de Candole, our Defence Attaché in Pretoria in 1982, recalled that there was an unusually strong contingent of Israeli attachés in South Africa at that time. He said: 'You could be forgiven for wondering why this was, until you understood just how closely the two countries co-operated in the field of arms production'. He added that, unusually, none of the Israeli attachés joined the Attachés Association. It would seem that for the Israelis it was all business and no pleasure.

Andrew Duncan had preceded John de Candole in the job. He recalled that, during his time in South Africa, the number of South American attachés serving there trebled. Special tours were regularly arranged for them to visit Israeli defence industry facilities, and the non-South American attachés were excluded. He said: 'The Israelis were very keen to sell to South America, and consequently their attachés received privileges that the other attachés did not. Even in my time – before the Falklands War – there was a great deal of activity connecting Israel and South Africa, as well as strong rumours and confirmed reports of equipment going to Argentina via South Africa.'

There was an Armscor facility not far from Johannesburg in the 1980s, constructed to resemble a concentration camp and about as difficult to access, in which the South Africans were attempting to build a helicopter simulator (the embargo precluded them from being able to purchase one from abroad). The facility was stiff with Israeli technicians helping the South Africans with their project. It was further evidence of the ways in which the two countries co-operated in the area of defence equipment.

John de Candole confirmed that there was invariably a heavy Israeli presence in many of the Armscor facilities in South Africa.

Jack Worth was the Naval Attaché there. He had been specifically sent at the request of Admiral Leach. The Royal Navy and the South African Navy had once had an excellent relationship, and Jack's brief was to maintain and, if possible, strengthen the ties.

He was actively involved in tracking Armscor's activities, and he confirmed that equipment was sent to Argentina during the war. He was equally sure that the South African Government would not have had to give approval, and would have been quite content to let it happen. He said:

Because of the sanctions in force, it would probably have taken the view that Armscor should just go ahead and do it... The French and Germans were actively side-stepping the arms embargo and Armscor's attitude was 'the more the merrier'. A number of countries that were sanctions-busting worked with Armscor via the Israelis. The UK was not sanctions-busting though. Armscor was employing many ex-pats then, some of whom had been in the (British) armed forces. Some of them became very useful points of contact, but they were employed for their technical expertise, and would not have been aware where equipment or arms were destined.

A final comment he made was particularly interesting. He said that Israel and South Africa's relationship was very much a commercially-oriented marriage of convenience. Israel always tried to extract everything it could from South Africa. There were never any good deals for a country that dealt with Israel, and that included South Africa.

Sir John Nott, when asked if Simonstown was ever seriously considered as an alternative to Ascension Island, said:

We approached the South African Government several times to ask if we could use the base there, in the event of needing a bolt-hole for wounded personnel, or disabled ships. However, the South Africans had no intention of co-operating with us, and never agreed. Indeed, it was well known within British Government circles that South Africa and Israel were co-operating with Argentina, and sending aid and arms. South Africa was determined to do its best to frustrate us whenever possible. It was all being regularly reported to us by our SIS representatives.

Sir Ewen Fergusson was the British Ambassador in South Africa in 1982. He was an ex-Scottish rugby international, and recalled that whilst he was in South Africa, he was not allowed to attend any rugby matches. In June 1977, the signatories of the Gleneagles Agreement had focussed on sporting contacts with South Africa (amongst other things) and agreed to 'discourage contact or competition with sporting organisations' (i.e. as long as the South African Government pursued its policy of apartheid). Choosing his words with care, Sir Ewen said:

> The South African Government played it carefully during the Falklands War, being very aware of the sensitivity of the subject to many white, English-speaking South Africans. So, it was a balancing act, really: not wishing to offend them, but at the same time, being none too happy about the ongoing arms embargo. The government would always have had an interest in looking for outlets for its products – i.e. from the arms industry – and our war in South America presented an ideal opportunity... but, being ever-anxious not to upset the English-speaking community, it played down its involvement during, and after, the war. The government had good relations with Israel at the time.

The question of precisely what was sent to Argentina, and when and how, and via which country, still seems to throw up contradictions and unanswered questions and, of course, denials. The experience of Captain Julian Mitchell (our Naval Attaché in Buenos Aires until the Embassy closed and he was forced to relocate to Montevideo), was an example of this. He said that many people 'knew' what was going on, or were 'quite sure', but evidence was always hard to come by.

South Africa probably did send arms to Argentina, and Israel was closely involved with South Africa at the time. Neither country had any great affection for Britain then, and both were driven by the desire to take any opportunity offered to sell their equipment to other countries. Britain's war with Argentina offered a ready market, which promised further opportunities in South America in the future.

Exocet

Scarcely anything else conjures up memories of the Falklands War quite like the word 'Exocet'. It was the single most potentially decisive weapon system possessed by either side. They had it. We feared it. The Royal Navy was caught out by it. Later, it became clear just how fortunate Britain was that Argentina had received only the few missiles it had before the war, and not the balance of the order it had placed. It probably became quickly even clearer to the Argentine military junta that, if they had not brought forward the invasion date but had waited until more missiles had been delivered, things might have turned out very differently for them.

There were basically three versions of the missile on offer in 1982: a surface-launched version; one that could be launched from a submarine (that was still under development); and the feared AM39 air-launched Exocet missile. All versions employed the same basic principles of operation; that is to say they were 'fire-and-forget', and skimmed low over the surface of the sea towards the target.

The French firm Aerospatiale supplied the missile, but could not take all the credit for the on-board technology. John Stephenson had spent much of his working life in the aerospace sector. He had worked in English Electric's Guided Weapons (GW) Division, which later became part of British Aircraft Corporation (BAC) and then British Aerospace (BAe). In the early 1980s, BAe bought out Sperry Gyroscope, the navigation, mines and underwater warfare specialist. John said: 'At the time, whilst I was with BAe, Stevenage, the gyroscope guidance system, which was installed in all versions of the Exocet missile, was of a US design. BAe took the design and manufactured the gyroscope – probably hardly changing the design at all – which was then sold to the French to be integrated into all versions of their Exocet missile.' The French then sold the finished product, the missile, to Argentina to use against the British. Quite an international effort! John added that the USA had a

71

range of good gyroscope designs at the time, whilst Britain had a reputation for being good at building them.

Perhaps, in a curious and small way, we got our own back on Argentina. When HMS *Sheffield* was being built for the RN, there was a fire on board which caused some damage. Close by, work was also proceeding on Type 42 destroyers for the Argentine Navy. It was decided to 'rob' the back end of the *Santisima Trinidad* and weld it on to the damaged *Sheffield*. As *Sheffield* was later destroyed by one of Argentina's Exocets, perhaps it could be argued, with tongue firmly in cheek, that they actually destroyed a ship that was part Argentine.

The squadron designated to receive the Exocets was the 2nd Air Naval Fighter and Strike Squadron of the CANA (Argentine Naval Air Command), commanded by Captain Jorge Colombo. The navy had ordered fourteen Super Etendard aircraft and fourteen Exocet missiles, and the first five aircraft and five Exocets were delivered in November 1981. Britain was fortunate that the balance of Argentina's order was delayed by the French in order to honour a larger, more lucrative order from Iraq first. Later, the French embargo prevented the delivery of any further aircraft or missiles until after the war. Pilots and technical personnel had spent several months in France in 1981, learning about the aircraft and missile systems. The pilots returned to Argentina with up to 50 hours flying time each on the aircraft type.

The Super Etendard is a single-seat, French-built naval attack aircraft with an in-flight refuelling capability. On the anti-ship missions during the Falklands War, the aircraft carried 2 × 30mm cannons, a single Exocet missile under the starboard wing, and a fuel tank under the port wing. The aircraft was able, if required, to carry alternative weapon loads, including bombs and air-to-air missiles.

A typical mission against ships of the Task Force would have involved a pair of aircraft (with, ideally, a serviceable back-up aircraft in case of an unserviceability before take-off), a KC-130H tanker aircraft, and a Neptune (maritime patrol) aircraft. The role of the latter, operating at altitude, was to seek the British ships using its radar, and to guide the attack aircraft to the Exocet release point. The mission also required accurate pre-mission intelligence information on the Task Force's movements and suitable weather, both at the Río Grande air base and in the target area. There were, therefore, a number of elements that had to come together at the right moment. Each missile, of the few available to Argentina, had to be made to count.

Normally, the Super Etendards would refuel en route to the target area and again on the return flight, but this was not always necessary. The Neptune aircraft were available only for the initial Etendard missions. Later on, due to age and unserviceability, they were withdrawn from service; the Etendards then relied upon target information received from radars located on the Falklands (which became the targets for the Vulcan involved in the Black Buck 6 mission).

The role of the Neptune aircraft, and later the ground radar, was to guide the Etendards, which flew at low altitude to avoid detection by the ship's radar, to a point about 30 miles from the target ship. Having acquired and locked on to the ship, and passed its co-ordinates to the missile, the pilot would then release the missile and turn immediately away to return to base. The missile meanwhile, using the target information now stored in its own built-in computer, carrying over 350lbs of high explosives and travelling in excess of 600 knots, would continue on to the ship. Flying approximately 15 feet above the waves, it was designed to impact the ship around the water-line. Even if the missile failed to detonate, the combination of its kinetic energy, unspent fuel, and the residual, combustible gases, had the potential to be devastating.

Peter Ginger, formerly a Royal Air Force air defence pilot, became a test pilot at BAC, Warton. He had tested and evaluated the Agave air-to-surface radar that was installed in the Jaguar aircraft. He also delivered the first of fourteen Jaguars that BAC had sold to Ecuador, in January 1977. He said: 'The French (Thomson CSF) Agave radar in the Argentine Super Etendard aircraft was the same as that installed in the Jaguars, so we already knew it well, which was useful. There might have been one or two minor changes in the display, or presentation, of information but basically it was identical.'

Quite apart from Peter's comments, the French were co-operative and forthcoming in giving us information regarding the aircraft and missile systems. One of the reasons we were able to obtain the information from the French so easily was the excellent personal relationship that CDS had with his French opposite number (and confirmed by David Brook). Peter also added: 'The French were particularly proud of the Super Etendard aircraft and its Exocet missile, and rightly so. It was acknowledged as being a formidable and successful weapons system.'

Perhaps this understandable pride lends some credence to the claim that the French technicians who remained in Argentina during the Falklands War were interested only in ensuring that their product operated satisfactorily, and did not specifically support Argentina. Equally, one can forgive those who are slightly sceptical of this view.

British Concern

There was a great deal of anxiety at the Ministry of Defence, from the early days of the war, with regard to the Exocet missile. Bill Bale was (as a Lt Col) with COSSEC (the Chiefs of Staff Secretariat). He recalled: 'There was a considerable amount of discussion and concern about Exocet, and its potential to harm our efforts. The possibility of trying to buy up as many as we could, to prevent them getting into Argentina's hands, was also discussed at some length. This was considered a good, viable option.'

The Royal Navy's best defence against Exocet depended upon receiving the earliest possible warning of the missile's approach, and then following a well-rehearsed procedure. Although different ships were equipped with various combinations of gun and missile, most Royal Navy captains appeared to share the view that an early awareness of the Exocet heading their way, followed by rapidly taking the correct evasive action, realistically gave them the best chance of survival.

Most RN captains had appreciated the potential danger presented by the Exocet system at an early stage in their journey south to the Falklands, and regularly rehearsed the procedures they would have to adopt in the event of having to counter an incoming missile threat. Captain Chris Craig (HMS *Alacrity*) said:

We spent a great deal of time working up our procedures. We were pretty confident about the threat posed by the A4 Skyhawks' iron bombs, but Exocet was taken very seriously. Admiral Woodward provided good, hard-nosed leadership. He had all the captains on board *Hermes* and told us it would be a close-run thing; that it would not be easy and we could lose between four and six escort ships. Exocet, he said, was the main concern and we had to be ready for it. We should not forget that we were in their territory.

Captain David Pentreath (HMS *Plymouth*) said:

We realised the significance of the Exocet threat within days of leaving Gibraltar, and started working up our drills and procedures for countering it. I think I would have used the 4.5-inch guns, but essentially the procedure was to turn downwind, throw up chaff and try to remain in the middle of the chaff 'cloud'. The Sea Wolf missile, although available to some, was rather unreliable.

Captain Brian Young (HMS *Antrim*) said a number of captains felt that Argentina was not yet ready to fire an Exocet, and it took the loss of HMS *Sheffield*, which surprised everyone, to concentrate their minds. He, and some of his colleagues, Brian said, had not been very impressed with the way HMS *Sheffield* had reacted. It had assessed the threat of an Exocet attack as low, and the satellite communication system (SCOT) was being used inadvisedly at the time. Brian added:

> Some ships had various combinations of gun and missile. The Phalanx gun put up a wall of lead but was essentially a short-range, last-ditch response to an Exocet. If the missile was already that close, you were in big trouble. The Sea Wolf was a short-range missile and the same thinking applied. Many of my colleagues didn't believe it provided any defence against sea-skimming missiles and it wasn't regarded as being very reliable, anyway.

Nick Bradshaw, an officer on HMS *Invincible*, remembered that there was an awareness of an Exocet threat before the journey south even started. He said that Captain Jeremy Black briefed everyone 'from time to time' via the on-board TV screens. The procedure they practised in the event of an Exocet attack was to turn to face the missile (as distinct to turning downwind regardless), throw up a cloud of chaff and launch a Sea King helicopter. The Sea King was briefed to hover a ship's length astern, which would appear to extend the length of the carrier, thus increasing the chance of a near miss. Another *Invincible* officer added that, of course, the Sea King could equally well have been deployed ahead of the carrier.

The officers and men took these briefings very seriously. The loss of *Sheffield* especially, and of *Atlantic Conveyor* later, made a huge impact on the Task Force, and the minds of everyone on every ship were sharply concentrated. This relatively inexpensive, sea-skimming missile seemed capable of inflicting so much damage. Comparisons were inevitably made between the great warships of the past, which were able to take so much punishment without catching fire, and their modern descendants.

Anthony Dymock (later Vice-Admiral) served with Brian Young on HMS *Antrim*. He said: 'We practised our procedures on the way south, but there was a feeling at the time that the land-based version of the Exocet missile was likely to present the more significant threat. Many thought that Argentina wasn't yet ready to threaten us with the air-launched version.' He also agreed, as had others, that if either *Hermes* or *Invincible* had suffered an Exocet strike, it could have meant an end to

Britain's efforts to repossess the Falklands, although 'if our troops had already landed, it would have been a different calculation.'

The management of the on-board GEC Marconi Satellite Communications Terminal (normally referred to as SCOT) became an important factor when there was a risk of an Exocet attack in the area.

SCOT had already been fitted to most, if not all, of the major warships prior to Falklands but, according to Captain Brian Young, 'not to frigates and below'. SCOT provided secure voice communication and teleprinter facilities, and became the primary means of communication with Northwood. It was forbidden to use SCOT for making personal calls (e.g. to family members back in England), although Naval Attaché Julian Mitchell said it was used by some ships on an 'if permitted by the Captain' basis (i.e. there was a loose interpretation of the instruction).

HMS *Endurance* had the merchant version, INMARSAT (International Maritime Satellite Communication System), as did the RFAs, and most of the other larger ships taken up from trade. INMARSAT was not secure and ships fitted with it were told not to use it except in emergency. Brian Young was very angry when he learned from his own radio intercept team that the crew of *Endurance* had been chatting on INMARSAT to families and friends at home whilst the Task Group was making its supposedly covert approach to South Georgia. Brian said: 'This might have explained how the BBC World Service was able to announce our arrival the day we got there...'

Atlantic Conveyor had a military radio room, with satellite communications equipment that had been installed in Plymouth prior to departure. The use of the room was restricted to only the most senior personnel, and the equipment was operated by an RFA Radio Operator, Ron Hool (who sadly died when the Exocet missile hit the ship).

A SCOT terminal was also engineered into the QE2 in short order prior to its departure from Southampton on 12th May. Installed at a cost of over £1 million, it promptly failed on the very day Major General Jeremy Moore embarked at Ascension Island with his eighty-strong staff, and joined 5 Commando Brigade (which had been enjoying the good life on board since embarking at Southampton). This inopportune failure made the task of command almost impossible initially for the General.

The problem associated with operating, or using, SCOT when an Exocet threat existed had everything to do with the fact that SCOT's frequency of transmission was very close to that of the radar used by the missile, thus masking the missile's detection.

David Fletcher was Managing Director of GEC Marconi in 1982. He recalled that after the *Sheffield* disaster his workforce had to work round the clock to produce an effective answer to the problem. The aim was to devise some form of active decoy which 'would seduce the missile away from the ship,' he said. Time was not on their side.

A great deal of 'clever' research work was being carried out at that time in the ECM arena, at Marconi's Stanmore Headquarters. The *Sheffield* disaster accelerated the effort and gave it a new urgency. David Fletcher said:

> The disaster should never have happened. We had already recommended that SCOT should be switched off if there was an Exocet threat in the area. Several meetings were held at the MoD during the year preceding the Falklands War, during which we pointed out the proximity in frequency of transmitters like SCOT to the radars typically used on anti-ship missiles, thereby masking their detection. We said that improved ESM and missile decoy systems were needed to reduce the high vulnerability to missiles like Exocet.

He did not know, of course, how this information had been disseminated, or what guidance had been given to the captains of RN warships. He added: 'Our advice was disregarded with tragic consequences. In fact, the explosion – as the Exocet hit *Sheffield* – was heard on the tapes at Northwood (when they were replayed) because *Sheffield* was transmitting on SCOT at the time.'

Working flat-out, the Stanmore laboratories produced a solution in less than six weeks, code-named SKYSHADOW (its name in 1982). The war was about to end anyway or just had, when it was ready. It effectively picked up the signal of the incoming missile (any type of missile) and sent it straight back to confuse and deflect the missile. It has been greatly developed and refined since then.

Atlantic Conveyor

In the 1970s and 1980s, Cunard had two sister ships in the Atlantic Container Line fleet operating in the North Atlantic, *Atlantic Causeway* and *Atlantic Conveyor*. At the time, they were regarded as being state-of-the-art roll-on, roll-off container ships. In 1982, they were requisitioned by the MoD to carry supplies (e.g. Wessex and Chinook helicopters, Harrier and Sea Harrier aircraft etc) for the task force. John Brocklehurst was on *Atlantic Causeway*, until transferring to *Atlantic Conveyor* on 19th April as Chief Officer. He recalled that she set off from Devonport at the end of April:

On the journey south we were given intelligence briefings but the content depended upon the job one was doing, and need-to-know. We were certainly made aware that Exocet was the main threat. We didn't have chaff launchers on *Atlantic Conveyor*; just a couple of general-purpose machine guns (GPMGs) and, on the run south from Ascension Island, an RN Sea Harrier with Sidewinder missiles fitted, on permanent standby. This was, we were told, mainly in case an Argentine B707 aircraft came within range.

In the event that an Exocet missile came our way, the drill was to turn away from it as rapidly as possible and present the stern of the ship to it. The stern ramp and door were especially strongly constructed on the two *Atlantic* ships.

On 25th May, the Exocets were intended for another ship, probably the carriers, but the chaff cloud fired off caused one of the missiles to break lock and home in on us instead. It was fast approaching the port quarter. I had just been down to the stern deck to get a Chinook airborne, but in the event, for some technical reason the flight was cancelled. Another Chinook was already airborne and survived the Exocet attack.

Suddenly, within minutes of having returned to the port bridge, the air raid warning sounded, at the same time giving the threat direction. I later estimated that the missile had been fired at a range of thirty to thirty-five miles from us, and had probably taken two to three minutes to reach us.

When the missile struck us, I was approximately fifty feet above and fifty feet forward of the point of impact. We were still in a starboard turn to present the stern to the missile, but hadn't had time to complete it. We were doing about fifteen knots at the time, and it was late afternoon with the light beginning to deteriorate. It was then a race against time to get everyone, especially the casualties, off the ship before it was dark.

Atlantic Conveyor had been carrying Harrier aircraft but fortunately, these had been transferred to the carriers a week before the missile strike. It had also been carrying four Chinooks, and a number of Wessex helicopters, all of which were urgently needed on the Falklands by our forces there, to facilitate the movement of men and equipment. All the helicopters were lost except for the single Chinook that happened to be airborne (carrying out an air test) at the time of the strike. The ship was also carrying plant and equipment needed by 11 Field Squadron RE to build an airstrip for the use of Harrier aircraft at Port San Carlos. All this was lost too, but the airstrip was built anyway.

The pilot of the single airborne Chinook helicopter, Dick Langworthy, flew to HMS *Hermes* and then on to the Falklands. The Chinook was a tough and versatile machine, with an impressive load-carrying capability which was urgently needed by the forces on the ground, especially because the terrain of the Falklands made movement by any other means extremely difficult. The Chinook that survived the *Atlantic Conveyor* disaster, *Bravo November* (BN), was still flying, in Afghanistan, twenty-five years later. It holds the record (or did in 2007) for the highest number of people ever carried in a Chinook (eighty-four including the crew), most of whom were Gurkhas and Scots Guards picked up at Goose Green.

Tim Gedge, the Fleet Air Arm (FAA) Sea Harrier pilot, was on deck alert on HMS *Invincible* at the time of the Exocet attack. He recalled:

I flew two missions that day, the 25th May, one in the morning and the second just after *Atlantic Conveyor* was struck. I witnessed Sea Dart missiles being fired from *Invincible*.

My own reaction was one of dismay as I had brought 809 Naval Air Squadron south from Ascension in her, transferring to *Invincible*, via *Hermes*, only a week earlier (on 18th May). I had come to know her Master, Ian North, well during the twelve-day passage, and had shared his day cabin.

Admiral Woodward later expressed the view that had *Atlantic Conveyor* – which was just 4 miles from the Admiral's carrier, HMS *Hermes*, at the time – not been the missile's eventual target, *Hermes* could have been struck instead. This could have happened if *Atlantic Conveyor* had been carrying chaff dispensers and successfully deflected the Exocet missile.

Both Admiral Woodward and John Brocklehurst acknowledged, after the event, that if the Exocet missile had struck HMS *Hermes* instead, it could have spelt the end of British efforts to repossess the Falklands.

Sadly Ian North, the popular Master of *Atlantic Conveyor*, was one of those who lost their lives that day. He was in the sea and trying to get to a liferaft when he disappeared. Nick Bradshaw, who had served as an officer on HMS *Invincible* in 1982, recalled that Ian North had rapidly acquired a reputation as an exceptionally good station-keeper, not an easy task in a ship that was very difficult to manoeuvre.

John Brocklehurst assumed command of *Atlantic Conveyor* for the brief time remaining before the ship went down. Following its loss, he became the Chief Officer standing by the construction of the new replacement *Atlantic Conveyor* which entered service in 1984. He was promoted to become its Master in 1991.

The Land-based Version

As soon as it was learned that the Argentines might have succeeded in adapting a sea-launched Exocet to be launched from the back of a truck (i.e. to become the land-based missile to which Anthony Dymock had alluded), it was recognised that this could present a significant threat to British ships tasked to shell the Falklands. Early in June, this became a new and worrying consideration, and Harrier aircraft from the carriers were launched to seek out any such missiles.

Argentina, however, did have some success. After some initial teething problems, two Exocets were flown to the Falklands one night in a C130 aircraft, and in the early hours of 12th June the County class destroyer, HMS *Glamorgan*, was hit by one of them, fired from a standard flat-bed trailer onshore. She was heading away to the east at the time, having delayed her departure from the area in order to continue giving naval gunfire support to 45 Commando ashore. What was a significant success for Argentina was a disaster for Britain. Thirteen men died, many others were injured, and the ship was badly damaged.

That Exocet missile was the last to be fired during the Falklands War. The Argentines, thanks to the persistence and ingenuity of a few officers, responded magnificently to the call to develop a land-launched Exocet missile in short order. Contra Almirante Bezzola was Head of Electronica Naval, and personally became deeply involved in the project. He, like some of the engineers who worked for him (e.g. Captains Pedro Auge and Calandre), were very professional and also 'anglicised', in the sense that they had a healthy respect for British engineering and equipment.

The following short story (a précis of the original), was related by

Falkland islander Fred Clark who, after attending an Aerospatiale engineering training course in 1972, spent nearly eight years working on Aerospatiale equipment and components. It suggests that, at the end, the Argentines may have had more missiles available than perhaps many realised at the time. It was Fred's own experience and it occurred on 9th June, approximately three weeks after the British forces landed on the Falklands. The Argentine occupation still had a few days to run. He said:

It was very early, and the first light of dawn was not yet evident. Normally, the streetlights would have been illuminated, but the Argentine Army of Occupation had switched them off. It was a typical June morning, very cold and icy, and with an air temperature that was still well below freezing. Normally, I wouldn't have been out before the end of curfew, but I wanted to see a cargo that had been landed unusually early, which might have been important.

A small group of my friends had managed to get hold of a short wave radio to pass messages to the advancing British troops and warn them of any possible dangers. Someone had spotted a ship entering the harbour just before the night's curfew started. He had reported that it was a white-painted vessel with a Red Cross painted on its side. As we had been tipped off that the next ship would be bringing in non-medical supplies, we were naturally interested but someone had to go down and have a look. This created certain difficulties; firstly, the jetty was in a military area and therefore out of bounds to the locals, and secondly, the ship discharged its cargo during the curfew hours. As I had a pass to access the area and knew it well, I volunteered to investigate. A pass wasn't going to help me if I was caught out after curfew, and certainly not if I was found in the military zone.

I left the house just after five o'clock when all seemed quiet, and managed to get to the jetty entrance without detection. Work on the ships had finished, and as I watched, the crew battened down the hatches and prepared to go to sea. I could just make out wheel tracks in the ice, and they all led to a long shed with wide access doors at each end on the east side of the jetty. I approached the nearest end and peered in. There was some light at the far end so I risked a forty-five yard trip down the open jetty to get in at the other end. I saw no sign of a guard, but could see the footprints on the ice where he had passed earlier. There was a light in a shed at the end of the jetty. It was the jetty foreman's hut that was used for shelter, warmth and, no doubt, the occasional brew of *mate*, their favourite beverage. I decided to walk steadily along the icy jetty and hope for the best. I reached the other end of the shed and dived for cover beside some empty crates.

No one came, so I crawled to the closed doors, which were unlocked. Moving cautiously, I finally had a good view of what was inside. A long trailer painted in camouflage green with double wheels on the back axle, and slightly oval in cross-section, indicated a heavy load. On it were two long square metal cases painted green with writing on the ends in French. It even had tell-tale pressure indicators on the ends, each showing green. I was looking at two Exocet missiles in their transit containers. I had to get this information back to be transmitted to the British. I was about to stand up when the door opened and two guards appeared. They came towards the doors where I was lying. I quickly rolled over and lowered myself over the side until my feet touched the wooden cross members of the jetty structure. I then crept silently along in the shadows.

I lay there for what seemed a long time, but as the tide was rising I knew I had to move. I hadn't heard any patrols, and dawn was breaking. It was now or never, so I pulled myself up on to the concrete and made my way to the corner of the shed. Nobody was in sight so I decided to walk quickly back along the side of the shed and cross the street into the nearest garden. It was then that I came face to face with a guard. He brought up his rifle and, aiming at me, tried to pull the trigger. I stood there completely numb, without a thought in my head, expecting a loud bang but nothing happened.

We looked at each other. He was only about eighteen years old. We both looked at his loaded rifle; he had meant to shoot, but was still wearing his quilted gloves to keep his hands warm. They didn't allow his finger to go into the cold trigger guard and pull the trigger. I slowly raised my hand to my chest pocket and took out a packet of cigarettes. We both smiled. I opened the pack, gave him one and took one for myself. I quickly produced my lighter and lit both cigarettes. I didn't want him to take off his cold weather gloves. I turned quickly, waved, and ran across the road into the nearest garden. I was anxious to escape from this brief encounter with the enemy. The first rays of sunlight broke across Stanley Harbour. It was a good morning to be alive.

Fred remarked that the use of the ship with the Red Cross insignia painted on the side was 'very unethical'. Some years before the Falklands War, he had lived in France and his work for Aerospatiale (as a qualified aircraft engineer) had enabled him to identify the missiles for what they were.

They were a version of Exocet that had been adapted for launching from land towards a ship out at sea (like the missile that struck HMS *Glamorgan*). In any case, there were no Argentine aircraft on the Falklands capable of carrying the AM39 version.

After the discovery, he made contact with a colleague who, operating a clandestine radio, notified the Task Force direct. The two missiles were never used and were still in Stanley on Liberation Day. They were, he said, guarded by 2 Para until they were finally removed, and were still in their boxes on 16th June.

Argentina's Efforts to Acquire the Missile

Argentina fully appreciated that it had a weapon system capable of turning the war in its favour, if just one of the precious few missiles it possessed could sink, or even seriously damage, one of the two British aircraft carriers.

It therefore gave a high priority to obtaining, by whatever means, more Exocets from any possible source. Apart from the office in Paris run by Captain Carlos Corti, which was dedicated to trying to track down and procure more missiles, there were many stories of missiles promised and never delivered, of cash paid and lives lost, and scams.

Captain Guy Holman was the Naval Attaché in Copenhagen. His story was not untypical. He said:

One day I received a telephone call from a Swedish gentleman. He said he had access to two Exocet missiles and these could be made available at a suitable price, thereby denying the sale to Argentina. Was I interested? I agreed to meet him in the foyer of a well-known hotel. It would constitute 'neutral' ground. We would then discuss terms etc.

I informed the Ambassador, who in turn felt we should inform the Danish Intelligence Service to get extra help (as we were rather short of numbers). Unfortunately, they went 'over the top'. The Swede didn't show up for the meeting. I suspect he took one surreptitious look, found a foyer full of men wearing dark glasses, all pretending to be reading their newspapers, and bolted.

We'll never know if he actually had any missiles to sell, but probably not. It may have been just one of the many scams doing the rounds.

Many stories, which vary in detail, link Peru with efforts to procure Exocets to pass on to Argentina. Some refer to chartered aircraft arriving at Lima airport with missiles to offload. The Ambassador, Charles Wallace, the Defence Attaché, and other diplomats in the British Embassy at the time, are all adamant that they knew nothing of any Exocets going through Peru. They were aware only of the fairly well-known attempt to send some missiles on a merchant vessel from the French port of St Nazaire to Peru which, at the request of the British Government, the French stopped at the eleventh hour and turned round. If it hadn't, Britain had been prepared to send in Special Forces to stop the ship and prevent the delivery.

The tragic loss of the container ship *Atlantic Conveyor* on 25th May, following HMS *Sheffield* on 4th May, had brought renewed demands from some MPs for retaliation. Some wanted Britain to bomb air bases on the Argentine mainland, but this was vigorously rejected by the government. Not only was it not feasible militarily, but it could also have caused many South American countries openly to support Argentina instead of just paying lip-service. The British Government was also very anxious to confine the conflict to the Falklands alone.

The two losses also underlined the need for airborne early warning, and reminded some that the last naval early-warning aircraft, the Gannet, was scrapped, along with the *Ark Royal*, in 1978. The Royal Navy finally said farewell to its last Gannet early in 1979. The Task Force had nothing to provide the ability to look over the horizon for a threat such as a Super Etendard with its Exocet missile. There was a sudden flurry of activity as naval officers searched, on both sides of the Atlantic, for any Gannets that might still be airworthy. The search produced nothing; in any case finding enough of the rare Rolls Royce Double Mamba turbo-prop engines, which had not been used by any other military aircraft, would have been another difficult task.

More significantly, the successful Super Etendard missions intensified the search by British agents for Exocet missiles across the world. Whilst the Defence Intelligence Centre (DIC) was organised to monitor Argentine military activities, an arms traffic cell concentrated on Argentina's attempts to procure arms and equipment from foreign countries. There were many rumours and many false trails, and Exocet was, for everyone at that time, the main concern.

France was helpful and informed us to whom it had sold the missile, but some of them had been redirected to other countries. There is no doubt though that President Mitterrand's support, and the French arms embargo, were important factors in preventing Argentina from obtaining further Exocets in time to turn the tables on Britain.

Many SIS (MI6) agents became actively involved in the search for Exocet missiles. One, who had served in the British Embassy in Buenos Aires, said:

We had a pretty good idea which countries had them. What was not so clear was which countries might have slipped one or two to another country, or to a less scrupulous third party, for a good price. I'm sure the French were probably honest about who they had sold the missile to, but probably didn't always know the final destination, if different. Also, if they did, they might have neglected to tell us. The whole operation was not so much 'Do you have any Exocets?' but rather 'Is there any nefarious person out there to whom you have passed one on to?' No one could be absolutely sure, and this was the situation right up to the final day of the war.

Another said:

Britain procured some Exocets, and we traced many more that could have fallen into Argentine hands (i.e. that might have been sold on to Argentina).

Others that were considered safe could also have been sold on. There were no guarantees that we would always get it right. There was at least one successful sting operation, and one Exocet was 'doctored' so that, if it had been fired, it would have blown up the Super Etendard (however, it never reached Argentina).

A considerable amount of effort was expended and compressed into just a few short weeks. Judgements had to be made, and it was impossible to state categorically that all Exocet missiles had been traced. I would guess that we accounted for about ninety per cent of them, and that was to a large extent thanks to French assistance.

Meanwhile, during the same frenetic period, Argentines like Captain Corti in Paris, were working equally hard to persuade nations and individuals around the world to part with their Exocets. Just a single missile would have been welcome, and would have attracted a good price. The normal price for an AM39 Exocet was slightly under half a million dollars in 1982, but Argentina would happily have paid two or three times that price for a missile that just might turn the tide of the war.

With all this behind-the-scenes activity taking place, and in the aftermath of the HMS *Sheffield* and *Atlantic Conveyor* disasters, it is hardly surprising that there was mounting concern, particularly in London and throughout the Royal Navy. Not only did Argentina still possess its fifth and final missile, but also the possibility existed that it could acquire a further missile, or missiles, and this possibility would exist until the war ended.

It was against this background of concern and uncertainty that, during the month of May, a considerable amount of thought went into the planning of a military operation which aimed to insert Special Forces into Argentina to destroy the Super Etendard aircraft, any Exocet missiles Argentina still possessed (or had latterly acquired), and to kill the pilots.

It was a bold idea and not without considerable risk. Very few were allowed to know what was being planned. It was given the name Operation Mikado. Royal Air force C130 aircraft would be involved, to convey the Special Forces to the Río Grande air base in Tierra del Fuego where the Super Etendard aircraft were based. The crews would have to be carefully selected, and they would require special training for a mission that would be unlike anything they had ever undertaken before.

Operation Mikado – The Royal Air Force Prepares

No discussion of the ways in which the war touched mainland South America would be complete without mention of the ill-fated Operation Mikado. Although much has been written on the subject, two aspects deserve further treatment: the sequence of events from the time the Sea King crew, who participated in Phase 1 of the Operation, crossed from Argentina into Chile; and the Royal Air Force's preparation for its involvement. The former, including the role played by the British Embassy in Santiago, is discussed separately in Part Four.

The Threat

The lethal combination of Argentina's Super Etendard aircraft and its Exocet missile probably constituted the most potentially decisive weapon system possessed by either side during the war. Just one successful attack against either of our two carriers, *Hermes* or *Invincible*, could have forced the Task Force to withdraw and dealt our efforts to repossess the Falklands a fatal blow. This was a view widely held at the time, and the minds of any doubters would have been sharply concentrated when HMS *Sheffield* was attacked on 4th May. This incident dramatically demonstrated the missile's effectiveness and gave further impetus to the idea of mounting an operation to destroy the aircraft, and remaining Exocet missiles, before another disaster occurred.

Although Argentina had taken delivery of five Super Etendard aircraft and five Exocet missiles from France in November 1981, more than twice that number of missiles had been ordered. The balance of Argentina's requirement had been delayed by the French to satisfy the more lucrative Iraq contract. We will never know how hugely important that delay might have been to the outcome of the war.

If Galtieri had waited a little longer before launching his invasion, he might not only have received some or all of the remainder of the missiles due to Argentina, but he might also have acquired a missile or two from another source. It was estimated that well in excess of 1,000 Exocets of the same air-launched variety had already been sold by France to countries around the world before the war started. These unknowns do not take account of other considerations that impelled the junta to act when it did, but perhaps we were fortunate, nevertheless, that Iraq placed its order for the missile when it did.

On 19th April, the Super Etendard aircraft were relocated to their operational base at Río Grande in Tierra del Fuego in the south of Argentina. Work to mate the missiles to the aircraft had been completed. Four aircraft were still intact and the fifth was being 'cannibalised' to provide spares for the others. Of the five Exocet missiles delivered before the war, Argentina still had three available when Mikado was first mooted – enough to cause us considerable concern.

The Options Available

Various ways of approaching the problem of how to destroy the aircraft and missiles, with the Super Etendard-qualified pilots thrown in for good measure, were considered and dismissed. Harriers were too few and too precious to be risked. The Vulcan could not guarantee the pin-point accuracy required for a vital mission that could never be repeated in the event of failure. A 'Cockleshell Heroes' raid, involving Special Forces (SF) disgorged from a submarine offshore, was briefly considered later on and had possibilities.

The favoured solution was to send two Royal Air Force C130 transport aircraft carrying SF down to Río Grande to carry out an Entebbe-style assault mission. The operation, code-named Operation Mikado, would consist of two distinct phases. Phase 1 would be an intelligence-gathering mission, involving the insertion of SF personnel into Argentina by means of a Sea King helicopter from HMS *Invincible*. They would have the task of establishing the disposition and strength of Argentine forces engaged in the defence of the Río Grande air base, the weapons at their disposal, the precise location of the Super Etendards and Exocet missiles, and even where the aircrew slept at night. This information would be passed back to the UK by means of satellite communication.

Subject to the adequacy and quality of the intelligence received, Phase 2 would then be implemented. Two C130 aircraft would land at Río

Grande at night, each carrying two 'Pink Panther' armoured long-range Land Rovers and approximately thirty men of B Squadron, 22 SAS (Special Air Service). After landing the SAS would quickly seek out and destroy the aircraft and remaining missiles, and kill the aircrew. The C130s would be waiting for the SAS with engines running, hoping to take off again before the whole base was alerted and all hell broke loose. That was the plan.

If such a daring plan was to succeed, then much careful planning, preparation and training would have to be accomplished in a short period of time. A clear understanding of each other's roles, and agreement throughout the process, would also have to be established between the two principal elements involved, the RAF crews and the SF personnel.

A little while before Operation Mikado assumed the urgency it later did, discussions were held between these elements with a view to mounting another similar operation elsewhere. The detailed planning and intensive training for that mission proved later to be very relevant to Mikado.

No 47 Squadron SF (Special Forces) Flight

Missions that involved crews and aircraft of the RAF's C130 fleet working with Special Forces (i.e. SAS, Special Boat Squadron [SBS] or the Submarine Parachute Assistance Group [SPAG]) were assigned to a Flight dedicated to such work.

In former times, each C130 squadron had an element specialising in tactical work in support of UK Special Forces. In the mid-1970s these elements were brought together into a single dedicated unit, No 47 Squadron SF Flight. To be a member of this Flight was a sought-after honour. You could volunteer, but you had to be good and your face had to fit. If you were selected, there was specialist training to be carried out. In April 1982, No 47 SF Flight had just five crews, including Max Roberts, the recently-appointed Flight Commander, and Harry Burgoyne, the Flight's longest-serving and most experienced SF pilot. David Musgrave and Jim Cunningham were their respective navigators.

Early in April, Max was asked to go to Hereford where he met Brigadier Peter de la Billiere, Colonel Mike Rose and other SAS officers for the first time. From what he learned that day of their thinking, and of the part they envisaged the SF Flight would play in some of their future missions, Max decided that clandestine assault training should start immediately, and in earnest. It was clear that No 47 SF Flight would be called upon to participate in missions for which they were as yet singularly unprepared. In Max's words: 'The SAS wanted to elevate SF Flight's game to a level unknown before, for which I knew the crews would need extensive training. I also knew that this was nothing they couldn't cope with.'

SF Flight set to work. Their training concentrated at first on single aircraft assault landings and rapid offloads, but was quickly stepped-up to two aircraft missions. Within a short time these were being flown at low level and at night. Time was not on their side.

During this period of intensive work-up, the nature of the first mission the Flight might be called upon to take part in became clearer, but the specifics, i.e. 'why and when', were not yet known. Even so, the little they did know, or worked out for themselves, was not to be discussed outside the two crews. Security was of the essence.

Then one day it became official. Harry and Jim were instructed to report to the Station Commander's office at RAF Lyneham. They were told to attend a highly-classified briefing in the station's secure facility. In the briefing room the Station Commander, Group Captain Clive Evans, and a Squadron Leader from HQ 38 Group briefed on a requirement to insert, or drop, a small SAS intelligence-gathering cell on to the Falklands. Its task would be to monitor Argentine activity, by gathering information about troop strengths and dispositions, and to report back to the UK via satellite link or high frequency (H/F) radio. An outline plan had been prepared to accomplish this. It involved the covert insertion of a patrol in a designated area in the west of East Falklands. The patrol would also have, as was normal in these situations, the task of creating a little havoc where and when the situation presented itself.

The range of the C130 at that time made it impossible to reach the Falklands – or indeed anywhere else in the South Atlantic – unless the aircraft staged through South America. The plan therefore envisaged mounting the operation from Chile's Easter Island, whence the C130 would fly down to Punta Arenas, ostensibly to deliver military supplies to the Chilean Air Force. The aircraft would also carry its own engineering pack-up (known as a 'Ranger Pack') consisting of several large boxes. On this occasion the Ranger Pack would be supplemented by several extra boxes, which would conceal eight parachutists plus their equipment whilst the aircraft was on the ground at Punta Arenas. A standard download time would normally be between 90 minutes and 2 hours.

After take-off from Punta Arenas the C130 would route, as expected, back towards Easter Island until out of radar coverage. It would then descend to low-level, turn and fly over the sea round Cape Horn to the Falklands, carry out the insertion, and then return to Punta Arenas to refuel before continuing on to Easter Island.

As a cover for this part of the operation, normal air traffic control (ATC) H/F radio position reports would be made, as if the aircraft was heading towards Easter Island. At the appropriate moment, it would be 'discovered' that an important box that should have been offloaded, was still on the aircraft. The aircraft would therefore have to return to Punta Arenas. The radio call to explain this would be made at a time that would coincide with the aircraft's return from the Falklands, when it would reappear on the radar again returning from the west.

Harry and his navigator checked the plan and proposed timings and found that the approximate time of 8 hours from Punta Arenas to the dropping zone (DZ) and back again was roughly the same as Punta Arenas to Easter Island. The plan was feasible.

They had a concern, though. An intelligence briefing on the Argentine Order of Battle given a few days earlier had indicated that they had an excellent H/F direction finding (D/F) capability. The worry was that if the C130's radio transmissions during the Punta-Falklands-Punta leg were D/F'd by the Argentines, they would be found to be originating in the South Atlantic, and not from the Pacific somewhere between Punta Arenas and Easter Island. Harry suggested therefore that a second C130 should accompany his aircraft to Punta Arenas. It would then continue on to Easter Island, maintaining the radio transmissions for both aircraft after Harry's aircraft parted company and set off for the Falklands. This amendment to the original plan was accepted.

The next few days were spent conducting detailed route-planning and evolving techniques that would permit the dropping of parachutists in winds of up to thirty-five knots, i.e. much higher than the normal limits.

The route to the DZ was chosen with care, using radar coverage map overlays provided by the Royal Radar Establishment and other SF sources. It was calculated that they should be able to get in and out of the DZ at low level (i.e. 250 feet above ground level [AGL]) and stay below any enemy radar. In order to increase the chances of success, the mission would be carried out at night. Harry said later:

When we started our detailed planning, one of the potential problems identified was the winter climate and, in particular the high winds which were regularly twenty to thirty-five knots; indeed, forty to fifty knots was not uncommon. We realised then that we had a major hurdle to overcome if we were successfully to carry out this parachute insertion. The existing low-level military static-line parachutes had little or no steering ability, which meant that the effect of wind-drift on the parachutist could not be countered. This restricted their use to ground level winds of about eighteen knots maximum and led us to consider the steerable, square parachutes used in free-fall drops.

For the drop, the aircraft would therefore have to climb smartly to 2,500 feet AGL, to allow the parachutists to jump using their new (and not yet cleared for use) military free-fall parachutes. The aircraft would therefore be briefly exposed and vulnerable until it descended to 250 feet.

The route chosen would take the aircraft from a promontory on the west side of the northern entrance to Falkland Sound – easily identifiable on the aircraft's radar in the event of bad weather or poor visibility – and thence to the San Carlos inlet and, finally, via a gap between two hills, approximately 1,000 feet high, to the DZ. After the drop the aircraft, having descended to low level, would exit the area to the northwest. The routing was designed to utilise maximum cover and be as covert as possible.

Harry and his navigator were instructed to report back to HQ 38 Group to present their detailed plan. They were told it was too complicated and should be simplified. In their view this would inevitably mean that the approach to the DZ would be less covert and consequently more risky. They were not at all happy about this new development and agreed amongst themselves that they would stick to their original plan.

When they deployed to Ascension Island in mid-May, the mission was still an option on the table. By that time, the C130 fleet was heavily focussed on the long-range resupply of the Task Force using in-flight refuelling. A few days later, however, Harry received a highly classified message warning him that the mission would go ahead shortly, but using a single C130 only and operating from Ascension Island. He would fly directly to the DZ and then recover to an airfield that 'had yet to be determined' (but not Ascension Island). The general consensus was that it would probably be Punta Arenas, where they would refuel before continuing on to Easter Island.

They would never find out though, as Harry's mission was suddenly cancelled. 'We assumed,' Jim said, 'that it was because of mounting concern that the normally excessive wind strengths would preclude a safe (and therefore, successful), parachute drop'. Harry just thought that events had probably overtaken the mission. The Task Force had arrived in the Falklands area, and it might have been decided that the SAS and SBS teams should be inserted on to the islands by helicopter or RIB (rigid inflatable boat). In the end, the SAS troops were quietly inserted by RIBs from the Task Force, and the information that they gathered indicated that the number of Argentine troops in the Falklands had been greatly underestimated.

Much of the training and planning that had been carried out by the C130 crews, however, would not be wasted, and would shortly be put to good use in the context of another all-important mission, Operation Mikado.

Operation Mikado

Max Roberts was summoned back to Hereford for further meetings; this time to discuss Operation Mikado, which had assumed a greater urgency after the Argentine Exocet attack on HMS *Sheffield* on 4th May. This mission would now clearly be even more challenging. The training and preparation already carried out would still be relevant, but there would be a need for further planning and much refining.

It was immediately made clear that, apart from David Musgrave, no one else was to be told even of the existence of this mission, let alone any of the detail. This included not just the crew of the second C130 that would participate in the mission (Harry's), but even other members of Max's crew.

This heightened level of security presented some problems. Normally, the burden of planning for any C130 mission was shared between the navigator and the co-pilot, but on this occasion even co-pilot Nigel Watson was not allowed to know of the mission's existence until some time later. Max alone had the full picture and David was only gradually fed what he needed to know for planning purposes, which initially he had to do alone.

In Max's words: 'We were forced to operate in little bubbles, which inevitably led to some confusion and affected morale.' Even so, he was being diplomatic. Much had to be discussed and there were many problems to be resolved, whilst the level of secrecy imposed constraints which impeded the process of training and problem solving. Sometimes what was perceived by Max and David as being crucial to success, was not necessarily a view shared by the SAS.

Many of the issues to be resolved involved providing the designated aircraft with equipment not normally carried by the C130 fleet. Accurate maps for the final low-level approach to Río Grande proved hard to find, but precise navigation would be essential, the aircraft would have to avoid detection, and the landing would have to be from the first, and only, approach. Air Chief Marshal Sir Michael Armitage was Director of Service Intelligence in 1982. He recalled: 'One day we were asked to produce, in short order, a map of the Río Grande area, clearly indicating Argentine radar coverage. This would enable the C130 crews to plan the safest low-level approach to the airfield whilst, hopefully, avoiding detection.' He set his staff to work.

Certain non-standard items had to be found and installed, including radar warning receivers, chaff-dispensing systems, decoy flares, seat armour and suitable parachutes in case an emergency necessitated abandoning the aircraft in the vicinity of the Task Force. The need for explosion suppression foam had been discussed before the war and was again requested. It could have been a lifesaver but in the event was not approved.

There were many other issues too and items had to be begged, borrowed or 'acquired' by whatever means necessary. Much lateral thinking went into purloining items not normally available. A few 'illegal' modifications to the aircraft were also tolerated in these exceptional circumstances. And everything, of course, was needed immediately!

A new generation of night-vision goggles had just become available and these were acquired for crew members. They were an enormous improvement on those previously available – so much so that, in David Musgrave's view, they probably changed the possibility of failure into a probability of success. Some 'rather exciting' low-level training was carried out in Scotland using them down to 150 feet – and over Dartmoor at night down to 250 feet. A safety pilot, also wearing night vision goggles, was carried during these flights and radar altimeters had to be serviceable.

If, during Operation Mikado, there happened not to be a moon, or the light level was insufficient, the mission would still have to go ahead, probably flying 500 feet above the highest known obstacle in the area and relying heavily on several pairs of wide eyes. It was decided at some point that both aircraft would carry extra crew members. That would certainly be a help.

94

Towards the middle of April it had become apparent that one of the C130's main tasks would be the resupply of the Task Force, but by then it was already at the extreme range of even the Ascension-based aircraft. It was clear that the range of the aircraft had to be extended.

Tony Webb was on a ground tour at the time and, as an ex-C130 pilot, was given the task by HQ 38 Group of determining how many C130s should be fitted with a probe. He recalled: 'We decided there should be two Probe Long Range (PLR) aircraft with probes and extra internal fuel tanks, followed by ten further aircraft with probes only. A further four aircraft would be equipped to give them the capability to act in the role of tanker aircraft.'

Once the decision to proceed with an air-to-air refuelling (AAR) capability was taken, Marshall of Cambridge, the internationally-renowned aerospace engineering company, set to work with enthusiasm. It had been appointed in the mid-1960s as the first overseas service centre for the US company, Lockheed. This resulted in a contract that was to continue for decades, providing design, repair and modification facilities for the RAF's Hercules C130 transport fleet. In 1982, the firm was short of work and welcomed a government contract to provide C130 aircraft with an in-flight refuelling capability.

Things moved along quickly. The first C130 fitted with a probe arrived at Boscombe Down towards the end of April. Modifying those aircraft selected to offload fuel would take a little longer. At Boscombe Down, RAF test pilot Ian Strachan checked out the aircraft systems and handling aspects. Ian said: 'The C130's probe was in front of the co-pilot which made AAR easier for him, but slightly less straightforward for the captain. The trouble was the captain invariably wanted to do it!'

The next day, Max and Harry arrived at Boscombe Down where they were quickly trained in C130 AAR. Max was nominated as the first Hercules AAR instructor. He established the Hercules AAR Flight and set about passing on his newly-acquired skills to the other SF pilots with gusto. None of Max's pilots had carried out AAR previously and they had little time in which to become proficient. It was a steep learning curve for everyone.

The crews later spoke very highly of the support they received during this work-up phase, and the rapidity with which everything appeared or happened. The general view was that the RAF 'system', and RAF Lyneham Station Commander, Clive Evans, had moved mountains to ensure that the Mikado crews had the highest priority and swiftly received what they needed. Clive Evans commented recently: 'During the

Falklands War, I lost control over my SF flight crews and aircraft when they were on SAS missions. The SAS top order had the ability to communicate directly to the *highest* level!'

After the war, he served a spell in the Falklands as Deputy Commander and, in 1990, became the first senior officer to visit Argentina after the war. He was sent to pave the way for a return to normal relations. Shortly after his visit, Group Captain Patrick Tootal, also an ex-C130 pilot, arrived in Buenos Aires to become the first post-war Defence Attaché.

The Special Forces

The Special Forces, vehicles and equipment necessary for Operation Mikado had to be equally distributed between both aircraft. What one aircraft could carry would be insufficient to ensure the mission's success. It was decided therefore that, in the event something major occurred to prevent either aircraft continuing on to Río Grande, the mission would be aborted immediately.

One of the subjects discussed at Hereford was the possibility of finding French technicians at Río Grande (there was a strong rumour that a number of them had remained in Argentina to support the French-supplied aircraft and missiles); and, if they were found, how to handle the situation. David summed it up rather neatly. He said: 'There was a simple solution to that problem. There would be neither the time nor the inclination to deal selectively with anyone encountered. They would probably have been killed in the process of accomplishing the mission and getting out alive.'

At the initial Hereford briefings, Max and David formed the impression that the SAS were always under enormous pressure to succeed and, in consequence, were probably rather ruthless and not necessarily inclined to reveal all their cards. A particular area of concern related to where the C130s waited whilst the SAS troops 'did the business'. A few cracks started to appear between the thinking of the RAF and the SAS. David recalled:

Max and I quickly established that our preferred option was to stay on the ground with engines running. The SAS, however, proposed that the C130s should get airborne again after they had disembarked, and orbit a few miles away waiting to be called back in. This was thought to be totally illogical by the RAF crews, as it would dangerously expose the aircraft, especially as the element of surprise would already have been lost.

The SAS could also be very vulnerable whilst awaiting the return of the aircraft if their timing was not precise. In any case, if the mission was to succeed at all, the time available to the SAS would hardly have justified the C130s taking off again to orbit a few miles away. It is hard to imagine anyone surviving if the SAS needed much time to carry out their task, although figures between 3 and 15 minutes were bandied around. Jim remembered hearing someone claim that they would need only one minute. What was learned later about the extent to which Argentina had deployed ground forces to defend the airfield, served only to confirm the wisdom of the RAF's preference for remaining on the ground.

The two navigators decided they could be usefully employed, whilst waiting for the SAS to return to the aircraft, by positioning themselves outside their respective aircraft and providing a token defence with sub-machine guns. These ideas were eventually accepted by the SAS.

Max and David could not entirely shake off the feeling, however, that the SAS may have quietly decided not to reboard the aircraft at all, but to proceed overland to Chile instead. They might even have decided to disable the two aircraft to prevent them falling into Argentine hands, forcing the RAF crews to travel overland with them.

This was not an option the crews cared to consider. RAF crews are in their element in the air, doing what they are trained to do. They would have less appetite for an overland option, if it could be avoided. They were not trained, as were the SAS, to keep up a fast pace across difficult terrain. There was also a slight suspicion that, in the event that one of the RAF crew members could not keep up, or was injured and holding up the others, the SAS were perfectly capable of sacrificing the man to keep up the pace.

At one point it was decided that the crew members should all carry small arms. Someone felt this should be mentioned to the SAS. It turned out to be a bad move, however, and the idea had to be dropped amidst mutterings that 'we have enough to worry about without the increased risk of friendly fire!'

Various other options were considered from time to time, discussed and dropped. The possibility of landing the C130s on a straight, suitable stretch of road not too far from the airfield was debated. Whilst having some merit, since the C130s' chances of survival might have been improved away from a heavily-defended airfield, the SAS would have had the added problem of getting to the airfield, accessing it and then returning to the aircraft afterwards. It might have been feasible but would have required another layer of intelligence and the idea was therefore dropped.

There was also a reserve airfield not too far away from Río Grande, which had been developed by Argentina for aircraft dispersal in the event of a conflict with Chile. This, too, came under scrutiny but was not pursued; either because of inadequate intelligence, the difficulty for the aircraft of making a safe approach at night, or the problems associated with retrieving the SAS after their activities at Río Grande. The extent to which the airfield was defended, if indeed it was, would also have had to be determined, requiring yet more intelligence.

Ready to Go

Finally, the problem areas were sorted out to everyone's satisfaction, the RAF 'system' had surpassed itself and provided what was needed, and the crews were trained and ready. Harry and his crew left Lyneham on 13th May for Ascension Island, to take up the role of long-range resupply of the Task Force and await possible further SF tasking.

Cabinet approval for Operation Mikado was given, and relayed to Northwood, on 14th May, following which Harry's crew was tasked to take the eight-man SAS patrol destined for Phase 1 of Mikado down to the Task Force on 16th May. Harry recalled: 'During an epic flight of over twenty-four hours, we inserted the patrol and they were taken on board HMS *Invincible* to rest for twenty-four hours before being flown to Argentina in a Sea King.' Jim Cunningham added:

> For that flight south to the Task Force, we insisted on knowing its current disposition (known as Op Gen Bravo) for safety reasons. This included the sailing speed and direction of its elements. Normally this would not have been made available to us, but on this occasion we insisted that it should be and so, exceptionally, it was. When we reached the Task Force, we had to pass through a predetermined 'arrival gate' to reassure the RN that we were not an Argentine C130. It then required four passes dropping two SF personnel plus their equipment on each pass. After parachuting into the sea close to the designated ship, they were rapidly picked up by

RIB. The twenty-four-hour mission was accomplished with a single air-to-air refuelling.

Shortly after Harry landed back at Ascension Island, the Sea King helicopter, captained by Royal Marine pilot Richard Hutchings, took off from HMS *Invincible* with the SAS patrol. Phase 1 of Operation Mikado was under way.

On 19th May, Harry was joined by Max at Ascension Island. Together they waited to hear that the vital intelligence, which would allow Phase 2 to proceed, had been received from the SAS patrol flown to Argentina. On 20th May, Max was summoned to Air Headquarters to receive the Top Secret Operation Order that commanded him to lead a two-aircraft assault to the airfield at Río Grande. He noted with some disquiet that there was no recovery plan.

During the days that followed, rumours were rife that all had not gone quite as it should, and that perhaps Phase 1 had been unsuccessful. Nobody knew for sure. What was certain, however, was that being told that a perceived suicide mission is on, then off, and then on again, is not good for anyone's health. The strain was palpable. Jim Norfolk, the extra pilot on Harry's aircraft, recalled: 'We were all loaded up and ready to go. We just awaited the authority to proceed. Then we heard that Phase 1 had definitely failed.'

Some alternative, last-gasp ideas for gathering the intelligence were briefly considered. One envisaged 6 SF personnel parachuting from an altitude of 800 feet using a static line, 5 kilometres north of Río Grande and then proceeding to the air base. Information gathered would then be communicated directly to Hereford by satellite. The plan was abandoned, however. It would have involved a further delay of three to four days, and would have been very risky; perhaps unacceptably so.

On 25th May, an Exocet missile destroyed the *Atlantic Conveyor*, further emphasising the importance of Max and Harry's mission. On the following day, the Sea King crew arrived in Santiago, having walked from the crash site to Punta Arenas in Chile. Still Max, Harry and their crews waited.

Various schemes were considered to try and keep Phase 2 of Mikado alive. The worldwide effort to ascertain whether Argentina had managed to procure any further Exocet missiles meanwhile failed to come up with anything. At the end of May, one of the Super Etendards fired the fifth and last of the five missiles delivered to Argentina back in November 1981.

The war, as it turned out, still had two weeks to run. It could have been longer; *Hermes* and *Invincible*, and other RN ships, would in theory have been vulnerable until the bitter end. Although some would say that the SIS had comprehensively ensured that Argentina could not obtain any more Exocets, could anyone really be so sure? There were certainly many others who were less certain. Well over a thousand of these missiles had been sold to nations around the world, some of which were quite unscrupulous and might have preferred that Argentina won the war. There were also a great many totally unscrupulous arms dealers who would have done anything for the sums of money such a deal promised.

Mikado is Cancelled

The powers-that-be finally made the decision, late on 30th May, to lay Operation Mikado to rest. Another option, to attack Río Grande by other means, was briefly considered. It envisaged the infiltration of SF personnel by inflatable boats from the submarine HMS *Onyx*. The men would be disgorged a few miles offshore with their equipment and weapons, including anti-tank rockets and explosive charges. A few brief rehearsals had been carried out in San Carlos Water. The plan did not include getting the men out again. They would have to escape overland and across the border into Chile, no doubt hotly pursued by Argentine troops. That plan was also abandoned.

The uncertainty that the crews had lived with had made life very difficult for a while. Mikado had never been far from their minds. It was the first thing that they checked on after returning from their other missions. The crews of SF Flight were now able to concentrate on their other principal tasks, the increasingly urgent requirement for long-range supply drops to the Task Force, and planning the insertion of patrols as required into the Falklands.

Their reaction to the cancellation was nevertheless understandably mixed. There was considerable relief, but it was tempered with disappointment. It would, after all, have been one of those unique opportunities sought by real professionals in war. David said: 'As far as we were concerned, Operation Mikado was under way when we left Lyneham, having said goodbye to wives and children we believed we might never see again. We understood the risks, but the crews were ready for it.' Although the expression was rarely used, it was regarded by most as being a suicide mission.

The finger of blame for the failure of Phase 1 should certainly not be pointed at the Sea King crew. They did exactly what was required of them, and would have been as disappointed as were the C130 crews that Operation Mikado did not take place – with, of course, a successful outcome.

As Richard Hutchings said years later: 'The Argentine military were as aware as we were that they had a potentially devastating weapon system. They had anticipated a raid, and planned accordingly.' It was later discovered that a substantial defence force of marines and infantry, under the command of Brigadier Miguel Pita, was deployed at Río Grande at the time of the proposed operation, both on the base, and surrounding it in depth. There were minefields too, anti-aircraft artillery, surface-to-air missiles, and the perimeter fence was patrolled day and night.

As if all those measures were not enough, two Argentine destroyers had been positioned in the area to beef up the firepower and provide radar coverage. The Argentines were also wise enough to disperse their Super Etendards from time to time off the base, to guarded revetments alongside the nearby coast road. There was no guarantee, therefore, that the aircraft would have been at the Río Grande air base when the C130s arrived. In this eventuality, the SAS would still have sought out the Argentine aircrew, ground crew, and technical support facilities, and destroyed whatever they could. Any recently-acquired missiles would certainly have been included.

Their mission, however, was fated to join the long list of those that, having been meticulously planned and prepared for, were subsequently cancelled and might have been quietly forgotten. Hopefully, the occasional mention serves as a reminder that many such missions, fraught with dangers and complications, were unhesitatingly taken on by courageous, dedicated professionals grateful for the opportunity to serve their country doing what they do best. Nevertheless, one imagines that Max and Harry must have hoped that the SAS would have been able to 'do the business' in no more than 3 minutes.

A VC10 Captain Remembers

One day, not long after Phase One was aborted, Rob Robinson, a No 10 Squadron VC10 captain, was relaxing by a hotel swimming pool in Dakar, Senegal, when he was summoned to the telephone. The brief call advised him that, instead of returning to RAF Brize Norton that evening as planned, he and his crew would be picked up by a C130 aircraft within the hour and taken to Ascension Island. Once there, he would be briefed on the reason for the change of plan. He said:

On arrival at Ascension Island, we were taken to a bungalow, apart from other RAF crews. We spent the evening speculating on what the next day would bring. In the early hours of the following morning, I was informed that someone wished to speak to me. I went out on to the verandah. Lurking in the bushes, I found Major Ian Cooke SAS. He said we were required to fly an SAS squadron to Belize. There was a VC10 aircraft waiting for us. In Belize, he said, the SAS would probably transfer to a civilian aircraft which would take them all to an Argentine fighter base, where their mission would be to locate and destroy Exocet missiles. If, for any reason, the civilian aircraft did not materialise in Belize, we would be required to fly them on down to Argentina.

I had more than the slightest suspicion that the civilian aircraft was never expected to materialise in Belize. Take-off was planned for 1400 hours that day. A quick call to HQ 38 Group in the UK confirmed my worst fears. I briefed the crew and we spent the rest of the morning planning the mission.

We had been waiting on the aircraft for about an hour, and all the SAS kit had been loaded, when we received a call from Operations ordering us to stand down. We learned later that the War Cabinet had decided that this dire measure was no longer considered necessary. It certainly would have been a desperate measure sending a VC10 on such a mission, especially with a crew that had not been able to train or prepare for it.

Rob added recently: 'Perhaps a civilian aircraft might have had a slim chance of landing at Río Grande unscathed, on the pretext of being in a Mayday situation, but it would never have taken off again! It was unlikely anyway that a civilian crew would have risked their necks, or certain imprisonment if they were more fortunate, just for financial reward.'

He and his crew were left with the distinct impression that, if the mission had not been cancelled, it would have been VC10 all the way! Rob and his crew were also involved in three of the casualty evacuation flights to Montevideo; a breeze by comparison, and with large red crosses painted on the aircraft by way of an insurance policy.

When Max Roberts and Harry Burgoyne learned, nearly thirty years later, that a VC10 had been contemplated for the mission they had so thoroughly trained and prepared for, they were, understandably, absolutely amazed.

Part Two
Chile – Our Cautious Ally

Chile

Why Cautious?

Various events over the years have shaped relations between Chile and its Latin American neighbours, and with Britain. They also help to explain the position taken by Chile during the Falklands War.

In the sixteenth century, the Spanish arrived in western South America searching for gold and silver. Instead, they found Indians and a region with good, fertile soil and agricultural potential. The conquest of Chile was carried out in 1550 and it became part of the Viceroyalty of Peru.

In 1810, Chile became an autonomous republic under the Spanish monarchy, but in the years that followed a strong mood for total independence developed. After a lengthy struggle under the legendary Bernardo O'Higgins (whose statue stands in Santiago today), Chile was proclaimed an independent republic in 1818. The decades that followed were characterised by the absolute rule of successive presidents, the power exercised by wealthy landlords, and the strong influence of the Roman Catholic Church. Social change was minimal and there was a sharp divide between the 'haves' who had the power, and the 'have-nots' who had very little, including no say at all in their own destiny.

In the 1880s, the British Crown was involved in a process which determined that three disputed islands in the Beagle Channel should belong to Chile rather than to Argentina. This proved to be a decision that left a festering sore in their relationship, which has persisted to this day. It was further aggravated by a Chilean decision to populate the islands with families that lived and worked on them.

From 1879–83, what became known as the War of the Pacific was fought between Chilean forces and those of an alliance formed between Peru and Bolivia. Essentially, the war started as a dispute over ownership of territory containing mineral-rich deposits and escalated rapidly. No one seems quite sure who started it, but it led to Chile's invasion of Bolivia's port city of Antofagasta. Chile went on to destroy Peru's navy and plunder Lima. It was mainly a guerrilla war after 1881 and a truce was finally signed in 1884. The war resulted in Chile acquiring parts of Peru and Bolivia and leaving the latter landlocked. Most importantly though, the war has left deep scars and bitter memories.

More recently, Salvador Allende became the first communist to win power in a democratic election, when he was elected president in 1970. His programme of nationalising the means of production and expropriating foreign-owned banks, corporations and industries badly damaged the Chilean economy and, with a little help from the USA which sought to exacerbate the situation, resulted in nationwide unrest and rioting.

In September 1973, when inflation was running at 900 per cent, General Pinochet led a military coup aimed at toppling Allende and communism along with him. The result was quick and inevitable. Allende was found dead in La Moneda, the presidential palace, and controversy has surrounded the manner of his death ever since.

The extent to which the USA was involved in the coup is also uncertain (though rumours abound), but it is unlikely to have been too upset to see a communist government fall in its own back yard.

After the coup, there was huge pressure on governments across Western Europe to cut links with Chile and to be less enthusiastic about selling defence equipment to it. At the time, Britain had lucrative orders to build or modernise warships for Chile, and the Wilson government resisted the pressure, insisting that existing contracts should be honoured.

President Pinochet soon replaced the initial junta with a system that gave him sole control and a Cabinet, two-thirds of which were serving officers.

During his tenure in office, the economy went from strength to strength, but at the same time the nation was plagued by atrocities. Countless numbers of people, whose only crime was to oppose or criticise his extreme methods, were rounded up, tortured and killed. Many simply disappeared. The disparity between rich and poor soon became greater than in any other country in South America.

The Sheila Cassidy Affair

In 1975, an incident occurred that significantly affected Britain's relationship with Chile for several years. For many it became known as 'The Sheila Cassidy Affair'. Her story really started on 15th October 1975.

Sheila Cassidy was, and is, a very personable and intelligent lady. She was apolitical and interested only in advancing her skills as a medical practitioner. She also held the not-unreasonable view that she wanted to practice medicine where she was most needed. It was logical therefore that she should accept an offer from a Chilean friend, whom she met and studied with in Britain, to go to Chile where a huge number of poor people were unable to get any medical advice or treatment. She was never in any way a member of, or in league with, any of the many anti-government or left-wing groups that existed at the time. She just worked in a poor, run-down urban clinic. Not unnaturally, her reputation as a caring person and a skilful doctor spread around the community.

On that fateful October day, a gun battle took place in a small country town some fifteen kilometres from Santiago. Members of Chile's out-lawed revolutionary party, the MIR (El Movimiento Izquierda Revolu-cionaria), had been surprised by the security forces and during the shoot-out, one man was killed and another received bullet wounds in the leg.

Several days later, Sheila Cassidy had a visitor. A Chilean priest, who was known to her, asked if she was prepared to treat a man with a bullet in his leg. Her reaction was a purely medical one. She said: 'I didn't hesitate; it was not my place to judge this man, but to treat him'. He was Nelson Gutierrez, a member of the MIR.

It is important to understand that in a police state like Chile at that time, it would have been quite impossible for the man to present himself at a hospital. Sheila, if she was prepared to help, probably represented the man's only hope of survival, at the very least of saving his leg. She therefore did what she could for him, before he was accepted into the home of the Vatican's diplomatic representative in Chile. He was then placed in the hands of another doctor. A few days later, on 1st November, Sheila was arrested by men from the DINA (the Directorate of National Intelligence).

The next two months were the most appalling of her life, spent partly at the infamous Villa Grimaldi, the torture centre on the outskirts of San-tiago, partly in solitary confinement and also, for some of the time, at an internment camp. Finally, thanks to British Government pressure, she was released and able to return to the UK.

Robert Gordon, Head of Chancery, said: 'Sheila Cassidy's treatment caused considerable inter-governmental furore. There was also a great deal of indignation in Britain that a British citizen should have been treated in such an appalling way for innocently helping an injured man.' The whole episode created a rift with Chile, which resulted in the Ambassador being withdrawn and the Embassy reduced to a thinly-staffed Consulate. The Chileans refused to apologise and this unsatisfactory situation started to improve only after Margaret Thatcher became Prime Minister.

Sir Reginald Secondé was the British Ambassador in Chile in 1975, at the time of the Sheila Cassidy affair. He said, many years later: 'We were successful in getting Doctor Cassidy out of jail eventually, but I made myself very unpopular in the process. I was then withdrawn back to the UK together with some other members of my staff. We didn't have an Ambassador in Chile for the next four years.'

Prime Minister Thatcher decided that Britain had made its point and it was time to mend fences. She sent John Heath out to Chile in 1980 to be our new Ambassador, with the task of repairing relations between the two countries. Robert Gordon, whose responsibilities included Human Rights issues and Chile's repressive tendencies, had already arrived ahead of him.

Fortuitously, all this occurred just prior to the Falklands War, by which time the two governments had managed to put those difficult years behind them. By the time Argentina invaded the Falklands, Chile was just about ready to be our cautious ally – but it was a close-run thing.

The Beagle Channel Dispute

Pinochet had already been president for five years when Chile and Argentina came to the brink of war over the disputed Beagle Channel islands in 1978. In November of that year, talks between the two countries predictably broke down. Argentina's Admiral Massera had been largely instrumental in steering his country towards the confrontation, and its military had organised a propaganda campaign to prepare the population for a 'just war against Chilean territorial encroachment'.

The two countries also took the opportunity to argue over the position of the border running through the Andes, and the Chilean Alpine Troops, equipped with a rare and very robust breed of horse, the only one which could cope with the difficult mountainous conditions, were deployed.

The Rev. Terry Brighton was an agricultural missionary in Argentina at the time. He recalled the Alpine Troops of both countries being deployed, and the tension in the air. 'But,' he said, 'very quickly the mood changed and there was a feeling amongst the troops that they didn't really want to fight at all. There were many stories doing the rounds that the troops of both countries, as they faced each other across the border, communicated

110

and even shared food, and that many thought the islands not worth dying for.'

War was only narrowly averted by some skilful diplomacy on the part of the USA. The Pope was asked to intervene, which he quickly and wisely agreed to do. He despatched a cardinal to South America who banged a few governmental heads together, and the crisis was de-fused.

The Argentine Navy in particular was unhappy that the opportunity had been lost, but most ordinary people in both countries were hugely relieved. The British, of course, were happily selling arms to both sides anyway!

Many Argentines might say today that, whilst seizing the islands would hardly justify the loss of life, it should nevertheless remain an objective to be realised in the longer term. Few believe it will happen in their lifetime. The sad fact is that a ruling made in Europe back in the nineteenth century has resulted in over a hundred years of dislike and mistrust between the two countries.

1982

Although the British Embassy would say that the worst of the brutality of President Pinochet's Chile had become a thing of the past by 1982, there were still violent demonstrations against the government from time to time. Left-wing opposition had certainly not been eradicated and those arrested were frequently dealt with harshly. However, the economy was doing well, copper prices were rising and most of the population were reasonably content.

John Cummins, Consul at the British Embassy, Santiago, recalled being sent to Buenos Aires in January 1982 on official business. He said: 'There was no suggestion at that time that anything as dramatic as an Argentine invasion might happen, even though the junta was perceived as being somewhat erratic.'

The following month, he went down to Punta Arenas to organise the first visit by a Royal Navy ship to Chile since the Sheila Cassidy affair. Military co-operation between Britain and Chile had stopped completely after that episode. His task had been to ensure that the visit by HMS *Endurance* went smoothly. A new Naval Attaché had been appointed, but he was not due to arrive in Santiago until later in the month. Punta Arenas was chosen for the visit for being rather off the beaten track, enabling a fairly low-key start to getting visits going again.

'I remember very clearly that Captain Nick Barker had expressed his concern regarding the atmosphere in Argentina, where he had just been,' John said. 'Unusually, he and his crew had been cold-shouldered in Ushuaia and not made to feel at all welcome. There were hints of worse to come as well.'

Shortly afterwards, Argentina started to act provocatively. The cruiser *Belgrano* sailed up and down the Beagle Channel, crossing the invisible line down the middle of the channel into Chilean waters. Argentina seemed to be suddenly pushing the boundaries, perhaps testing to see if there would be any reaction. This was only a few weeks before their invasion fleet set sail for the Falklands. In the climate of mistrust that prevailed between Argentina and Chile, the two countries exchanged military attachés, but any form of co-operation between their respective armed forces was non-existent. They did not carry out joint exercises together, and officers did not attend each other's courses (e.g. staff college). Although Chileans regarded Argentina as their main threat, relations with Peru and Bolivia were poor as well.

Captain Malcolm Johns arrived in Santiago as Naval Attaché in April 1982. Recalling his impressions of the Chilean armed forces at that time, he said:

I was very impressed with the general level of preparedness. They were well-equipped and trained, ready for anything, kept their forces at constant readiness and were meticulous about servicing and maintenance. The Chilean Navy was probably marginally superior to Argentina's. It had excellent facilities including a dockyard and a floating dock, which were comparable to anything you would find in Portsmouth.

The Argentine Air Force, though, was probably slightly superior to Chile's and its pilots better trained. Their armies were comparable, but the Chileans were more likely to take the fight to the last man. I found the Chilean Army very Germanic and not easy to relate to, unlike the Air Force, which was kind, helpful and generous. The Navy, which had many ex-Royal Navy ships was, not surprisingly, very straightforward to deal with. Each of the armed forces had its own intelligence branch headed by a general (or equivalent). There was also a completely separate civilian intelligence service.

The intelligence services were approachable and worked well with us. When Britain needed to know all about Argentine air movements at the air base at Río Grande, the Chileans agreed to co-operate but said they didn't have a suitable radar to monitor them, so we flew one in (Graham Finch's C130 brought it out from the UK and took it down to Punta Arenas).

Chile's Reaction to the Argentine Invasion

Robert Gordon recalled that in 1979, not long after arriving in Chile, he drove across the border to Comodoro Rivadavia in Argentina. From there, he went to the Falklands to attend the wedding of a friend. This friend contacted Robert from the Falklands on 2nd April 1982 by ham radio (via a Chilean contact), and informed him that the invasion fleet was arriving. Robert believes he may have been the first person outside the Falklands to learn of the fleet's arrival; information which he duly, and hastily, passed on.

When news of the invasion broke, the Chilean Ambassador in London was instructed to urge the British Government not to allow Argentina to get away with it. Chile was concerned that if Argentina gained control of the Falklands, she (Chile) would lose an ally with a presence close to South America.

The Ambassador was also directed, by way of making an early gesture on Chile's part, to offer Britain the ex-Royal Fleet Auxiliary (RFA) *Tidepool* for the Task Force. She had already been sold to Chile, and was off Peru heading south on 2nd April. The offer was gratefully accepted, and *Tidepool* turned round and headed for Ascension Island instead.

The Naval Attaché's new car was on *Tidepool* at the time, also on its way to Chile. He recalled many years later: 'Mercifully, *Tidepool* survived the war, having successfully dodged bombs and Exocet missiles. Eventually, just after the war, it reached Chile and was accepted by the Chilean Navy... and I finally received my car!'

Chile also offered to delay acceptance of HMS *Norfolk*, destined for its navy as well, but the British Government decided to let that go ahead as planned.

From a British perspective, the southern cone was politically and economically significant, and it was therefore important that the balance of power between Chile and Argentina should be maintained. The way to achieve that was by Britain maintaining a credible presence in the Falklands – and never allowing Argentina to imagine that a military adventure there would be tolerated – whilst having good relations with, and selling defence equipment to, both countries. Britain also knew that if she should be unsuccessful in repossessing the Falklands after an Argentine invasion, an adventure on Argentina's part in the Beagle Channel would most probably follow. That, however, was not the immediate problem.

Chile remained officially neutral throughout the war. It dutifully paid lip-service at times to the notion of Latin-American solidarity – as did all the countries in South America, including Brazil – but its concern was always not to give Argentina any reason to invade it. Chile's Foreign Ministry understood that a public showing of neutrality was essential and that their armed forces should not become actively or obviously involved in our war. That need not, however, preclude Chile from quietly giving Britain some assistance in other ways.

When Argentina's invasion fleet sailed, Chile, by its own admission, was taken by surprise. Ambassador John Heath said: 'Chile was caught napping, but as the Argentine junta was rather unstable, some action like that to consolidate its position should perhaps have been anticipated.'

Many years later the then-retired General Matthieu, Chief of the Chilean Air Force in 1982, said that although they knew the possibility of a Falklands adventure existed, they did not really believe Argentina would be that stupid.

Notwithstanding fears that the war could so easily spill over in their direction, the Chileans played a careful game, endeavouring not to upset either Argentina or Britain. When the *Belgrano* was sunk, Chile unhesitatingly sent a ship to aid Argentine rescue operations.

Nevertheless, the armed forces were quickly brought to a high state of alert. Members of the British Embassy staff at the time have since commented that, whilst this was a perfectly understandable response, there was British concern that Argentina could interpret this as being unnecessarily provocative. John Heath said, many years later: 'We urged Chile to proceed cautiously', a view echoed by Robert Gordon. From Chile's perspective, a country that could act as unpredictably as Argentina had, clearly needed to be carefully watched by a close neighbour that also had much to lose.

Since the general view was that Chile's armed forces were well-trained, well-equipped, and highly motivated, diplomats and attachés in our embassies in both Chile and Argentina agreed that any war between the two countries would be hard-fought, and the result difficult to predict. The element of surprise would therefore always be particularly important. This suggests that the highly-acclaimed Chilean Intelligence Services might have been a little embarrassed at not having anticipated the Argentine invasion. It also helps to explain why Chile not only swiftly placed her armed forces on high alert, but also deployed them along the long border with Argentina.

Chile always denied that she had had any intention of using her troops offensively, or of taking advantage of Argentina by attacking from the rear whilst she was fighting Britain. The explanation for deploying her troops at all, which Chile was anxious to convey via Argentina's Embassy in Santiago, was that 'they were a prudent measure in case of accidents'.

Given the extent of the mistrust that existed between the two countries at the time, Chile's oft-repeated joke that 'it was covering Argentina's back' might have caused some anxiety, but many Argentines have since commented that no one seriously thought Chile would attack them. Britain, for her part, would have been content that Chile's forces tied-up two of Argentina's top marine infantry brigades, keeping them well away from where the war was being fought.

Nevertheless, as the repossession of the Falklands headed towards a successful conclusion, Britain was very anxious that there should not be any misunderstandings. A plan to stage a major Chilean exercise close to its border with Argentina was therefore scaled down to avoid the possibility of unwanted, or unintended, incidents.

Apart from keeping an ever-watchful eye on Argentina, Chile would have been aware of the rumours, or possibility, of an Argentine/Peruvian alliance, or of a Bolivian/Peruvian alliance attempting to reinvent the War of the Pacific. In either case, the motive would have been to seize the moment to enable these historically aggrieved countries to get their own back on Chile. Peru, and in particular the military, was known to have been strongly against the British position during the Falklands War and might have been persuaded to assist Argentina.

Bolivia, on the other hand, would have been less inclined to stick its neck out for Argentina, but was possibly interested in grabbing an opportunity to regain lost territory which would once again give it access to the Pacific coastline. Fortunately, nothing came of the rumours.

The British Embassy view was: 'If the war had spilled over on to the South American mainland, Peru and Bolivia might have been tempted to support Argentina in some way, perhaps even invading Chile from the north. Argentina did hold tentative discussions with Peru at one point.' Ecuador, which did not have any grievances with Chile – and relations between the two countries were good at that time – might have then decided to support Chile and invade Peru from the rear. There were many possibilities.

Whilst Britain was pre-occupied with Argentina during the war, it would also have been aware of the uncertainty that existed throughout South America during those few brief weeks. Not too surprisingly, therefore, the British Embassy in Santiago sent strong signals back to London saying: 'Treat South America with great care... ', the implication being that the situation across the continent was potentially explosive, and the effects possibly far-reaching and with the potential to involve several South American countries.

Part of the reason that so many countries were distinctly edgy can be attributed to Galtieri's 'Invasion Speech', when on 2nd April he informed an unsuspecting nation of the invasion then in progress. The speech contained the threatening message that occupying the Falklands was only the first step in a process of recovering Argentina's lost territories, suggesting to an exuberant (then, but not later) population that after 'Malvinas', Argentina might settle another old score by seizing the disputed islands in the Beagle Channel.

In fact, many people in Chile did not learn of the contents of this speech until a couple of weeks later, when it appeared in the Chilean press for the first time (when, allegedly, it was attributed to a Brazilian source). There had been an assumption initially that the British Government would not be sending a Task Force, which had persisted until the force appeared on the horizon. That assumption had immediately fuelled fears throughout Chile that, in due course, a fight for the Beagle Channel islands was very likely.

Thus, the mood was one of great apprehension at first, but also pro-British. Robert Gordon remembered his wife going to the market shortly after the invasion, and being mobbed by enthusiastic Chileans urging Britain to respond firmly. He said: 'They didn't want us to bluster or make gestures. They were deadly serious, because they understood the consequences of Britain failing them (as they saw it). When the news broke that the Task Force was on its way, the mood in the country was one of huge relief and gratitude.'

This would have been a particularly difficult time for those Chileans living in Tierra del Fuego in the south of Argentina. If Britain had invaded this Argentine province, an idea that was briefly mooted in the very early stages of the war, and quickly snuffed out when the political ramifications were weighed up, then life would have been even more difficult for them. The region boasted an oil-field and two airfields, one of which was the all-important Río Grande base where the Super Etendards were later deployed. Fortunately, the dangers attached to taking the war to the mainland were quickly understood. Quite apart from offending nations around the world that might otherwise have supported British efforts to retake the Falklands, a British occupying force would have been within range of aircraft operating from Argentine air bases.

The British Embassy

There had not been an SIS representative in the British Embassy in Santiago during the years preceding the Falklands War. In Ambassador John Heath's words: 'The Embassy had not needed one. The Chileans were always very co-operative anyway. It was, in any case, a military dictatorship and therefore very intelligence-orientated, and it would not have been a very good idea if we had decided to operate behind their backs. So we played it absolutely straight, in an open way, and if we needed to know something, we simply asked.'

After the invasion, it was discovered in London that nobody knew anything very much about the Argentine Air Force. At the same time, John Heath identified a clear need for an Air Attaché in Santiago. Although Malcolm Johns' responsibilities included covering air matters, as a Royal Navy engineering officer he lacked the necessary experience and contacts to do the job in a war situation; also, he did not speak Spanish. A senior RAF officer, fluent in Spanish, was therefore quickly despatched to Chile, where he established himself and started working closely with the Chilean intelligence services to acquire the information needed.

When 'S' (the RAF officer) arrived in Chile, the nature of his job required him to set himself apart from other Embassy staff. He had a small office, but did not integrate much with the other diplomats, wore civilian clothes, avoided social occasions and operated directly with his contacts in the Chilean Air Force and Intelligence Departments. He was never an officially accredited Air Attaché, but became a vital link between Britain and Chile at a time when each needed the other, and deals had to be struck, determining which country provided what to the other, and what was expected in return.

Though he spent much time in Santiago, he also operated from within a Chilean underground command post at Punta Arenas, where signal and radio communication information from various listening posts was displayed, together with data collected from Chilean radars. The information was presented graphically and clearly, and was also communicated back to Northwood via a satellite communication link.

A powerful radar, which provided information on Argentine air movements, was supplied by Britain and flown down to Punta Arenas, where it was sited close to the Argentine border. The information obtained from it was also relayed back to the UK, and thence to the Task Force, providing early warning of Argentine aircraft heading towards it.

Though the degree of co-operation was invaluable to Britain, it was a marriage of convenience. Each side was cautious, there were strings attached to assistance given, limits beyond which Chile was not prepared to go, and an air of nervousness pervaded; a fear that if Britain erred in any way, Chile might suffer the consequences.

'We received a report from the Americans during the first week of the war,' Sir John Nott said years later. 'It was concerned with the likely reaction of the other South American countries to the invasion. With the single exception of Chile, they all declared their support for Argentina.' Even allowing for the fact that some of those countries were only towing the South American party line and would have been hoping they wouldn't be called upon to do anything too daring in support of Argentina, clearly Chile would be the only possible candidate for allowing us the use of an airfield from which to mount operations.

John Heath obtained agreement from the Chilean military authorities that Britain could use Punta Arenas, subject to RAF aircraft always bearing Chilean markings. Graham Finch, C130 pilot, later remembered the flight to Punta Arenas with the surveillance radar. He said:

> I spent about two and a half weeks in Chile on that particular mission. Our main task was to transport an airfield surveillance radar down to Punta Arenas, where it would fill a vital gap where there wasn't any airborne early warning (AEW) available. In particular, we were very anxious to have the capability to monitor Argentine air movements from their Río Grande base in Tierra del Fuego. After we had delivered the radar, we became involved in No 39 Squadron's (a Canberra photographic reconnaissance unit) activities in Chile.

The British Embassy was very concerned that the Chileans were communicating with their Embassy in London on Falklands-related matters, and using insecure means. It was also known that these communications were being intercepted in Argentina. The Ambassador therefore asked the Chileans if they would henceforth use the British Embassy's secure facility when discussing the Falklands. Unfortunately, the Chileans declined to co-operate.

'Normally though,' Malcolm Johns said, 'those of us in the Embassy who had to deal regularly with Chilean officials found them helpful and friendly, including those who worked for the various intelligence departments. They were clever though, always helpful, but wanting or expecting more than they gave!'

Early in the war, President Pinochet had discussed his own position with General Matthieu. The Head of the Air Force told him that matters could stay in the hands of the military and not become political. Pinochet agreed to step back and leave it all to his military chiefs, and thereafter had little further involvement in the war.

As far as the Air Force chief was concerned, their dealings would henceforth be largely with 'S' specifically, rather than with the British Embassy. This would keep everything within military circles and outside political interference. John Heath had been in complete agreement that matters should be handled in this way.

Punta Arenas

The British link was strong once in parts of Chile. Punta Arenas, which played its part during the Falklands War, lies on the Chilean shores of the Strait of Magellan, and was known as Sandy Point to early British settlers.

British sheep farmers, missionaries, and others who sought a new life there helped to develop the wild, desolate region at the bottom of South America. There is not much evidence of them now, although a few, like the descendents of Thomas Bridges, who left Harburton, Devon in the mid-nineteenth century to settle there, still rear sheep and cater for the few tourists who pass their way. The British Club in Punta Arenas, once a focal point for the small community, was forced to close down just before the Falklands War. For a long time now the 'British' School has only had Chilean pupils.

The beginning of the end of the good days occurred when the Panama Canal was completed in 1914. At a stroke, the passage time and distance for ships travelling between the Pacific and Atlantic Oceans were dramatically cut. Suddenly, there was no need for them to take the long and often dangerous route through the Strait of Magellan, or round the Horn. The outbreak of war in 1939 further exacerbated the situation, together with the slump in meat exports, and the land reforms, which resulted in the break-up of the larger ranches.

During the Falklands War its proximity to the Argentine border, and Argentina's assets in Tierra del Fuego, brought Punta Arenas back into the limelight from time to time. It might have been a logical place from which to mount the Canberra PR missions, had the plan materialised. There were visits from RAF C130 aircraft from time to time (e.g. carrying the SAS and the radar that was to monitor Argentine air movements on the other side of the border), and it became the point of arrival for the Sea King crew and the SAS who participated in Phase 1 of Operation Mikado. The Chilean Air Force maintained an F5 fighter detachment there for the duration of the war.

Not too surprisingly, therefore, it became a place where elements of the Chilean armed forces, the local Chilean population, British journalists, Argentine spies, and passing members of the British armed forces all occasionally rubbed shoulders.

Despite its strategic location, and the traditional links that existed between the Chilean armed forces and the local civilian population, Punta Arenas was a far from secure location and for the duration of the war, the Chileans endeavoured to keep contact between civilians and the military to a minimum. Other measures were also taken, such as obscuring the windows of the airport building, and ensuring that all civilian aircraft kept the blinds closed over their windows during take-offs and landings.

After the War

The outcome of the Falklands War undoubtedly ensured that Chile's relationship with Argentina would enter a period of relative calm and co-operation, untroubled by any Argentine adventures in the Beagle Channel. However, as long as Argentina refuses to accept Chilean ownership of the islands, few believe that the issue will not surface again one day. This prospect, however remote, will ensure that the Chilean and Argentine armed forces will continue to be maintained, trained and equipped with each other in mind. Argentina will be well aware that any rash move on its part will be met by strong Chilean resistance.

Richard Wilkinson was the British Ambassador in Chile 2003–5. He agreed that:

In the short to medium term, the Falklands War produced, as an unintended by-product, a calming-down of the Beagle Channel dispute. However, as long as it remains unresolved, it will not be forgotten by either country. Chile could afford to heave a sigh of national relief after that war because it knew that the worst possible outcome of Argentina's invasion of the Falklands would have been that it was allowed to get away with it.

Chilean nervousness, whilst it co-operated with Britain during the few brief weeks of conflict, will be remembered as a price worth paying, and Chileans will hope that any future British Government will have the same determination to respond in the event of another Argentine venture in the Falklands.

For some time after the war, both Britain and Chile were reluctant to admit publicly that the two countries had co-operated. Sir John Nott recalled some years after the war that: 'The importance of Chile, with its long-standing rivalry and fear of Argentina, was... very great,' and '... in several respects the Chilean link proved very valuable to us.'

The feeling that Chile was our one cautious ally at that difficult time was felt elsewhere as well. Jane Boucher was our Defence Attaché's wife in Tel Aviv. She recalled: 'During the war, the diplomats and their families in the British Embassy were forbidden to socialise with any of the South American countries, except for Chile. I gave English language lessons to the wives of diplomats from many different South American embassies, but during the war I was only allowed to teach Chilean wives. Of course, immediately after the surrender, it was business as usual!'

John Heath confirmed years later that President Pinochet had been easily persuaded that matters could stay in the hands of the military, and need not, therefore, become political. Thereafter, he had little further involvement, even when the Canberra and Nimrod visits were being discussed. This meant that the British Embassy was less involved than it otherwise would have been.

Although the Chilean military had dealt to a great extent with 'S', the level of co-operation that had existed between the two countries had been impressive, and should be judged in the context of Britain's disapproval of Chile's record of human rights abuses, and Chile's nervousness at being caught helping Britain against a neighbour it would have to live with long after the dust of the Falklands War had settled.

At the end of the war there was a nationwide feeling of huge relief in Chile that, because it had urged the British Government to respond strongly, and Britain had, Galtieri and his cronies had been ousted. Chile then felt more secure, and many other countries in South America also felt reassured.

Chilean help had been cautious and discrete. It had to be. If Argentina had taken the war to Chile, the effect could have been explosive, with far-reaching consequences, and could have involved other South American countries. Not surprisingly the Chileans were praying that the Task Force would be successful.

Intelligence Gathering

The Nimrod R1 is Considered

The role of the Nimrod R1 aircraft at RAF Wyton was studied as part of the Chief of the Air Staff's (CAS's) examination of the ways in which the RAF might be able to support the overall military effort. This process led to discussions with the Chilean Government, which resulted in tentative agreement that a Nimrod could operate in their airspace. It was part of an arrangement whereby, in exchange for supplying Chile with certain aircraft and equipment, it would help us to gather vital intelligence.

General Fernando Matthei, Chief of the Chilean Air Force in 1982, summed it up many years later: 'What they (the British) were most interested in was intelligence. They had not been at all concerned about Argentina, (although) they knew everything there was to know about the Soviet Union.' Implicit, perhaps, was a view that we had been caught napping by Argentina.

In theory, the Nimrod would have to be in transit (just visiting) although, in practice, the aircraft would be accorded the use of a covert base and its facilities from which to operate. As it was 'just visiting', the aircraft would keep its normal RAF markings throughout.

The General also claimed that, as part of the arrangement, a couple of Chilean military observers had been on board the aircraft during its missions. This was denied, however, by members of the Nimrod crew. Even on the Chilean base, everyone other than Nimrod squadron personnel was kept well away from this extremely sensitive aircraft.

The Chileans would, of course, benefit from the intelligence gathered. This was of utmost importance to them at a time when they knew Argentina could equally well launch an attack against them, especially if it acquired evidence or even suspected that Chile was assisting Britain in any way.

The Chilean Government would also be unlikely to forget the clear message contained in General Galtieri's 'invasion speech' to the Argentine population on 2nd April. He had said that: '... reclaiming the Malvinas would be just the first step in a process of taking back lost territories...', a clear enough statement of intent that the three disputed islands in the Beagle Channel could be next on the agenda.

That speech, not too surprisingly, had a chilling effect in Chile and accounted significantly for the high degree of nervousness that prevailed throughout the war. This was detected not only by Embassy and RAF personnel at the time, but also by British personnel visiting Chile after the war.

The Chileans had two small turbo-prop aircraft in their inventory for intelligence-gathering purposes. They had been modified to carry equipment that could detect, analyse and classify radar signals, but were severely limited by their inability to operate at high altitude. Any intelligence that could be passed on from Nimrod missions would therefore be very welcome.

So it was that a Nimrod R1 aircraft of No 51 Squadron took off from its base at RAF Wyton on 5th May and flew, via Belize and Bermuda, to a small island in the Pacific Ocean, 600 miles northwest of Santiago. It was the remote Chilean island of San Felix. The Officer Commanding No 1417 Harrier Flight recalled the Nimrod passing through Belize:

> It arrived around midnight, without any lights. The airport, which was never normally open during the hours of darkness, was heavily guarded. The aircraft door remained closed. It just refuelled and continued on its way. No one disembarked and it was on the ground for only about thirty minutes. A number of us watched this 'secret' operation from a distance, it being impossible to avoid a leak in such a small community.

Choosing a Suitable Base

British Ambassador John Heath was involved in the negotiations for a suitable base for the Nimrod. 'I pushed hard,' he said, 'for one offering maximum security, allowing the aircraft to approach from the Pacific and operate at high level on the Chilean side of the border with Argentina.' In any case, the Chileans had every reason for wanting to provide a remote, secure base that would raise no eyebrows.

Air Marshal Sir John Curtiss said recently: 'We were never really successful in getting a proper deal or agreement with the Chileans to use one of their airfields. Although the Nimrod was permitted to operate briefly from the remote offshore island of San Felix, it was on the understanding that this was to be regarded as a visit.'

John Nott, Secretary of State for Defence at the time, endorsed the Air Marshal's view and added: 'We tried to do a deal with them to station combat and support aircraft (in their country) but were not successful; nevertheless, the Chilean link proved very valuable to us.'

San Felix was offered as being the most suitable base from which to mount the Nimrod missions. As the aircraft would be approaching the South American mainland from a point way out in the Pacific Ocean, it was about as remote as anything Chile could offer and would allow the missions to remain as covert as possible.

It was, however, a considerable distance from the aircraft's operating area and the aircraft did not have an in-flight refuelling capability. It therefore had to refuel at a military base on the mainland en route to its operating area. Although the aircraft normally had a range well in excess of 2,000 miles and an average sortie length of between 8 and 9 hours, the mainland 'top-up' helped to ensure the most effective use of each mission. On completion of the mission, the aircraft flew directly back to San Felix.

Whilst some of the information gathered was acquired at high altitude on the Chilean side of the Chile/Argentina border, the aircraft also went around the bottom of South America. One crew member's estimate was that about seventy-five per cent of the overall task was achieved at altitude from the Chilean side of the border.

Martin Lampitt was a C130 pilot on the Operational Conversion Unit (OCU) at RAF Lyneham in 1982. He recalled being sent out to Chile with no prior warning for an unspecified mission but, unusually, flying out from RAF Brize Norton in an old, unmarked B707 freighter aircraft. The crew members appeared to be civilians and declined to say who they worked for or where the aircraft came from. Martin suspected that CIA personnel were on board as American accents were very much in evidence. Fuel en route was paid for in cash. On arrival in Santiago, he took over Graham Finch's C130 and learned for the first time that his mission in Chile had several purposes, support for the Nimrod R1 at San Felix being one of them.

Martin later described San Felix as: '... a chunk of bare rock a long way offshore with an airfield and little else. The airfield had a good runway, little in the way of aids and certainly didn't have any radar. Not much was said on the radio either. Easter Island was the only diversion if ever one was needed.'

San Felix was indeed a quiet and secretive island in 1982. There were no civilians there, just a handful of Chilean military personnel. It boasted a single vehicle and a small twin-engine aircraft. The Chileans were never permitted near the Nimrod and normally only the aircraft captain dealt with them on all matters, operational or domestic. Aircrew and ground crew accommodation was nearby, and a Chilean was detailed to be on hand to cook meals for RAF personnel whenever they were required.

Meteorological information for the Nimrod's missions was rather basic too, according to members of the crew, and came from the UK by signal. It was based upon estimates 'which were not wonderful; for example, the high altitude winds were often very inaccurate and tended in practice to be much stronger than had been forecast,' one crew member said.

For all its shortcomings, though, most of the RAF personnel there in 1982 would probably admit that San Felix was a wholly appropriate choice for the Nimrod during its brief two-week stay in Chile. It was well out of range of prying eyes and ears and enabled the job to be done.

The Aircraft's Characteristics

The Nimrod aircraft had been chosen to replace the Comet 4C to carry out the SIGINT and ELINT (Signals and Electronic Intelligence) roles. Three aircraft had been ordered and the first one was delivered to No 51 Squadron at RAF Wyton in July 1971. At Wyton, the aircraft were fitted out with the most sophisticated electronic equipment available. They were then designated the Nimrod RI. The first aircraft delivered happened to be XW 664, the one that went to Chile in 1982.

The R1, though not unlike its cousins the MR1 and MR2 (maritime patrol aircraft) in appearance, had the ability to eavesdrop on enemy communications, identify electronic transmissions, pinpoint the location of radar systems and gather vital information on an enemy's activities by 'listening' to command and control centres. It was for these reasons that it was decided to send a single Nimrod R1 to Chile.

To carry out its missions, the aircraft had an array of antennae above and below the fuselage. It also carried RAF-trained Spanish-speaking tactical interpreters (TIs) on each mission (the US armed forces were greatly impressed by them during the Gulf War). Normal squadron practice was to have one aircraft fully serviceable and available, and another on standby in case it was required. The third aircraft was usually undergoing some refit or major servicing.

Although British Aerospace responded magnificently to the RAF's sudden requirement to have eight Nimrod MR2s modified for AAR (the first few aircraft were modified and delivered to their base at RAF Kinloss in less than three weeks), fitting a refuelling probe to XW 664 and giving it an in-flight refuelling capability was probably never an issue. Not only was there insufficient time to modify the aircraft before it left Wyton, but it would not have had RAF tanker support in Chile, nor could the Chileans have provided it.

However, the aircraft was temporarily fitted with auxiliary fuel tanks in the weapons bay to increase the fuel capacity. Initially at San Felix, the ground crew also experimented with refuelling the aircraft from fifty-gallon drums, but this proved to be laborious and time-consuming. Once or twice, too, a passing C130 assisted by passing fuel aircraft-to-aircraft. After all this rather tedious experimenting, the decision was taken to refuel at a mainland Chilean base. If required, the aircraft could also operate for long periods on only two engines for greater economy.

Apart from not having the AAR capability that many of the MR2s had received, XW 664 was also not modified to carry Sidewinder air-to-air missiles like the MR2s. It would therefore have been vulnerable had it ever encountered Argentine fighter aircraft. However, the aircraft's usual area of operation, coupled with its ability to operate at high altitude, made this eventuality less likely. It was also fitted with a Missile Approach Warning System before it left the UK, although, when such warnings are received, it helps if the aircraft has the ability to take rapid avoidance action. This would not have been one of a Nimrod's strong points.

When operating a long way from home base with as few ground crew as possible, and not being able to take spares to cover every eventuality, one prays for a measure of good luck. In spite of any prayers offered up, there was a short period of high drama when it was discovered that the aircraft required an engine change. The problem was passed back to the UK where it reverberated around the MoD, and a C130 was rapidly dispatched with a replacement engine and a few extra ground crew.

After each mission, during which as little as possible was ever said on the R/T (radio) and nothing was said in English anyway, the aircraft would send off its post-flight report to the UK. For this purpose, the aircraft was equipped with a Satellite Communication System. The report was received at the same time at the MoD and GCHQ Cheltenham.

Authorising the Missions

Back at the MoD, within the Directorate of Operations (Electronic Warfare and Reconnaissance), Group Captain Fen Allen had three Wing Commanders working for him, with responsibility respectively for No 39 Squadron, Disinformation, and No 51 Squadron. Bill Black, a navigator, looked after No 51 Squadron. Fen recalled that in April, on the Tuesday following Easter weekend:

> Things started to move quickly and a decision in principle was taken to send a Nimrod R1 to South America. Nimrod maritime patrol aircraft operating from Ascension Island were already obtaining a certain amount of intelligence on the Falklands side of Argentina, but not SIGINT/ELINT. They were not equipped for that, and they were also limited in range at that time because the MR2s had yet to be fitted with an AAR capability.

Bill Black's job involved communicating with GCHQ, which was closely involved in framing the mission intelligence requirement. This represented the requirement as perceived not only by GCHQ but by other agencies as well. Bill then had to liaise closely with the squadron to work out the schedule and calculate what was possible, or not, as the case might be.

Fen Allen had then to seek authorisation at the highest level for each individual mission. This would, under normal circumstances, have been obtained from Secretary of State John Nott, but as his wife Miloska was a foreign national from Maribor, Slovenia, it was delegated to his Minister of State. Although the missions were tasked by the MoD and with an obvious input from GCHQ (and other agencies), HQ 1 Group at Bawtry also had a small tasking cell and was closely involved. The MoD, GCHQ and Bawtry were also all interested parties when the post-flight intelligence reports were transmitted back from the aircraft at San Felix after landing from each mission.

The Chileans' Demands

In exchange for helping us to acquire the intelligence we needed, and for allowing the Nimrod to operate from a Chilean base (albeit briefly), the Chileans gave the British Government a shopping list of aircraft and equipment they wanted. They were certainly interested in acquiring

128

Hunter, Canberra and C130 aircraft. RAF personnel visiting Chile at that time were given the distinct impression by their hosts that they believed some of these aircraft would be gifted to them, even that some operating in, or transiting, Chile might be retained and not permitted to return to the UK. Canberras were supplied after the war anyway, but we did supply some Hunter aircraft early on in the war as part of the arrangement.

The Chileans had already been operating the Hunter for some years, dating back to a contract signed in 1966, when fifteen single-seat and three two-seat aircraft were supplied. Some of these aircraft were used to attack President Allende's Palace during General Pinochet's coup of 11th September 1973. The coup resulted in President Allende's death.

In April 1982, Britain supplied a top-up batch of twelve FGA9 Hunter aircraft. They were reported at the time as having been transported out to Chile in a US-based B747 aircraft, taking six aircraft on each of two flights. As defence sales to Chile had been stopped by Britain's Labour government when General Pinochet seized power in 1973, and subsequently restored by the Conservatives in 1980, the Hunter deliveries represented one of the first steps towards normalising relations on the defence sales front. 'Sales' is perhaps slightly 'tongue-in-cheek' as the aircraft were allegedly sold for the princely sum of one pound!

After the war, the RAF sent a few Hunter-qualified pilots to Antofagasta in northern Chile, where the Chilean Air Force Hunters were based, to serve brief (one-year) flying tours alongside Chilean pilots. It was part of a 'thank you' on our part for the Nimrod arrangement. Peter John went to Chile in 1984. He was a Qualified Weapons Instructor with plenty of skill and experience to offer the Chileans and was given a modest allocation of 85 flying hours for the year.

Peter recalled that the Chileans did not have a Hunter flight simulator then; new pilots flew back to RAF Brawdy in the UK to carry out their training. In the mid-1980s, Rediffusion Simulation Ltd bought the aircraft parts from the RAF Brawdy simulator, once it was no longer required, and built a Hunter flight simulator for the Chileans. It was installed at Antofagasta.

Peter also went down to Punta Arenas once on detachment and even then, over two years after the war, was carefully briefed not to be obviously an RAF pilot, including not sporting any give-away markings. 'There was,' he said, 'still a great deal of nervousness on the part of the Chileans. The detachment was part of a policy of making an occasional show of force, or sabre-rattling. There was still hostility and friction between Chile and her neighbour.'

He also remembered an Argentine soldier firing shots across the border just to create an unsettling effect, a 'wind-up' not actually intended to hit anything. Peter felt that, although the Chilean military were extremely professional and well trained, they were at the same time very definitely not over-confident regarding the outcome of any conflict with Argentina. It was also clearly understood by all that it would not take much to set off a train of events that might be hard to stop as long as the Beagle Channel issue continued to foment simmering resentment.

An Important Contribution

The Nimrod R1 made a brief, but nevertheless important, contribution to the vital business of gathering urgently-needed intelligence during the Falklands War. It was also a positive and successful example of the co-operation that existed at that time between Britain and its one cautious ally in South America.

Chile's undoubted nervousness throughout the Nimrod's brief stay at San Felix clearly brought the arrangement to a premature conclusion. In any case, from the British point of view the scale and urgency of the requirement reduced once our troops had landed on the Falklands. Nevertheless, three successful intelligence-gathering missions were flown on the 9th, 15th and 17th of May. The intelligence was, in the usual way, linked to that gathered from all other sources, including the USA and satellites, to obtain the best and most accurate overall picture.

Admiral Woodward is believed to have wanted further missions between the 19th and 21st of May. The Chileans, however, had asked that they be discontinued after the 17th of May mission, and the aircraft was withdrawn before any others could be flown (assuming, of course, that they would have been authorised). The Nimrod returned to RAF Wyton, via Belize and Bermuda, arriving on the 22nd of May.

Ian Strachan, an RAF test pilot at Boscombe Down at that time, later remembered the R1 being sent to Chile and added : 'Boscombe tests were always carried out on Nimrod MR2s. The R1 aircraft, being full of sensitive equipment, were never sent there. As the airframes were prac-tically identical, I am sure that, for certain clearances, whatever we did on the MR2s would have been read across to the R1.'

'Robbie' Robinson, BAe Woodford's Chief Test Pilot for many years, was as qualified as anyone to discuss modifications proposed for Nimrod aircraft during the war. He remembered flying a one-hour sortie in

XW 664 on 2nd June, only a week and a half after it returned from Chile. No 51 Squadron's Derek Brice was the captain. Robbie said:

> Because of the sensitive nature of the Nimrod R1's missions, all modifications were carried out on the station. I recall that this aircraft had been fitted with an AAR probe just before the sortie we flew that day. The flight checks we carried out were designed to check stalling characteristics and directional stability and were required because, prior to going down to South America, the aircraft had been fitted with large wing-tip ECM pods. The aircraft had not, however, had time to obtain the necessary CA (Controller of Aircraft) Release before departing the UK. Presumably this was regarded as acceptable as the aircraft was deemed essential to the war effort. Alternatively, the RAF may have assumed a read-across from the Nimrod MR2s to the R1 until the war was over.

Quite apart from the sensitive nature of the role performed by the Nimrod R1, the specific arrangement with the Chilean authorities demanded that utmost secrecy should surround the aircraft's task throughout its stay on the island of San Felix and afterwards. Indeed, No 51 Squadron's activities have always been tightly controlled and on a need-to-know basis. Each of the aircraft's missions during the war was authorised at a very high level and a cover story was always available if required. This was usually along the lines of a 'radar proving sortie'. Only after the passage of much time has enough information become available to tell the story of the RAF Nimrod R1's contribution during the Falklands War.

A Request for Photographic Reconnaissance (PR)

During the early days of the war, Major General Jeremy Moore, Royal Marines, was an Adviser at Northwood before being appointed Land Force Commander (LFC) in mid-April. He appreciated the importance of, and the pressing need for, aerial PR to identify Argentine military dispositions on the Falkland Islands and, importantly, ahead of any British effort to repossess the Falklands. Photographic evidence of what was happening there was urgently required and, if possible, before the Task Force arrived in the area. Any Argentine ships that happened to be unloading at Port Stanley would also be of interest. The possibility of acquiring useful intelligence from satellites was certainly understood at that time, but it was felt that it might be rather thin.

Shortly after taking up his new appointment, the General discussed this requirement with the Air Commander, Air Marshal Sir John Curtiss, and a meeting was quickly set up on 16th April to include them both, and the Officer Commanding No 39 (PR) Squadron, Wing Commander Colin Adams, who recalled:

> The Air Marshal was clearly persuaded by the case for PR put forward by the General. He did not feel there was any need to delay, and the decision was taken there and then to send a pair of Canberra aircraft. I was instructed accordingly.
>
> It was made clear to me that the requirement was immediate and that a forward party should be dispatched as soon as possible. A pair of Canberras would depart for Belize shortly after, and hold there until given the go-ahead to proceed on to Chile. This would happen when a suitable operating base had been identified, and the necessary political clearance obtained. It was also made clear that the mission would be open-ended. The aircraft would return when the job had been done and they were no longer required.

He added that there had never been any suggestion that the aircraft might be retained by the Chileans afterwards as part of some political deal. Nor did he recall ever having been given a cover story to use if challenged. 'Indeed,' he said, 'that would not have been necessary as we could always have employed the old faithful... that we were carrying out a mapping survey. Basically, the Air Marshal wanted to know if we could get the aircraft down to Chile and, once there, that we could do the job.'

The Canberra PR9

At that time, No 39 (PR) Squadron, based at RAF Wyton and equipped with the PR9 version of the Canberra bomber, was operating worldwide in both the strategic and tactical PR roles. The PR9 operated with just a pilot and navigator, whereas the bomber versions had carried three crew members.

By definition, strategic PR is normally carried out at higher altitudes employing both oblique and vertical photographic techniques. Although the Canberra was normally associated with tactical PR, using a variety of cameras and flying at 10–15,000 feet altitude, the missions to the Falklands might have to be carried out at high altitude. An alternative scenario, employing a high-low-high profile, i.e. descending from high altitude to carry out the photography, and then climbing back to high altitude for the return flight, was therefore carefully considered.

There was an acute awareness of the vulnerability of the Canberra. It did not carry any defensive armament and the risk posed by Argentine fighter aircraft would be considerable. For this reason the aircraft would prefer to be at high altitude whenever possible, where its ability to cruise at around 60,000 feet would give it its best chance of survival against fighter aircraft that would be unable to reach and operate at such altitudes. It would also be very important to be as invisible as possible on these missions. Mere identification of an RAF Canberra without an air-to-air refuelling capability in the Falklands area, even if interception proved difficult, would suggest the complicity of Chile. If for any reason photography at a lower altitude became necessary, the high-level oblique camera could be used at the lower altitude. However, this would necessitate flying at only 180 knots (the speed necessary to carry out the mission at that altitude) and the Canberra would be at its most vulnerable.

The vertical cameras were operated by the navigator, who directed the pilot on to the appropriate track; however, the large oblique camera required the pilot to fly the aircraft to hold the camera on the target line.

This was not always an easy task, and the amount of cloud cover was also a critical factor.

After the aircraft landed from a mission, the ground support team would normally process the films, which would then be passed on to the photographic interpreters (PIs) for analysis. It could then be established if the mission had been successful. If not, that part of the mission might have to be repeated. When away from home base, the ground support team normally took a reconnaissance/intelligence centre (RIC), a mobile facility within which the processing and analysis was carried out. A RIC was taken to Chile.

The Canberra PR9 could fly approximately 2,000 miles at altitude but the pilot would be getting a little anxious towards the end of the flight. The distances involved from various possible air bases in Chile to and from the Falkland Islands, the close proximity of its border with Argentina almost everywhere and the absolute requirement for total secrecy, were clearly all going to be major factors in determining how to operate, and from which base.

The PR9 did not have an air-to-air refuelling capability, and fitting a refuelling probe would have been technically out of the question. In any case, it would have been difficult to spare one of the precious Victor tankers from Ascension Island; a problem that, in the event, never had to be addressed. Certainly, the Canberras could not, and would not, have received any help in that respect from Chile.

So, as the Canberras prepared to leave Wyton, there were still many unanswered questions and the officer commanding the forward party would have his hands full getting some answers. The one thing that was quite clear was the nature of the mission.

The photographic evidence of Argentine dispositions would have to be sent back to the UK by the fastest means possible. Colin Adams thought that the diplomatic bag from the British Embassy in Santiago would probably have been the means used, but this had still to be settled when the Canberras left the UK. At that time, there was no system available to transmit the information by rapid electronic means, although a signal report might have been possible via the British Embassy. The possibility of dropping copies of the photographic evidence, suitably packaged and protected, to the Task Force after it arrived in the area, was also considered. This was, however, always of secondary importance to getting the information back to the UK and may not have been feasible anyway. Nevertheless, Colin kept this in mind and gave some thought as to how it might be achieved.

He recalled that, as a junior pilot, he had flown over his base airfield with a load of toilet rolls in the bomb bay. These were released at the appropriate moment. It was a Christmas prank that singularly failed to amuse his squadron commander at the time, but Colin felt that the idea could possibly be developed for dropping packages to the Task Force. From what we learned later on, the Argentine troops on the Falklands might have been delighted to receive a consignment of toilet rolls from the RAF by whatever means!

At some point early on in the planning process, Prime Minister Margaret Thatcher was made aware of, and approved, the plan to send the Canberras to Chile. In fact, she specifically asked to be shown the first photographs that arrived back in the UK.

Meanwhile, at around the same time, the British Ambassador in Chile, John Heath, was busy negotiating an agreement with the Chilean military whereby, in his words: 'The Royal Air Force could use the air base at Punta Arenas in the far south providing their aircraft were suitably adorned with Chilean Air Force markings.' He appreciated that there might well be good reasons why the arrangement might not be entirely satisfactory from an operational point of view, but it was at least a starting point and he was successful in his negotiations. The officer commanding 39 Squadron's forward party could take it from there.

The Forward Party

One of Colin Adams' first tasks, therefore, on returning to Wyton from Northwood was to nominate an officer to command the forward party. This duty fell to Squadron Leader Peter Robbie, Colin's Flight Commander, who was given little time in which to prepare before departing.

The party had to be large enough to support the Canberras throughout a detachment of unknown duration in an unfamiliar country. Apart from all the usual ground equipment and spares, it included a flying officer (PI) and three non-commissioned officers (NCOs) to operate the processing equipment and a RIC. Peter explained: 'The party had to include the most capable and experienced people we could find, and who would also be best able to handle difficult situations and solve the many problems we would inevitably encounter. At the same time we had to keep its size to the minimum possible.'

The party plus equipment required two VC10 aircraft to transport everything from RAF Wyton. Later, it was all cross-loaded to RAF and

Chilean C130 aircraft at Easter Island for the final leg of the journey to the Chilean mainland.

Peter Robbie understood that his task was to command the forward party, and prepare the way for the Canberras which would, all being well, arrive just a few days later. Most importantly, he would have to visit Chilean air bases and then recommend how, and from which base, the Canberras should operate to carry out their PR missions over the Falklands. It was also planned that he would fly the first PR mission as soon as the aircraft arrived. This would allow a suitable period of rest for the pilots who had flown them down.

When he arrived in mainland Chile, after staging through Easter Island, he immediately noticed a high degree of nervousness amongst the Chileans he met. They clearly feared it would take little to precipitate a hostile response from Argentina; and this undoubtedly included being 'caught out' helping Britain in some way. This was, of course, precisely what we were asking them to do by allowing our PR aircraft to operate from a Chilean air base.

Not too surprisingly, he found that a Chilean Air Force liaison officer had been appointed. Colonel Gonzales (who was part of a Chilean team that went to Wyton after the war) was more in the nature of a 'minder'. Anything that Peter wanted to do, such as visit an air base to assess its suitability, had to have his approval. Permission even had to be sought to visit the British Embassy in Santiago; when it was approved, it was a furtive journey undertaken under blankets in the back of a car. Because of the great distances involved, visits to Chilean air bases were sometimes made in an RAF C130 with Chilean Air Force markings, and always with the Colonel never far away.

On the first trip to look at Punta Arenas, the idea was that Peter should brief the Chileans on the nature of the RAF's mission and the importance of the PR task, and that they, in turn, would brief him on local considerations. As he later recalled:

They were very sceptical, and tried to discourage the idea of operating at all from Punta Arenas, citing (and often exaggerating) the problem areas; for example the bad weather factor, very strong winds, likelihood of snow, proximity to the border with Argentina, movements only possible at night, and so on. I had the distinct impression that the Chileans would have liked to be more helpful; but their obvious nervousness caused them to be progressively less so, to the point where they were clearly trying to scupper the whole idea.

If one tries to see the problem from a Chilean perspective, having studied the geography of the area and noted the proximity of Punta Arenas to the Argentine border, and taken into account that it was, allegedly, bristling with Argentine spies, it becomes easier to understand the Chilean point of view and why they were so apprehensive. Peter said:

> The Chileans insisted that they must be represented during the planning and briefing of the first PR mission if it was flown from Punta Arenas (which was indeed what he eventually recommended). They were afraid the aircraft would head east after take off and 'blow it'! Another problem was the presence of an Argentine picket ship, equipped with search radar and positioned just south of Chile, which had to be avoided. Its task was to identify and report all aircraft movements in the area.

Whilst dashing around trying to answer the immediate questions of how and where the Canberras should operate when they arrived, communicating with the outside world was just one of the many other problems that also had to be solved. When, later, the Canberras arrived in Belize, Peter Robbie found that he could not communicate at all with his CO, Colin Adams, who was waiting for his news. No secure telephones were made available to him and he had only a brief ten-minute 'window' each evening when he could communicate with Northwood, via Hereford. He was later to discover that his messages and queries had not always been passed on to Belize.

There were also some health issues in the forward party, mainly intestinal problems causing sickness, and, unhelpfully, he was given the distinct impression that some sort of a 'political deal' was in the air and that possibly either the Canberras or two C130s, or maybe both, would be remaining in Chile when the war was over. Certainly, remarks were made by some Chileans to this effect, which was rather unsettling for an RAF officer whose job it was to leave the politics to others and who was, anyway, completely in the dark and unable to comment himself.

The Chileans' comments arose because, as Ambassador John Heath later confirmed: 'The country wanted Canberras in exchange for help given on the intelligence front; it was not long before this was interpreted as a *fait accompli*, a "done deal" at all levels.'

The UK Secretary of State for Defence, John Nott, was in no doubt. He had been closely involved in negotiations with the Chileans over the use of Nimrod and Canberra aircraft, and felt strongly that the Chileans' desire to have some Canberras was used as a trade-off in exchange for us being able to operate a Nimrod aircraft from a Chilean base.

General Matthieu later revealed that an arrangement between Britain and Chile allowed them to provide us with intelligence in return for which we would supply certain items, including Hunter and Canberra aircraft. In the event, the Hunters arrived with little delay; the Canberras were supplied after the war.

Finally, having looked at no less than five Chilean air bases, Peter's assessment, and his recommendation to Group Headquarters in the UK, was that the Canberras should operate from a highway in the north of the country. They should then stage through and refuel at Punta Arenas, en route to carrying out their operational PR missions over the Falklands. Routing and timing to and from Punta Arenas during the hours of darkness would require careful planning.

C130 Support

Graham Finch was the captain of one of the two C130 aircraft that supported Peter Robbie's Forward Party. He said:

> We took off practically empty from RAF Wyton. Later on, we met up with two VC10s, which carried the bulk of the party's ground crew and ground equipment, at an air base in California where much of the equipment was cross-loaded to the C130s.
>
> The rest of the men and equipment were cross-loaded at Easter Island but, as there was too much for the two RAF C130s to carry, a couple of Chilean Air Force C130s took the balance. Easter Island was as far as the VC10s would go before returning.
>
> The Chilean C130s also arrived with military personnel who converted the RAF C130s to Chilean Air Force markings; something that HQ 38 Group was apparently not too happy about. In the process, a word was misspelt on the fuselage of one of the aircraft, a mistake that was picked up by countless people, including some journalists, during the following days.

Easter Island had a joint civil/military airfield and a long 2,500-yard runway. The crews stayed in a guest house during their brief stay, the purpose of which was to prepare them and the aircraft before continuing

Top: Lt Sergio Fernandez (second from right) and his company attending the Blowpipe missile course at the Infantry School, Campo de Mayo in November 1979. John Reddick, the British instructor, is third from left.

Below: Chief of the Air Staff, Air Chief Marshal Sir Michael Beetham, meets his Brazilian opposite number, Tenente Brigadeiro Abreu Coutinho, in Brasilia in July 1981. He also met the Air Minister and a good rapport was established.

Top: No hint of what is to come! The author and his wife with the outgoing Argentine Air Attaché at the latter's farewell dinner in January 1982.

Below: Captain Nick Barker welcoming Captain Moya, CO of the Argentine navy's Mar del Plata submarine base, aboard HMS *Endurance* in February 1982.

Top: Captain Mitchell (Naval Attaché) and Colonel Love (Defence Attaché), and his wife, at the Argentine/Uruguayan border leaving Argentina on 3rd April 1982 after the embassy closed.

Below: Happier days! The author (far right) with other South American attachés just before the war.

Top: Chiefs of Staff meeting assembled after the outbreak of war for the photograph (note no paperwork and, unusually, in uniform). The Chiefs are in the foreground with supporting staff behind.

Below: No 39 (PR) Squadron Canberra PR9 and Harrier over San Pedro, Belize. The Canberras, in the end, did not continue south to participate in the war.

Operation Paraquat

Top: Guy Sheridan (standing) with his command team opposite King Edward Point (S Georgia) as the white surrender flags are sighted.

Below: Chris Nunn, OC M Company 42 Commando RM about to board HMS *Antrim's* Wessex 3 helicopter for the assault on Hestesletten on 25th April 1982.

Top: Alfredo Astiz signing a surrender document on board HMS *Plymouth* on 26th April 1982. Captain David Pentreath is seated extreme right, with Captain Nick Barker, HMS *Endurance*, on his right.

Below: Astiz (head only visible) in the helicopter, about to be returned to HMS *Endurance* after the surrender signing ceremony. Richard Buckland (observer) is nearest to the camera.

Top: C130 Hercules aircraft taking fuel from the Victor tanker.

Below: View from the tanker of the C130 aircraft looming large behind.

Top: Sergio Fernandez's watercolour depicting him firing the Blowpipe missile that destroyed Jeff Glover's Harrier on 21st May 1982.

Middle: Sergio Fernandez's watercolour of the Harrier crashing nearby.

Left: Harrier pilot Jeff Glover being rescued from the sea by the men who shot his aircraft down.

on to mainland Chile. The crews were given Chilean identities, uniforms and flying suits. Graham said he became 'Mendes' for the duration! They were also given Chilean 'minders' who remained with them throughout their stay in Chile; a constant reminder of the country's concern that any assistance given to Britain at that time could have unwelcome repercussions. They were told that there were some Argentine employees working on Easter Island, who had to be locked away out of sight whilst the C130s were there.

Whilst there, they also met for the first time the senior RAF officer who had a special role in Chile during the Falklands War. He arrived to meet the crews and seemed very agitated. Graham thought that this was due to the fact that a Soviet satellite passed overhead every 90 minutes, each time necessitating a temporary halt to the cross-loading from the VC10s to the C130s.

When all was ready, the C130s and crews, all suitably disguised, continued on to mainland Chile; initially to Santiago and then on down to Punta Arenas.

The Canberras Depart

Shortly after the forward party left Wyton, a pair of Canberra PR9s also took off, led by Colin Adams and his navigator, Brian Cole. The two crews were selected for the mission as being those best able to handle difficult, unforeseen situations. At this stage, the plan had received only tentative approval from the Chileans. Doubts started to creep in only after the aircraft reached Belize.

Ian Wigmore was the navigator on one of the two C130 aircraft that had supported the Canberras on their journey south. He said:

The requirement came out of the blue without any prior warning. There was only time for the barest of briefings, and even then we were told nothing of the nature of the Canberras' mission. We left on 20th April, flying quite independently of the Canberras, and arrived in Belize on 22nd April, having staged through Gander and Bermuda. This route had been chosen as the aircraft were not permitted to land in the USA.

The Canberras arrived in Belize on the same day, and Colin Adams was ordered to wait there until he received instructions to proceed south to

Chile. Meanwhile, whilst Peter Robbie in Chile was trying to sort out the details of how and where the Canberras should operate after their arrival, the Chileans appeared to develop steadily colder feet.

Colin and Brian had to consider very carefully the route they should take south from Belize, bearing in mind both fuel considerations and the sensitivities of Chile's neighbours at this time. Colin said:

> The route south from Belize would be the longest ever undertaken by a PR9. Fuel would be so critical that the aircraft would either have to be topped up after taxiing to the end of the runway for take-off, or towed out. Every drop would count. All RAF markings on the aircraft would be replaced by Chilean Air Force markings for the flight south but, on arrival in Chile, RAF markings would be restored and used for all the operational missions.

The plan, Colin Adams learned, was that the pilots would have to locate and land on a specific stretch of Chilean highway somewhere just to the south of Chile's border with Peru. They would then rendezvous on the ground with a waiting RAF C130, which would refuel both aircraft. After refuelling, they would take off again and continue south, probably to Punta Arenas where Peter Robbie and his party would be waiting. Peter would then jump into one of the Canberras and fly the first of the PR missions.

The plan sounded reasonably straightforward but it was, in fact, fraught with difficulties and uncertainties, not the least of which would be persuading the Chilean Government to give it the final go-ahead. Brian Cole said:

> The Ministry of Defence had wanted the aircraft to land in the dark in Chile, but this was plainly unacceptable. The aircraft would not only be very low on fuel after the long flight, but would have to make a visual approach to land on a totally unfamiliar stretch of road (something not regularly practised by Canberras). Reasonable visibility would be essential, but there was no prospect of obtaining reliable, up-to-date weather information for the destination before take-off. There would also be no radar assistance available. A compromise was therefore reached that the arrival would be at first light.

The Chileans were obviously very apprehensive that the Canberras might be identified by unwelcome eyes.

The idea was that after this long flight, during which the two aircraft would have a fifteen-minute separation, the pilots, having descended to low level, would radio ahead when fifteen miles from the landing point. Some form of lighting would then be switched on and Verey Cartridges fired to aid the final approach to land. After landing, the aircraft would taxi to a hidden, prepared area off the main highway, where the RAF C130 would be waiting to refuel them. The crews were briefed that in the event of having to eject during the final stages, the aircraft should be pointed out to sea and abandoned whilst still over land.

Another major problem was which route the aircraft should take. Countries along the route south were, to varying degrees, sympathetic to Argentina's position. Peru, in particular, had to be avoided at all costs. Colin wanted to fly a hundred miles off the Peruvian coast, but Brian argued that fifty miles offshore would offer an important fuel saving. Colombia, although less hard-line than Peru, had also to be avoided. Honduras, part of Nicaragua and also Costa Rica would have to be briefly overflown. There was much to be carefully considered.

As the Canberra crews were planning their flight down to Chile, and just as the C130s were about to leave Chile, Graham Finch received word that there was another job to do. With a few Chilean Air Force 'minders' on board his aircraft, plus the crew from the other RAF C130 and 39 Squadron's Peter Robbie, he was to fly north to locate and land on a stretch of the northbound Pan-American Highway leading up to the Peruvian border. This would be closed to road traffic. The aircraft would retain its Chilean Air Force markings.

'The purpose of the flight,' Graham was told, 'was to carry out a reconnaissance, and familiarise with the location prior to a rendezvous with a couple of RAF Canberras, possibly the next day or soon thereafter, in a clearing just off the highway.' He said:

I was warned that the Canberras would be very short of fuel and that I would be required to refuel both of them from the C130. I had the fuel to do that and you can cross-refuel from a C130 without difficulty. I was briefed to arrive in the north in low-light, dawn conditions, presumably to simulate the time of day that the Canberras would arrive. The flight duly took place on the following day. All the time we were engaged in this rehearsal, we were carefully watched by our Chilean friends and they wouldn't let us wander far from the aircraft. Throughout, their apprehension was very evident from their body language. Having said that, the closure of the highway and its rapid conversion to a runway was handled with slick precision. It was obviously a procedure that was regularly practised by the Chilean Air Force during exercises. A day or so later, whilst we were still waiting for the Canberras to materialise, we were suddenly told that we must leave Chile as quickly as possible. The rendezvous with the Canberras was cancelled.

Mission Cancelled

Colin Adams and Brian Cole both clearly recalled the day in Belize when they went to bed believing that, on waking, they would be taking off and heading south for Chile. However, they awoke to be informed instead that the mission had been cancelled. No reasons were given. The expected green light had not been given. Colin returned to the UK in a VC10, but his aircraft and a replacement pilot remained in Belize for a further couple of weeks in case the mission was resurrected. It never was.

Nor was it ever explained to Graham Finch and his crew why the rendezvous with the Canberras had been cancelled, or why they had to leave Chile in such unseemly haste. Their departure (both C130s) was so rushed, in fact, that they arrived in Tahiti on 5th May completely unannounced and without diplomatic clearance.

'The consequence of all this was that I received a dressing-down from a French Admiral there, who impounded the aircraft for five days,' said Graham. 'It was left to London and Paris to sort the mess out! We then continued on to Hawaii, where I received fresh orders to return to Chile. The other C130 continued on to the UK.'

Why was the mission cancelled? There were certainly many possible reasons and many theories were advanced during the weeks that followed. Broadly, they could be assembled under two headings; those that would have caused Britain to cancel the mission, and those that could have resulted in the Chilean Government deciding not to allow it to proceed. There was probably a degree of overlap between the two.

The squadron had a plan and no doubt felt that the mission could have been accomplished, although not without some difficulties. Punta Arenas was uncomfortably close to the border with Argentina and Argentine eyes and ears were everywhere. The picket ship also presented a difficulty. In any event, Punta Arenas could never be more than a refuelling stop en route to the Falklands. A secure base further to the rear also had to be found.

Chilean nervousness regarding the use of Punta Arenas, however brief the various aircraft stop-overs, could well have been a decisive factor, as also could have been the perceived lack of a suitable base, within comfortable range, to the north. Operating from the highway might have worked for the first mission; but range, and consequent fuel considerations, would have created concerns in the event of frequent use. Also, the Chileans would certainly have been unhappy about the use of the highway on a frequent basis, establishing a pattern that might attract unwelcome attention.

The difficulties associated with the flight from Belize down to Chile might, on balance, have been considered unacceptable. The risk of arriving perilously short of fuel and having to find an obscure destination in an unfamiliar area, and without radar assistance or reliable weather information, might have been judged too great. The possibility of being identified en route south by one of Chile's neighbours could have resulted in Argentina being tipped off and the mission being 'blown' or, even worse, the aircraft being intercepted with tragic consequences.

Whilst the Canberras remained in Chile, long flights close to the Argentine border would have been necessary; and the risk of identification would have been ever-present.

All these risks carried consequences, not just for the Canberras but also – and probably more significantly – for the Chileans as well. They would have to live with the daily fear that at any time a slip, some misfortune or miscalculation, or perhaps a sighting by unwelcome eyes, could result in the presence of the Canberras being exposed. That would suggest, as far as Argentina was concerned, that Chile was assisting Britain in its efforts to repossess the Falklands.

Sir John Nott, when recently asked the reason for the cancellation, gave a good politician's answer, coming as close as he could bring himself to being helpful, without actually answering the question. He said:

If we had been able to use a South American airfield from which to mount the missions, it would have made the whole operation easier. The importance of Chile, with its long-standing rivalry and fear of Argentina, was very great. We tried to do a deal stationing combat and support aircraft there, but were not successful. The Chilean link nevertheless proved very valuable to us.

Air Marshal Sir John Curtiss said:

Unfortunately we were never successful in getting a proper deal or arrangement with the Chileans whereby we could, for example, use one of their airfields. It had to be kept on a 'visit only' basis. Yes, Chile had to be very cautious, being part of the South American family. It certainly helped that they were on our side. I think their greatest disappointment was that we didn't sink the entire Argentine navy!

John Wilkinson MP was John Nott's PPS at the time. He said: 'The whole plan had become too overt for the Chileans' liking. Chile was most anxious that our war should not spill across its long border with Argentina; and was concerned that any leak might suggest evidence of co-operation between our two countries.'

Colin Adams recalled that the extreme sensitivity of the mission demanded that in Belize only the Commander, British Forces (a Brigadier) should know the reason for the arrival of the Canberras. 'Unfortunately, and unhelpfully, it became more generally known amongst the executives there,' he said. 'The mission became an open secret, although that was unlikely to have been a factor in the subsequent decision to cancel.'

There was some concern in Chilean quarters at that time that Argentina might initiate a foolhardy attack on Chile, possibly even aided by Peru and/or Bolivia, to divert its population's attention away from a worsening position in its war with Britain, and its ever-deteriorating economic situation. Chile would not have wanted to risk tipping the scales in favour of any such action being taken.

Even if Argentina had no such plans, there was always the chance that it might learn of Chilean complicity and take punitive measures. There were many Argentines living and working in Chile, in Punta Arenas and elsewhere. There were eyes and ears everywhere. Our Naval Attaché in Santiago, Malcolm Johns, discovered a little while after moving into his new home that he had an Argentine neighbour. He had neglected to establish who his neighbours were before choosing the house and moving into it.

Group Captain Fen Allen was at the MoD during the war. One of his three Wing Commanders had responsibility for No 39 Squadron's activities. Fen thought the mission might have been cancelled because the route from Belize to northern Chile could not have entirely avoided taking the Canberras through the airspace of countries sympathetic to Argentina's position. They might have been subjected to a hostile interception or Argentina could have been informed of their presence.

Whether the reasons for the cancellation were linked to the difficulties of getting the aircraft down to Chile, or operating them whilst they were there, together with the risk of them being intercepted by Argentine fighter aircraft during their missions to the Falklands, we may never know.

It is most likely that it had more to do with ever-mounting Chilean concern that, at some point, the Canberras would inevitably have been identified by unwelcome eyes for what they were. This information would surely have been passed to Argentina, confirming Chilean complicity. The Chileans simply could not have risked provoking Argentina to the point where it might have attacked them.

After the War

It was not clear whether some kind of political deal had been struck which might have resulted in a few Canberras (or a C130) remaining in Chile. Some members of No 39 Squadron's forward party were certainly given this impression by the Chileans. In the event, as the Canberras did not materialise, a party of Chileans arrived at RAF Wyton after the war to take delivery of three PR9 aircraft.

Brian Cole was involved in the training of the Chilean crews, a pilot and navigator for each of the three aircraft, who would then fly the aircraft back to Chile. He said:

The Chilean team included Colonel Gonzales, who had been Peter Robbie's Liaison Officer in Chile. He apologised for the treatment of Peter's party whilst they were in Chile, giving the reason as the nervousness of just about every Chilean who had anything to do with the Canberras, including the government and the intelligence services. He said all RAF personnel therefore had to be tightly controlled all the time.

In contrast, the Chilean crews were very well treated at Wyton. They had their wives with them, were allocated officers' married quarters to live in for the duration, and were frequent visitors to the squadron.

Philip Spencer, another squadron member, recalled that the Chileans later lost one of their three aircraft in an unfortunate accident, probably attributable to a maintenance error. The aircraft was flying over the Andes in turbulent conditions, when the pilot's ejection seat spontaneously fired. The navigator, whose seat was located in front of the pilot's, heard a 'bang', and on looking round (which is possible if the straps are loosened), discovered that he was alone in the aircraft and wisely decided to eject too. Both men survived their ordeal, although the navigator was injured when his parachute snagged on a cliff face. Owing to bad weather and inhospitable terrain, it was a long time before the crash site was located.

The Chilean Air Force soldiered on with the remaining two aircraft for many years. In the early 1990s, the RAF sent a team out to Chile to inspect the aircraft with a view to a possible buy-back, or even using them for spare parts. The view of the team though was that the aircraft were 'too far gone' to be of any interest to the RAF.

Meanwhile, after the Falklands War, No 39 Squadron was reduced to five aircraft. The squadron, which was formed in 1916 and equipped with Canberras in 1958, was finally disbanded on 28th May 1983 at RAF Wyton, its base since 1970. The parade was reviewed by Air Marshal Sir Alasdair Steedman. No 1 PRU (Photographic Reconnaissance Unit) was then formed and continued to operate the remaining aircraft for a few more years.

No 39 Squadron served the RAF with distinction for many years, but sadly was denied the opportunity, in the twilight of its life, to play a part during the Falklands War.

A Sea King Crew Arrives

Many years after the event, Admiral Woodward recalled being contacted by Admiral Hallifax – Admiral Fieldhouse's Chief of Staff at Northwood – and being asked to prepare a plan for sending a Sea King helicopter, with Special Forces (SAS) on board, from the Task Force to the Argentine mainland. This one-way mission became more usually known as Phase 1 of Operation Mikado (the rationale for which is discussed in Part One). The task of the SAS was to gather vital intelligence before Phase 2, an assault on the Río Grande air base, could be launched. The Admiral said:

> I was asked to send the plan by signal. After I sent it, the reply came back that D/SAS (Director SAS, Brigadier Peter de la Billiere) didn't like it. This went on for several days. In the end, it was all sorted out to everyone's satisfaction. The only problem was that the unnecessary delay it caused to the proceedings meant that a good weather window had been missed.

After the Admiral's plan finally received the seal of approval, the SAS who were to be inserted were flown south to the Task Force.

Richard Hutchings, a Commando helicopter pilot serving with 846 Naval Air Squadron, had volunteered to fly the Sea King IV helicopter on the mission. As a Royal Marine pilot, he also had the special skills and training to operate and survive behind enemy lines. His crew included Alan Bennett and Peter Imrie.

Two other options for inserting the eight SAS men had been briefly considered, but abandoned. One of them involved dropping the men offshore from a submarine, and leaving them to get to the shore in RIBs. This idea was abandoned as the water off Tierra del Fuego was judged to be too shallow to allow a submarine to get close enough to the shore. Another option, to parachute the men in, was quickly discarded as well,

147

as the aircraft would probably have been detected, destroying any hope of the operation being successful. The Sea King option was preferred.

The operation was scheduled to be mounted from HMS *Invincible* on 17th May, but was delayed 24 hours to give the SAS troops, fresh from the UK, more time to rest. As the need for utmost secrecy was paramount, even the Sea King crew were not privy to the details of the follow-on operation, Phase 2 of Operation Mikado, which, hopefully, would result in the destruction of the Super Etendard aircraft, the remaining Exocet missiles, and even the pilots on the air base.

The Flight to Argentina

On the evening of 18th May, Captain Jeremy Black moved HMS *Invincible* as far west as he dared, to a point south of the Falklands and some 300 miles from mainland Argentina. The Sea King, with the SAS troops on board, flew off the carrier later that night, which then turned to rejoin the Task Force far to the east before first light.

The plan was that the Sea King would fly to a designated area and drop off the Special Forces, who would then be on their own. They would head for Río Grande to gather the information required before setting off overland to Chile. Meanwhile Richard Hutchings and his crew would fly the Sea King to the Chilean side of the Argentine/Chilean border, destroy it, and head for civilisation, where it was planned they would make contact with the Chilean authorities.

It inevitably proved to be less straightforward than that. Poor visibility meant that precise navigation was difficult, and the SAS were set down a few miles short of the planned position. The SAS captain then controversially announced that he was aborting the mission, believing he had not been given the correct position of the aircraft, i.e. his starting point for their trek to the air base. The SAS were therefore taken back on board, and flown on to the first of three designated landing sites on the Chilean side of the border, where they were put down to proceed independently. The Sea King crew had no further contact with them.

The Sea King flew on to a lake, where it was planned to ditch the aircraft. Unfortunately, it proved unwilling to sink. Richard managed to take off again and fly to a beach at the edge of the lake, where the three men set fire to the aircraft with the aid of petrol, explosive devices and distress flares.

With daylight imminent, they then set off for Punta Arenas, eleven miles away to the north. They hoped the burnt out wreckage would not be discovered for at least two days to give them a good head start. Their orders were to avoid detection and capture for eight days before attempting to contact the British Embassy. They moved only at night; the terrain was difficult, and progress was predictably slow.

After five nights walking, Richard Hutchings and his colleagues saw Punta Arenas from a hill top, but it was another two days before they walked into the town, on the afternoon of 25th May. After being challenged by a local policeman, Captain Torres, who knew immediately who they were, they accompanied him to a police station where they were questioned. It was, Richard said later, a mere formality and red wine was consumed by all. He gave the Chileans his well-rehearsed cover story, which was essentially:

> We were conducting a patrol off the Argentine coast, searching for ships, when we had an engine failure. With the possibility of the other engine failing as well, we decided to head for the nearest friendly country. We headed west until we were short of fuel and decided to land. We destroyed the aircraft in case we were in Argentina, and then set about trying to determine which country we were in...

Meanwhile, back in the UK, D/SAS, on learning of the fate of the Sea King, had initially wanted Operation Mikado to proceed without the reconnaissance phase. This caused considerable concern and some dissent, until the idea was dropped. Whilst various alternative options were being considered at Hereford, B Squadron SAS, which was scheduled to participate in Phase 2, arrived at Ascension Island and the news broke in the British press that the wreckage of the Sea King had been discovered.

Britain Learns of the Sea King's Fate

The first the nation learned that something had happened to a British helicopter somewhere at the bottom of South America was on 21st May, on the BBC TV teatime news bulletin. Nobody knew at first why the helicopter had crashed. Nor had anyone heard of Operation Mikado. That came later. As it was planned as a one-way mission, the Royal Navy released a pre-arranged message after the news broke that 'the crew were missing but were believed to be alive.' BBC correspondent Brian Barron recalled:

> I was the Ireland correspondent for the BBC when the Falklands War broke out, but was suddenly asked to go to Chile to cover their end of things. I was in Punta Arenas when I was informed by one of our reliable intelligence sources that a British helicopter had crashed and was burning, about an hour's drive from Punta Arenas.
>
> At that time, there was fierce competition between the TV networks and all the foreign correspondents. I called the BBC team together, and we walked casually out of our hotel and drove away without any urgency, so that no one would follow us. After driving along a long, dusty road through the foothills of the nearby mountains, we rounded a bend and came upon a group of military personnel. On closer inspection we could see they had a bulldozer, and were burying the still-smoking wreckage of the helicopter in a pit beside the road. We had travelled about ten miles from Punta Arenas.
>
> We raced back to our hotel and I filed the report, which broke the news back in England. Later my Chilean contact filled me in with more details as they emerged. The Chilean military had been ordered to bury the remains of the helicopter as quickly as possible, in the hope that this could be accomplished before any media people (like me) turned up and also to minimise any embarrassment to the UK Government.

No doubt they had the Chilean Government in mind as well.

Shortly afterwards, Brian moved on to Santiago, leaving his vacated hotel room in Punta Arenas to Kate Adie, who had moved south from Uruguay. In Santiago, Brian attended, and reported on, the Embassy briefing when (a few days later) the Sea King crew members were paraded in front of the press and its cameras. He commented later: 'There is no doubt in my mind that Chile played an important role in providing material help and intelligence data throughout the conflict.'

Also in Punta Arenas at the time with his team was ITN's Jon Snow. He had been sent to Chile on the first day of the war with his five-man crew, had spent the entire war there and, in his words, had seen very little. Along with their rivals from the BBC, they had stayed at the Hotel Cabo de Hornos.

Jon said they had been desperate to get to the Falkland Islands, where the action was. At one point, they had seriously considered an ambitious scheme to fly there in a Catalina flying boat, but were persuaded that it would have been an insane thing to do. Brian Barron, as it turned out, had considered doing something similar, but in a light aircraft, which was even more bizarre. John Cummins, a Second Secretary at the British Embassy, had advised: 'Don't even think about it. The Chileans wouldn't approve it, and you won't get any help from us.'

One of the team's rare moments of excitement had occurred when Jon's Chilean navy contact knocked on his hotel room door and announced that the British helicopter had crashed nearby. They all jumped into a taxi and headed off to the crash site, but by the time they reached it, the Chileans had almost finished digging it into the ground. There had been little to see and no sign of the Sea King crew, which had long since departed the scene. Whether they had passed the BBC team going the other way, or who had arrived at the crash site first, is not on record! 'The ITN team,' Jon said, 'did not go on to Santiago to attend the Embassy press briefing. We had calculated that it would have been over by the time we could get there.'

He added: 'Although I had heard nothing about any Operation Mikado, there was a distinct feeling in the air that something was up. There were enormous tensions between the Chileans and the Argentines, so we were treated with great caution, just in case we did anything that might upset the Argentines and provoke a reaction.'

If nothing else, the Sea King incident provided the BBC and ITN crews with a few brief moments of excitement during their long weeks at the bottom of South America.

Santiago

Martin Lampitt was the captain of the RAF C130 that flew Richard Hutchings and his crew to Santiago. The aircraft and its crew were temporarily based at the Santiago Air Force base. Martin said: 'The helicopter crew never realised they were in a disguised RAF aircraft.' He recalled that he was required to have a Chilean Air Force pilot on board with him. This extra note of caution was evident at all times, and frequently commented on by British servicemen, press representatives and diplomats alike. The Chileans were in constant fear that someone, or something, would alert Argentina to the fact that they were co-operating with us in various ways.

It was well known by those who worked at the British Embassy that there were many Argentine spies operating in Chile. John Cummins said: 'The British Embassy itself was under constant surveillance, and we also knew there were many spies down in Punta Arenas.'

Richard Hutchings' recollection of the flight to Santiago was that it had taken about 5 hours, and they had chatted to some Chilean F5 fighter pilots who were also on the aircraft. He had learned that during the war, the Chilean Air Force maintained an F5 detachment at Punta Arenas, regularly rotating the pilots from Santiago. The Chileans had also expressed confidence that Britain would win the war. 'Nevertheless,' Richard said, 'they were also concerned that even in defeat, Galtieri might do something reckless, like invade the disputed islands in the Beagle Channel to appease a disappointed nation.' He confirmed that he was also under the impression throughout that they were flying in a Chilean Air Force C130. The crew arrived in Santiago on 26th May. Although the SAS team arrived a day or so later, their paths never crossed.

In Santiago, Ambassador John Heath had been forewarned by London, at about the time the Sea King set off from HMS *Invincible*, that he should expect the crew to surface about a week later and make contact. He was told they should be sent back to the UK as soon as possible, and have minimum exposure to the press.

He was therefore not too surprised when he was summoned to the Chilean Ministry of Foreign Affairs to be informed that: 'A British aircraft has landed without proper authority.' He said: 'It quickly became clear that no one was very upset because, with smiles on their faces, I was then asked: "When are you going to invade?" I was left in no doubt as to where Chilean sympathies lay, but of course gave them the usual solemn assurance that such an incident would not happen again!'

By the time the C130 landed in Santiago, every journalist within miles had arrived at the Embassy gates so there had clearly been a leak. When others gathered at the Ambassador's residence as well, he decided that the crew should be taken straight to John Cummins' house. It was, in fact, the third of three options considered. President Pinochet had invited the crew to spend the night at his residence. John Heath had politely declined that invitation, saying he needed to keep control over the crew's movements, and ensure they were kept out of the public eye and away from the press as far as possible.

He had then decided that the crew should go to his residence, but the gathering of journalists there quickly discouraged that idea. Finally, it was decided to quietly divert them to John Cummins' house. After a meal and a shower there, they were discreetly moved again to the apartment of one of the girls on the Embassy's staff, a move that successfully defeated the press pack. After resting there for a few hours, it was back to the Embassy again, where the crew were told of the Chileans' decision to hold a press briefing for assembled journalists.

The Ambassador had been rather surprised to be asked by the Ministry of Foreign Affairs to hold the briefing at the Embassy, and even more surprised to be told roughly what the ministry expected his statement to include. In fact, the Chileans' urgency was aimed at pre-empting any accusations of collusion on their part in the affair. Although some might say it was another example of the nervousness prevailing at the time, it was really just sensible handling of a potentially damaging situation.

Robert Gordon, Head of Chancery at the time, said: 'I was given the job of preparing the statement with Richard Hutchings. What we produced was along the lines that the Sea King had encountered technical problems whilst on a training mission and, being short of fuel, was forced to land in Chile... and the Chileans had kindly agreed that the crew should be repatriated, etc.' The statement was approved, with one or two minor changes, by John Heath.

There were about 100 journalists at the briefing, most of whom were Chileans, but also some British and a few Argentines. Richard Hutchings read out the prepared statement in English, and then promptly left the room with the other members of his crew. The Head of Chancery then announced that he would read a version in Spanish. This presented most of the journalists with a dilemma. Should they stay and listen, or try and follow Richard Hutchings and his colleagues who were being spirited out of a side door? Some of the British journalists left, but most of the Spanish-speaking journalists decided to stay.

Robert Gordon said recently that the move to get the crew to the airport as soon as possible was prompted by a genuine fear that efforts might be made to kill them, either in the Embassy area or, more likely, on the way to the airport.

The crew were taken initially to a 'safe house' to receive new passports and air tickets, before continuing on to the airport, where they caught a flight to Madrid en route to London. Probably the only thing left that could surprise them after the drama of the last action-packed week was their discovery that, on arrival at Gatwick Airport, there was no one from the MoD there to meet them.

Later, after the inevitable MoD debrief, and a weekend off with their families, they were put on notice that they might have to return south to the Task Force; however, the war ended shortly afterwards. The crew had known nothing of the movements of the SAS after they had parted company, although they realised that, having decided to abort the planned mission, the SAS would not have been able to acquire the necessary intelligence to allow Phase 2 of Operation Mikado to go ahead. The SAS had taken a different route to Punta Arenas from the helicopter crew, and had the added problem of having to cross the Strait of Magellan at some point. Eventually, when they too arrived in Santiago, they were accommodated in a 'safe house' and kept well away from the Embassy. After a few days rest, they also returned to the UK.

On Reflection...

Many years later, when he eventually wrote his memoirs, General Matthieu hinted that perhaps the episode had been a bit embarrassing for them. He admitted that Argentina had asked some awkward questions and the Chileans had given them lengthy explanations, swearing blind that they had not co-operated with Britain in any way. He said: 'The Sea King incident probably offered the only tangible proof that Chile had ever had anything to do with Britain during the war.'

John Heath said: 'His (General Matthieu's) memoirs were more a commercial exercise than a political one, but nevertheless demonstrated that the UK and Chile, for different reasons, had needed each other at the time. They also presented a truthful, accurate account of how we worked together. The manner in which the Mikado incident was handled was a good example of that.'

He summed up the whole incident as being: '... a bit embarrassing, but certainly not a catastrophe as far as the Chilean Government was concerned. It was well-handled by everyone. The Chilean Air Force in particular had quickly worked out what had happened, and throughout the whole episode had ensured that everything was dealt with quietly, efficiently, and without them appearing to have co-operated at all with us.'

The Chilean Foreign Ministry had dutifully issued the obligatory statement, indignantly protesting the helicopter's unauthorised incursion into Chilean territory, arriving unannounced and without any clearance, etc. Privately, of course, it was much more sympathetic. President Pinochet, apart from his invitation to the crew to stay overnight at his residence, had not been involved at all.

Part Three
Uruguay – Steering A Careful Course

Uruguay

The Uruguayan Perspective

As was the case with most South American countries, the frontiers of Uruguay, as we know them today, were established only after years of endless disputes and bitter, bloody fighting between the various colonial powers.

The land was inhabited by indigenous people until the Spanish first arrived early in the sixteenth century. The Spanish were met by fierce resistance and failed to find the hoped-for gold and silver they sought. Initially they maintained only a limited presence, during which they discovered that the terrain was ideal for cattle, which became an alternative source of wealth.

The Spanish steadily increased their presence during the years that followed and, during the seventeenth century, established permanent settlements from which to meet and thwart the expansionist plans of the Portuguese, who launched their forces from Brazil. The seventeenth and eighteenth centuries were marked by endless fighting between Spanish and Portuguese forces, during which Montevideo was established as a Spanish military base.

During the nineteenth century, British involvement grew steadily as well, as the three colonial powers sought to increase their influence and dominance in the region. At one point, British troops occupied Montevideo, using it as a base from which to launch an attack on the Spanish in Buenos Aires, part of Britain's ongoing war with Spain. In 1828, the Treaty of Montevideo, promoted by the UK, gave birth to Uruguay as an independent state and its first constitution was adopted shortly afterwards.

Peace in the region was still a long way off, however. The years that followed were marked by the so-called Great War, which became an international affair due to French and British involvement, and The War of the Triple Alliance, which pitched Uruguayan, Brazilian and Argentine forces against Paraguay for five years.

The endless fighting and land-grabbing mentality of the different colonial powers had seen their influence see-saw between them over a long period. This could only have hampered the development of Uruguay during its early years. It was probably with some relief, though, that Spain and Portugal welcomed Uruguay as a buffer zone between their respective military forces in Argentina and Brazil.

During the First World War, Uruguay opposed Germany's position. In 1917, it severed relations with Germany and declared its support for the Allies. It did not, however, play any active part in the war.

In the Second World War, it unwittingly became involved at an early stage. The Battle of the River Plate took place off the coast of Uruguay on 13th December 1939, when the German heavy cruiser, *Admiral Graf Spee*, was scuttled following a British attack. Many of the ship's survivors were interned in Uruguay and remained in the country after the war. The question of ownership, and salvaging rights of the vessel, caused considerable friction between Uruguay and Germany and, on 25th January 1942, Uruguay broke off diplomatic relations with Germany.

Recent Developments

More recently, during the early 1960s, an urban guerrilla movement, which became known as the Tupamaros National Liberation Movement, emerged as a result of growing political instability and poverty. They specialised at first in robbing banks and distributing food to the poor, but graduated to political kidnappings and more violent behaviour, in order to destabilise the Uruguayan Government and the existing social order.

As kidnappings were occurring with increasing frequency in South America, the British Ambassador in Uruguay, Sir Geoffrey Jackson, became the latest victim when, on 8th January 1971, he too was taken. He was fortunate to be released by his self-appointed Tupamaro jailors in September, after ten months in his underground prison. Some years later, he lectured would-be military attachés and diplomats heading for South America and other countries around the world to take up new appointments. The main thrust of his fascinating lecture was concerned with how to avoid being kidnapped in the first place and, if you were unlucky enough to be taken, how to conduct yourself and attempt to build up some sort of rapport with your captors to enhance your prospects of survival. This he certainly endeavoured to do, but his eventual release was also assisted by the payment of a sum of money by Edward Heath's government. Chile's President, Salvador Allende, helped to broker the settlement.

The Tupamaros were eventually defeated by the military in 1972, amidst a nationwide demand for a strong government that could put an end to the political instability. Sadly, although the Tupamaros ceased to be a threat in Uruguay, brutal tactics had been employed to achieve this and the country entered a dark period, during which many dissenters were jailed, tortured or simply 'disappeared'. International organisations denounced the country for the human rights violations, which continued until the mid-1980s. Democracy had thus been destroyed in a country once noted for its tolerance.

This, then, was the nature of the Uruguayan Government that was in power during the Falklands War; the government whose assistance we discovered we needed, and were fortunate to receive. The return to civilian rule was still a few years away.

During the Falklands War

The British Ambassador in Uruguay in 1982 was Patricia Hutchinson. She had travelled a great deal within the country, and continued to feel it was safe to do so throughout the war. The Embassy never had to close, and Britain maintained diplomatic relations with the host nation throughout. She did admit, however, that the Embassy's evacuation plan was updated and ready, in case the need arose. This was a sensible precaution, which probably would have been taken in all our embassies in South America. It certainly was in Brazil.

She said: 'Throughout the brief war, Uruguay continued to enjoy a good working relationship with both Britain and Argentina – a delicate balancing act and no mean feat – whilst the latter tried hard to persuade Uruguay to be less even-handed.' In spite of being under a great deal of pressure, the Uruguayan Government nevertheless managed to remain – in public anyway – effectively neutral in its stance.

The Uruguayan armed forces differed somewhat in their attitude. In general, they all had a good working relationship with Argentina's forces, held joint exercises, visited each other's staff colleges and attended courses together. John Bryant, who later served as Defence Attaché in Uruguay, thought their air force was the least pro-British of the armed forces and had a particularly close relationship with the Argentine Air

159

Force. The Uruguayan Navy was more friendly though; the army was generally rather indifferent, and inclined to see both points of view.

Julian Mitchell, the Naval Attaché in Buenos Aires, covered Uruguay as well throughout his tour of duty, and said that the Argentine Navy exercised regularly with the Uruguayans, even though it rarely did so with the other Argentine services, and had not done so at all during his time in Buenos Aires. 'It [the Argentine Navy] had a particularly poor relationship with the Argentine Air Force,' he said.

Most ordinary Uruguayans remained friendly during the war. No one in the Embassy recalled having had any particularly awkward or embarrassing experiences, or indeed hearing of any. Many Uruguayans resented the fact that numerous Argentines had second homes in their country. There was a considerable amount of friction over this issue.

Patricia Hutchinson endorsed these views and added: 'Many Uruguayans simply sat on the fence during the war, preferring the quiet life. There was little unpleasantness and certainly nothing of any consequence that I can recall.' She felt that the main functions of her Embassy at that difficult time were to calm fears, keep lines of communication open, and maintain a sense of business as usual. 'Most Uruguayans,' she said, 'were good, honest people, who were simply undecided as to whether or not they ought to support another South American country, especially one that was a close neighbour. That would have made them pro-Argentina only out of necessity. It was a difficult choice to make, so many did not bother to make it.'

Some Uruguayans, those with long memories, would not have forgotten that less than a decade before, Argentina had threatened Uruguay with war. Uruguay had refused to concede the small island of Martin Garcia, which lay closer to the Uruguayan side of the River de la Plata. The final Agreement, which many found distasteful, established the island as Argentine territory. Size matters!

Andrew Murray, who became our Ambassador in Uruguay a few years later, summed up their complex relationship succinctly:

The Argentine/Uruguayan relationship has been difficult since birth and we, the British, involved ourselves in the creation of this small country formed from bits of Argentina and Brazil, its two large and powerful neighbours. Uruguay owes its being to us, and its position between the two giants has always been an uncomfortable one. It has also, inevitably, always been economically dependent upon the fortunes of both its neighbours. When Argentina suffered

160

economically in 1981 and 1982, Uruguay was also very concerned. Things are easier today, and tourism is big business in the country. When we needed their help in 1982, it would have placed Uruguay in something of a dilemma, but they went as far as they could to help us, ever-mindful of their neighbour's size and strength.

Kate Adie summed up her view of the average Uruguayan admirably. She thought they were '... a mixture of the familiar European and the exotic South American... People looked as if they would be more at home in Paris or Madrid, and were distinctly un-American'. She also made the observation that, in general, Uruguayans were puzzled by the intense British commitment to a group of islands which lay off their shores.

When the British Embassy in Buenos Aires closed down, following the severance of diplomatic relations with Argentina, the diplomats and other Embassy staff had to leave the country. Some returned to the UK, but a few, including Julian Mitchell and Mark Heathcoat, both of whom had briefs to cover Uruguay as well as Argentina whilst they were in South America, went initially to Montevideo.

For those British subjects who chose to remain in Argentina, the uncertainty that prevailed there was an ongoing cause for concern. Newspapers in Buenos Aires reported one day that: 'The junta was preparing to take measures to control the residents from the enemy country'. There were certainly many of them in Argentina then.

British businessmen, company representatives, teachers at the English schools (which closed during the war) and many others, soon started to heed Foreign Office advice to leave as soon as possible. Most headed across the River de la Plata to Montevideo, which was regarded as a safe haven.

It was a trickle at first, and never quite became a flood, but the arrival of British subjects from early in April certainly resulted in a boom period for Montevideo's hotel owners. Although some went as a purely pre-cautionary measure, or for the sake of their families, there were a few death threats to spur on the undecided. Jimmy Burns, the *Financial Times* correspondent, received one such threat, and joined the flow with his wife. To his amusement and her consternation, she had to settle tem-porarily for a bed in a brothel; such was the demand for hotel beds.

The Rolls Royce representative in Buenos Aires, John Wemyss, recalled being told to 'take emergency action and initiate the evacuation of all personnel'. The plan involved loading up all their vehicles and

161

driving to Montevideo, but at the last minute the instruction was changed to 'take a flight to Rio de Janeiro', where the company had another office.

Shell had a large operation in Argentina, based in Buenos Aires, which included many Anglo-Argentine employees. When the war started, the company shifted its centre of operations to Uruguay, but there was serious concern regarding the allegiance of the workforce, and therefore its reliability. The Anglo-Argentine workers were forced to decide where their allegiance lay, and whether they felt predominantly Argentine or British. The vast majority said 'Argentine' and remained in Argentina throughout the war. Many of those who decided they were more British took no chances and opted for the trip to Uruguay.

Most of those who sought sanctuary in Uruguay regarded it as somewhere safe from where to monitor the developing situation to the south and east. The bars of Montevideo quickly filled with British arm-chair warriors who argued over the relative strengths of the two nations' armed forces. Their main enemy was boredom, and most were hugely relieved and ready to return to Argentina as soon as the war ended.

It has to be said that many others, who had elected to remain in Argentina, did not in fact experience any difficulties or harassment there, and never regretted that decision.

Arms for Argentina

There were strong rumours later on that arms for Argentina were being channelled through Uruguay from South Africa, possibly without the knowledge of the Uruguayan Government. It was known within the War Cabinet that South Africa and Israel were actively co-operating with Argentina at that time, and sending aid and arms. Sir John Nott said: 'South Africa was determined not to co-operate with us in any way and to frustrate us whenever possible'.

Dudley Ankerson was a diplomat in Buenos Aires just prior to the war. He said: 'Both Israel and South Africa were short of friends, so it would have been useful to both of them to befriend Argentina. Israel already had a good relationship with the Argentine Government and would have had commercial gain very much in mind (paradoxically, in spite of many Nazi criminals taking refuge there).'

South Africa was a pariah state, and relations between it and the UK were at an all-time low then, owing to the arms embargo. These were widely-held views at the time. The Israelis had also been co-operating with South Africa since the mid-1970s, and assisting with the building of its arms manufacturing capability. They were all hard-nosed opportunists, and neither country could be trusted at that time.

Julian Mitchell spent six weeks in Uruguay before being recalled to the UK. During that period, he was not only involved in the revelation that arms were being flown to Argentina from South Africa, but actively tried to have the flights stopped.

Although not offering conclusive proof, a Reuter report dated 24th May 1982 quoted a Johannesburg paper as saying: 'South Africa is supplying Argentina with weapons, including Israeli ship-to-ship missiles, for use in the Falklands fighting. The paper... quoted unidentified sources in Cape Town as saying that, in addition to Gabriel missiles, the weapons included spares for the Mirage fighter-bombers.' It went on to say that the weapons '... are loaded aboard a Uruguayan DC8 air-freighter in a remote corner of Cape Town's D.F. Malan airport and packed in ... pallets marked "Tractor Spares".'

One of the British Embassy's contacts in Argentina, an arms dealer based in Uruguay, had been an ex-French Foreign Legion man. He acted quite independently rather than for any government organisation. He was unable to prevent the first flight, which was thought to have landed in Uruguay, en route to Argentina, on or around 24th May, but was able to secretly observe the loading of the aircraft that made the second flight early in June.

Julian Mitchell, who was in the UK by then, received a telephone call from him on 2nd June with the information. He contacted the MoD Duty Officer immediately and asked him to pass the information without delay to the Foreign Office Duty Officer. The only hope of preventing the aircraft from taking off lay in the application of swift, high-level diplomatic pressure on the South African Government. Unfortunately, the trail went cold at that point, and no one has been able to explain what (if anything) happened after the MoD was informed. In the event, the aircraft was not prevented from taking off. It was probably a forlorn hope anyway – given the state of Anglo/South African relations at the time – that the South African Government might intervene. Julian's contact confirmed later that: 'at least two flights had taken place'.

In another sense this whole saga may actually have helped Britain, as publicity surrounding South African arms deliveries to Argentina served to strengthen black African support for Britain in the United Nations. Kenya was particularly sympathetic and helpful.

Uruguay can fairly be described as being in a difficult position geographically, sandwiched as it is between the two giant nations, Argentina and Brazil. Nevertheless, during the Falklands War, it demonstrated in the way it co-operated over such important issues as casualty evacuation and prisoner-of-war repatriation that it would decide for itself the extent to which it would work with Britain with regard to these all-important humanitarian issues. It would not be bullied.

The Repatriation of Prisoners of War (POWs)

There is no doubt that Britain needed a friend in the area in 1982 (in addition to Chile, on the other side of South America). Andrew Murray, the British Ambassador in Montevideo a few years later, said: 'Although this placed the Uruguayan Government in a difficult position, undoubtedly it did what it could under the circumstances. Apart from permitting the casualty evacuation process to proceed unhindered, Uruguay also ensured that British POWs released by Argentina were well-treated and granted safe passage through the country. Both issues were handled with care and sensitivity.'

The war casualties and the POWs (with one exception only) were transported back to the UK on VC10 aircraft of No 10 Squadron, based at RAF Brize Norton. The first VC10 flight left the UK on 3rd April to pick up those Royal Marines – of the Falklands detachment – who were captured when the Argentine invasion force arrived on the islands. They were flown to Montevideo on an Argentine Air Force transport aircraft on the same day.

Rex Hunt, the Governor of the Falkland Islands, also left the islands on the same Argentine aircraft. They all flew back to the UK on the following day, on the first of many VC10 flights that flew to Uruguay during the months of April through to the end of July.

The Royal Marines from South Georgia

The next prisoners to be released by Argentina were the Royal Marines who had been captured in South Georgia on 3rd April. Lt Keith Mills was the Officer Commanding the 22 RMs, made up of his own eleven-man detachment on HMS *Endurance*, bolstered by the addition of others from the Falklands detachment.

When the Argentine scrap-metal merchant, Davidoff, arrived on South

Georgia on 21st March, HMS *Endurance* received orders to proceed to the island and evict him. On arrival at South Georgia on 24th March, however, fresh orders were received, this time prohibiting Davidoff's eviction. After a few days, during which everything was on hold and rather unclear, HMS *Endurance* was ordered to return to the Falklands, leaving the RM detachment behind on South Georgia.

Keith Mills' orders were 'to be a presence to protect the scientists' (i.e. from Davidoff, his cronies and their military escort); also 'you may fire in self-defence or to save the life of another'. Officially, they were on venture training if asked, and no one believed an Argentine invasion was either imminent or very likely anyway; not, that is, until the evening of 1st April.

When Rex Hunt ordered the state of emergency on 2nd April, Mills ordered his marines to 'stand to' and wait for they knew not what! He had orders not to communicate with HMS *Endurance*, which was by then on its way back to South Georgia.

Also on 2nd April, the *Bahia Paraiso*, an Argentine navy supply ship, sailed into Cumberland Bay. The intention had been to invade the island, but as it was raining hard the Argentines decided to postpone their invasion. 'They sailed back out to sea again,' said Keith Mills, 'and called up on Channel 16 to say we should keep monitoring the channel, and they would be back again tomorrow. I decided to break R/T silence and send an encoded message to *Endurance* seeking instructions. There were various options open to the Argentines but I had only enough men to engage with small arms fire.'

He received a reply saying: 'When asked to co-operate, you are not to do so,' which was about as unhelpful as it could be. The next day, a further message said: 'OC RMs is not, repeat, not to take any action that might endanger life.' Faced with instructions like those, who can blame Keith Mills for putting the finishing touches to the defensive positions they had dug, and deciding to fight.

The action that took place later pitted the handful of Royal Marines against an Argentine force vastly superior in numbers and firepower. It included the frigate *Guerrico*, a submarine, two destroyers, a logistics ship in support, and helicopters. Keith Mills just had his twenty-two men. Before long, about 200 Argentine marines started to come ashore, whilst the shelling from the ships offshore was becoming ever more accurate. After a while, there being no escape route, and with one of the RMs badly injured, Keith Mills took the decision to surrender.

They were taken prisoner and transported to the *Bahia Paraiso*, where the Captain had the single casualty treated. Nigel Peters recalled: 'I was in the trench under fire when I was hit, and my arm was smashed. I was given morphine so wasn't really aware of events from then on. On the ship I was well looked after by the Argentine doctor. I was rather surprised actually, considering the amount of damage we had caused, and the casualties we had inflicted!'

The *Bahia Paraiso* sailed around for almost two weeks, whilst the Captain awaited orders. It then went to an Argentine marine training base in Tierra del Fuego, where the POWs were 'housed' for a few days in the changing rooms of an empty swimming pool normally used by conscripts. They were treated well and nothing very exciting happened, although an intelligence officer visited them one day for a fairly inconsequential chat.

On another day, they were taken to the Argentine Court of Justice, which caused some concern, fearing trumped-up charges of murder or something similar. In the event, they need not have worried, as they were confronted only by senior officers whose principal concern was how their own troops had performed.

For Argentina, the South Georgia action had been a disaster and an embarrassment – one ship badly damaged, a Puma helicopter destroyed and numerous casualties. Nevertheless, an Argentine Admiral shook Keith Mills' hand and promised: 'If there is anything you want, just ask.'

Nigel Peters was separated from his colleagues when they arrived on the mainland, and was sent to a hospital in Buenos Aires where his arm was treated. From there, he was taken to a 'safe house' on the outskirts of the city. He was given a radio one day, and remembers being able to pick up BBC overseas broadcasts. He said: 'It was thanks to that radio that we first learned a Task Force was on its way south'. He also recalled being interrogated whilst he was still alone. 'It wasn't a very professional effort. One or two armed guys in plain clothes tried, with little success, to engage me in conversation, but I stayed silent and pretended to be worse than I really was. They wanted to know what we were doing in South Georgia! They arranged a little barbecue for me and let me walk in a garden. There was no suggestion of any rough treatment. Nevertheless, I didn't sleep very well and was always alert. I felt very vulnerable until I was reunited with my colleagues after over a week alone. I had heard about the "dirty war"!'

On 20th April, the Royal Marines were flown in an Argentine military aircraft to Montevideo, where they were released to a warm welcome from the Ambassador and her staff. Patricia Hutchinson telephoned the

167

Prime Minister and informed her that they had safely arrived. She said: 'The Prime Minister then ordered me to put them in the best hotel in town and not allow them to talk to anyone, especially the press. They were to stay in their rooms until they finally departed for the airport'. Notwithstanding the PM's instructions, and the guards placed outside the hotel, Bob Ashton said that he was approached by 'a man who offered me a six-figure sum for my story!' They had been in Montevideo for just 24 hours when they boarded the RAF VC10 aircraft that took them back to England. Their ordeal was finally over.

Keith Mills' marines were joined in Montevideo by a further seven marines, who had been captured shortly after the invasion, but not until after they had spent several very uncomfortable days avoiding detection in the barren interior of the Falklands. When they were finally captured, they were taken as POWs to the General Roca Military Academy in the port of Comodoro Rivadavia, where they spent a couple of weeks before they, too, were taken to Montevideo for repatriation. With them were the thirteen scientists who had been working for the British Antarctic Survey on South Georgia.

They all appeared to agree that their treatment throughout the period of captivity had been very acceptable, and probably better than they had feared. The one adverse comment they made was that no news of their condition, or whereabouts, had ever been released by Argentina during the weeks spent in captivity.

The RAF VC10s also carried POWs in the other direction. After the recapture of South Georgia on 25th April, 180 Argentine prisoners were taken by sea to Ascension Island. From there, they were repatriated by VC10 via Montevideo.

Flight Lieutenant Glover's Experience

On 21st May, Flight Lieutenant Jeff Glover became the only RAF POW during the brief war. He was a pilot on No 1 Squadron at the time, flying the Harrier GR3 aircraft in the ground attack and photographic recon-naissance roles and was based on HMS *Hermes*. It is interesting to compare Jeff's recollections with those of Sergio Fernandez (in 'A General Remembers').

Jeff said: 'I was making a second low-level photo-reconnaissance run over suspected enemy positions at Port Howard when I was shot down. Although I was uncertain what had struck my aircraft, it was subsequently confirmed as having been a Blowpipe missile. Half the starboard wing had been shot away, and the aircraft had rolled uncontrollably, forcing me to eject. The aircraft crashed on to farmland, killing a horse in the process. The farmer later claimed £900 under the terms of a compensation scheme that was, in my view, extremely generous, as the horse was well past its prime!

'I came down in the sea about 100 metres offshore, and was too shocked to notice how cold it was. Having suffered a broken arm, shoulder and collarbone, I was in no shape to discard my parachute and felt myself sinking. Then, it started to get lighter again above me, and I was hauled out of the water and into a rowing boat. I was saved by the very soldiers who, minutes before, had shot me down.

'I was taken to an Argentine field hospital where I was the only British casualty. I found this rather unsettling, especially during the night. An Argentine doctor treated me very professionally, and clearly drew no distinction between British or Argentine casualties, something that seemed to upset some in the latter category. This only added considerably to my discomfort. During the three or four days I spent in the field hospital, I was kept incommunicado from the islanders in case they tried to help me to escape.'

Finally, Jeff was flown to the mainland, but not before the question of whether he should be placed in the care of the army or the air force had been hotly debated. He was greatly relieved when he learned that the air force had won the argument. Once on Argentine soil, he was taken to the Comodoro Rivadavia air base, where he was given drugs and a plaster cast, and thence to the Chamical air base near Cordoba.

At Chamical, Jeff spent the rest of the war in reasonable comfort. There was dusty desert all around and a good view of the Andes in the distance. The base had only one or two air movements each day and he spent most of the time completely alone. He did have one visitor though, a Swiss Red Cross Official who measured his room and gave him books and cigarettes. Other than that, a few Argentine air force pilots took an interest in him from time to time. Jeff commented: 'Some of them wanted to practise their English on me and one even gave me a bottle of wine. They were very pleasant really; in fact, far more welcoming than most of the RN pilots on *Hermes*!'

Jeff was interrogated twice, and each time only briefly; once while he was still on the Falklands, and then again on the mainland at the Comodoro Rivadavia air base. He said: 'Each time, it was pretty gentle stuff. The interrogators were senior air force officers who spoke good, educated English. They asked nothing about the Harrier, and one was interested to know if I had ever met Prince Andrew! There was never any attempt to brainwash me; nor was there ever any suggestion that anyone might get rough with me.'

On the 6th July, Jeff was sent back to the hospital in Buenos Aires, where he was informed that he was to be released the next day. After a further 24-hour delay, he was flown to Montevideo where he was finally released on 8th July. Later, he recalled his brief stay in Montevideo: 'I arrived at the Ambassador's residence late in the morning, where I made a phone call to my wife, had a few gin and tonics and then slept for ages. The next morning, I went into town to do some shopping, accompanied by a friendly SAS man. I must have been the only POW to go home with handbags for his wife and mother!'

Jeff was the last POW to pass through Uruguay. He had been in captivity for seven weeks, three of which were after the Argentine surrender. He said: 'Everything seemed to go very smoothly in Uruguay. In fact, I couldn't really fault the treatment I received from anyone, from the time I was rescued from the sea.'

Apart from the failure to release information about the safety and whereabouts of prisoners, Argentina can hardly be criticised for the way British prisoners were treated. Interrogations, if they happened at all, were low-key in nature, and of little consequence. Proper medical care was provided when necessary. It was all rather different from the treatment metered out to their own prisoners during the 'dirty war' years, something that was not lost on many apprehensive British POWs.

Uruguay's role in facilitating the return of POWs via Montevideo was also very much appreciated by Britain.

Casualty Evacuation

The casualty evacuation process involved both the Royal Navy and the Royal Air Force. To be more precise, the RN took the casualties to Uruguay, and the RAF then flew them back to the UK. The process worked well and unquestionably saved many lives and many limbs. It would not have been possible without the co-operation of the Uruguayan Government, and it was greatly facilitated by the British Embassy staff in Montevideo.

The SS *Canberra*, a 44,000-ton P&O passenger liner, and the second largest ship in the Merchant Navy, was requisitioned and joined the Task Force in April 1982. Nicknamed the 'Great White Whale', it was officially a troop-transporter and acted in that capacity on its journey south from Ascension Island. It was never a hospital ship but, in the words of Dr Peter Mayner, the P&O company medical officer on board: 'It was a "receiving station" for the duration of its stay in the South Atlantic.' It was not declared to Geneva and was therefore vulnerable to attack.

As a consequence, *Canberra* was forced to spend most of the war 200 miles to the east of the Falklands, to be out of range of Argentine fighter aircraft. On 21st May, when she took part in the mass disembarkation of British troops on to the Falklands, she had to be back 200 miles to the east again by dawn the following day. Admiral Woodward said later: '*Canberra* led a charmed life not being hit by the Argentines. They made the crucial mistake of going for frigates and destroyers, rather than amphibious ships and troop carriers.'

Peter Mayner, being a civilian, was known as 'the ringless one'. He had with him on board two nursing sisters, another doctor and comprehensive medical facilities. They could carry out amputations and had a blood transfusion unit. *Canberra* also transported the RN surgical support teams and doctors who later became part of the embarked force. On the whole, though, *Canberra* was under-utilised during the war.

171

Surgeon Commander Rick Jolly embarked in *Canberra* at Ascension Island, and stayed with her until he disembarked on 21st May to set up and run the field hospital at Ajax Bay. During the next few weeks he dealt with casualties from both nations and travelled frequently between the Falklands and *Uganda*.

Uganda had been converted from the P&O educational ship in Gibraltar in mid-April and became the official hospital ship, accommodating most of the doctors, nurses and medical facilities. It carried the Red Cross insignia and normally remained some 50 miles offshore, regularly coming in to Ajax Bay to collect the wounded from the field dressing stations (FDS). She had a designated Red Cross 'box' within which she could operate safely, although her markings should in theory have guaranteed her safety anywhere.

The wounded were flown out to *Uganda* in Wessex helicopters. Whereas those on *Canberra* remained on the ship, those that had been taken to *Uganda* became part of a process that eventually returned them to the UK when they were deemed fit enough to travel. Altogether, *Uganda* admitted over 700 casualties from the conflict zone during the brief war.

HM Ships *Hydra*, *Hecla* and *Herald*

The next stage of this process was the transportation of the wounded from *Uganda* to Uruguay. HM ships *Hydra*, *Hecla* and *Herald*, three RN hydrographic survey ships, were used for this task.

Dr Chris James served on HMS *Hydra*. He said: 'I was one of two young and inexperienced doctors on board. I had only been qualified for two years. We also carried five naval medical assistants and a couple of RN nurses. Some of our Argentine casualties thought they were in heaven! The three ships had been declared to the Red Cross, were painted white, and bore the Red Cross insignia. Militarily, they were quite useless as they lacked any weapons systems on board. The captain, a hydrographer, was also not accustomed to being in the firing line!'

With the co-operation of the Uruguayan authorities and British Embassy personnel, the three survey ships, acting as ambulance ships, made a total of eight return journeys from the Total Exclusion Zone (TEZ) to Montevideo. HMS *Hecla* made the first trip on 2nd June, carrying eighteen British casualties (nine of whom were survivors from HMS *Sheffield*), plus a further twenty-four Argentine casualties from the

172

Narwal. The badly-injured Argentine casualties were also normally evacuated to Montevideo. The final trip was made by HMS *Hydra* on 13th July, one month after the ceasefire.

On arrival at the dockside in Montevideo, the survey ships were met by the Uruguayan authorities. The Uruguayans were variously described as having been courteous, firm, helpful, ever-watchful and scrupulously correct. No member of the ship's company was ever allowed to step ashore.

Kate Adie, BBC correspondent in Uruguay (briefly, before she continued on down to Punta Arenas in Chile), described beautifully the arrival of one of the survey ships at the dockside. She said: 'A ship came into view – not battleship-grey, but white, signalling her purpose for everyone to see, and for the first time I felt that the war was coming to call in all its reality. She approached very slowly, and we could just make out people standing at the rails. It was a very quiet arrival – the Uruguayans wanted no fuss from someone else's war – and the waters of the Plata were flat silver, hiding the wreck of the German battleship *Graf Spee*, another reminder of another war. The men leaning over the ship's rails did not wave. As the ship grew closer, the evidence of their injuries became plain to see. The ship was a quiet reminder of the reality of war.'

No 10 Squadron, Royal Air Force

Argentine casualties, when there were any, were handed over immediately to Argentine officials. British casualties were passed to the Uruguayan medical services, and then transported to Montevideo airport, to a waiting RAF VC10 aircraft from No 10 Squadron.

No 10 Squadron's commanding officer was Wing Commander Gerry Bunn. He said: 'The VC10's main roles during the Falklands War included troop carrying, certain special supportive missions (e.g. to Chile's Easter Island), and flying to Montevideo to pick up war casualties or repatriated POWs. Normally, VC10s carried people and the C130s carried loads.' The VC10s had neither an air-to-air refuelling capability nor any defensive equipment.

Once the casualties started coming ashore, the VC10 flights were arranged as required. The aircraft always landed at night at Montevideo airport, refuelled, took the casualties on board and then took off again as quickly as possible. Most flights carried between fifty and eighty casualties, depending on the nature of the injuries. Obviously, stretcher cases took up more space than the walking wounded.

For these missions to and from Uruguay, the aircraft sported the Red Cross insignia on the fuselage. When Keith Mills and his Royal Marines were taken back to the UK, there were no such markings. Supposedly there were no war casualties at that early stage of the proceedings. Nigel Peters, whose arm had been shattered by an Argentine bullet whilst under fire in South Georgia, might have disputed that assessment.

Between 2nd June and 13th July, No 10 Squadron's VC10s flew eight ambulance flights, carrying over 400 casualties from Montevideo safely back to the UK. Some of the casualties were in a terrible state, with horrific wounds such as having shrapnel embedded in the head. The aircraft had an on-board operating theatre and carried a couple of doctors, an anaesthetist and two or three nurses so that surgical procedures could be carried out in flight. They were all RAF personnel.

If an in-flight operation was considered to be necessary, the doctor would ask the aircraft captain to descend to low altitude, to increase atmospheric pressure and thus the amount of oxygen available for breathing. Occasionally, this might be a problem if range became a critical factor. Having left Montevideo in the hours of darkness, the VC10s staged through Ascension Island in order to refuel, and then continued on to RAF Brize Norton with as little delay as possible. RAF casualties were then transferred to the Reception Centre at nearby Wroughton Hospital; Army and Navy casualties were transferred to their own service hospitals.

The flight from Montevideo to Brize Norton, including the stop at Ascension Island, took approximately 14 hours. The squadron took some pride in the fact that no individual evacuated by No 10 Squadron died of his wounds in the immediate post-war period.

The squadron was constantly at full stretch during the war. Sometimes there were barely enough people to do the job; occasionally it had been necessary to turn a blind eye to crew duty restrictions, and to manage on the basis of common sense and sleeping pills.

Inevitably, some of the VC10 flights were not without incident. Rob Robinson was the aircraft captain on three of the casualty evacuation flights, which brought casualties from HMS *Sheffield*, Goose Green and *Atlantic Conveyor* back to the UK. Mike O'Donovan was his co-pilot. Rob recalled those flights many years later:

We took off from Ascension Island on 12th June with a full medical team on board and the VC10 converted to a medevac (medical evacuation) fit. This fit, depending on requirements, could be up to fifty-six stretchers. Our flight duration was expected to be six and a half hours, and had been fairly routine until we were about two hours out of Montevideo, when we checked in with Recife (Brazil) air traffic control on HF radio. Recife was our Flight Information Region controlling authority, but the frequency was also monitored by Buenos Aires. We gave our position report to Recife, which included our point of departure and our destination. This was acknowledged by Recife, but was then immediately queried by Buenos Aires who told us, in no uncertain terms, that our flight was not accepted and that we were to turn back. We repeated our flight number, informing Buenos Aires that we were a hospital aircraft with a Red Cross International permit number. We waited for what seemed an interminable period, and then again we were told to turn back. It was at this point that Recife came on the radio to inform Buenos Aires that, as we were not under its control, they had no authority over us. We flew on without further incident and had no further contact with Buenos Aires. That did not stop us from peering out of the window in case any Argentine fighters had been sent up to trouble us!

We landed in Montevideo to discover that we were not going to be handled by civilians, as expected, but by the military. They were very efficient and polite, and within no time we were all on our way to the hotel in a large bus, and with military outriders.

The next morning, we returned to the airport to await the arrival of the casualties that had been brought ashore from *Uganda*. It was a very poignant sight to see so many ambulances in procession. The stretchers and walking wounded (dressed in Royal Navy dark blue trousers and light blue shirts) were brought on board, and we were soon on our way back to Ascension Island. I spoke to many of the casualties during the flight, most of them from HMS *Sheffield*, and many with horrific burns. They were all fairly euphoric though, and very happy to be on their way home.

On my crew's second flight to Montevideo on 16th June, we brought back the Para casualties from Goose Green. A discussion with one of the walking wounded has remained with me ever since. A young

175

soldier, not more than eighteen years of age, was brought up to the flight deck, supported by one of his mates. He had lost an arm and a leg in a mortar attack at Goose Green, but blamed himself for his injuries. He said that his sergeant had told all the young recruits, time and time again, that when under mortar attack, if another soldier is injured, do not under any circumstances crawl over to assist him, because the next mortar will land in the same spot! It did. He was happy to be alive and on his way home, but my thoughts were focussed on how this lad would be coping with life six months later.

On Rob's third flight, they brought back the survivors from the *Atlantic Conveyor*. The burn injuries made a huge impression on him. Whilst his second and third flights had gone without mishap, he noticed a progressive change in the attitude of the Uruguayans. On his second flight, the military presence had been less obvious than before, and on the third flight was completely absent. He said: 'On that occasion, the aircraft was greeted by a local dignitary and a huge crowd waving Union Jacks.' When Rob had mentioned to this dignitary the difference between the first and third welcomes he had received, she replied: 'The Argentine military junta had been looking for a way to focus the minds of their people away from the country's internal problems, and concentrate them instead on a national issue such as a war against Uruguay, Chile or over the Malvinas.' She added: 'It was a great relief (i.e. to all Uruguayans) that the junta had chosen to fight the British!'

Another VC10 flight that sparked a little controversy was the second one on the 5th/6th June. Captained by Brian Wheeler, with co-pilot Dick King, its task was to bring back injured sailors from HMS *Sheffield* and HMS *Coventry*, together with army casualties from Goose Green. In Dick King's own words (précised):

We had refuelled at Ascension Island and were en route to Montevideo. It is common practice for non-combatant aircraft to utilise the civilian air traffic control system when transiting through civilian airspace. We conformed to this procedure and passed our position reports on the HF long-range radio to Dakar and later to Recife and Porto Alegre in Brazil. As we neared the South American coast, some 500 miles or so out to sea, I called Porto Alegre in order to pass a position report. No answer. I repeated my call. Then, from out of the dark night a voice said: 'Go ahead Ascot 2645. This is Buenos Aires. I will relay your position to Porto Alegre.' Buenos

176

Aires is in Argentina. We were fighting a war against Argentina. I pretended I had not heard him, and we ignored the generosity of our enemy's friendly civilian air traffic controller.

Eventually we came within range and established radio contact with Montevideo. The lady operating the radio frequency advised us that we could not land in Montevideo as the visibility was down to fifty metres in thick fog. The only solution was to divert, but there are relatively few airfields in Uruguay suitable for long-range aircraft such as a VC10. The friendly lady air traffic controller then said we should divert to Durazno, which was approximately one hundred and fifty kilometres north-east of Montevideo. It turned out that Durazno was a relatively small training airfield for the Uruguayan Air Force. After landing, we were despatched to a small hotel in the nearby town, where we spent the night.

On our arrival back at the airfield the next morning, we were met by a large number of rather concerned people. Apparently, a box containing the personal effects of an RAF officer – who had left the aircraft at Ascension Island – had been found in the rear hold. In the box were several items that looked suspiciously like spare parts for Harrier aircraft, which should have been offloaded at Ascension Island. Happily, members of the crew were able to convince the Uruguayan authorities that it had been an innocent mistake, and the aircraft was allowed to take off again with its casualties on board.

This story has, over the passage of time, been distorted and blown-up out of all proportion. Needless to say, there is a Royal Navy version that suggests a whole Pegasus engine was hidden in the officer's personal effects! There was not; but no one could (or would) identify the officer whose baggage had included some Harrier spares.

As with the operations of the Royal Air Force's C130 fleet, little was said during the war about No 10 Squadron's VC10 activities, but many felt that the momentum of Operation Corporate, as the retaking of the islands had been codenamed, could not have been maintained without the lifeline provided by these two aircraft types.

Rick Jolly and his colleagues had always treated British and Argentine wounded alike, and without any regard to nationality. To be fair, that was also the attitude of the Argentine doctor who treated Harrier pilot, Jeff Glover, after he was shot down and captured in the Falklands. During the war, *Uganda* had liaised closely with the Argentine hospital ship to

177

which their casualties were often transferred, and from time to time the two ships helped each other out with medical supplies and drugs. The first Argentine casualties to be sent from *Uganda* were those (nearly eighty men) for whom British doctors assumed responsibility when Stanley was retaken. Many of them were operated on, under anaesthetic, on board *Uganda* before being transferred.

After the War

The ceasefire did not mean that the job had been done. On the 17th June, *Canberra* took her Argentine casualties and POWs, totalling 4144 men altogether, and deposited them at Puerto Madryn, once a small Welsh mining community in Argentina. One of those casualties was a Lieutenant Brown (Special Forces), whose grandfather had been an admiral in the Royal Navy. Lt Brown, like other casualties in British hands, had willingly given blood to help his compatriots. As previously mentioned, many of Argentina's casualties from *Uganda* had already been transported to Montevideo and handed over to Argentine officials.

The RAF VC10 ambulance flights also continued after the ceasefire on 14th June. No less than five further flights took place, bringing more wounded personnel back to the UK. By the end of July, No 10 Squadron's tasking started to show signs of returning to normality, but the considerable British presence on Ascension Island, and in the Falkland Islands, ensured that regular resupply flights would be needed for the foreseeable future.

After the war ended, Argentina segregated its war casualties and, sadly, some Argentine doctors denied that British doctors had treated their men at all. It was learned later that the Argentine Government had not wanted the word to get out that their wounded had not only received excellent treatment from the British, but were also extremely grateful. Many of them were effectively disowned by an ungrateful nation; others never received the disability pensions due to them. In some cases, returning casualties were consigned to a bleak future, begging to survive.

The diplomats and Embassy staff in Montevideo, encouraged by the Ambassador, saw their task as being one of mending fences and restoring a feeling of normality. Most agreed that this proved not too difficult to achieve. Britain had reason to be particularly grateful for the quiet, no-frills support given by the Uruguayan Government throughout the war.

There were, of course, one or two casualties of the war, and a hoped-for order for four Type 21 frigates for the Uruguayan Navy failed to materialise. Shortly before the war, the Naval Attaché had visited the agent in Montevideo to press for a decision. It was intended to be a barter deal – beef for frigates – and most of the pressure to conclude it had come from the agricultural sector rather than from the navy. Unfortunately it was not concluded. 'It was essentially a political decision,' one diplomat said. 'It was a victim of the war, because Uruguay had to placate Argentina at times, make the odd gesture, and never forget that the two countries had to coexist in the long term.' Efforts to sell the frigates were not pursued again.

One person whose visit to Uruguay during the Falklands War would probably have remained etched in his memory was Sir Rex Hunt, the ex-Governor of the Falkland Islands. Ambassador Patricia Hutchinson later recalled his arrival at the Embassy in Montevideo, following his hasty departure from the Falklands after the Argentine invasion. She said:

> His first duty had been to call the Prime Minister. He then had what can only be described as a one-sided conversation with Margaret Thatcher, who was singularly unamused at not having been informed immediately the invasion occurred. Eventually, she grudgingly accepted that he had tried to call her! He had not been looking forward to making the call, and was not in great shape for a while afterwards!

Part Four
The View from Brazil

Brazil

Brazil

Brazil's statistics are striking. It is a massive country – the fifth largest in the world – covering nearly half of South America. Its population in 1982 was 115 million and today exceeds 200 million. It is rich in natural resources, accounts for more than ten per cent of the world's fresh water, and is well supplied with hydrocarbons. It is still discovering huge reserves of oil in its offshore fields. It is the world's leading exporter of ethanol, beef, sugar and coffee.

These figures give a clue as to why Brazil's views and actions matter to its neighbours in South America, and frequently to the rest of the world too. That is the case today as Brazil, with the ninth largest gross domestic product in the world, gains increasing respect as one of the BRIC (Brazil, Russia, India and China) economies.

Brazil's opinions also mattered to Britain in 1982. How Brazil viewed Argentina's invasion of the Falklands, and Britain's response to that invasion, were important to us and of more than passing interest to Brazil's neighbours.

The country derives its language and culture from Portugal. When Pedro Alvares Cabral, the Portuguese explorer, arrived in 1500 and claimed the land for Portugal, he found an indigenous Indian population estimated today as having been between 5 and 7 million. Today, that figure is put at less than 200,000 and decreasing.

The colonisation of Brazil began in earnest in 1532. It became a Royal Colony in 1549, and gained independence in 1822, when Pedro I became Emperor of Brazil. He was succeeded by his son who, after some years of discontent, abdicated in 1889 following a military coup. A republican government was then established, and Brazil has been a federal republic ever since, interspersed with three periods of dictatorship.

From roughly the time that the colonisation process started and spread from the north, Brazil has been concerned also with developments to the south. The countries in the southern cone of South America have

183

a history of violence; disputes between them dominated much of the nineteenth century. They were all involved in wars that have defined the map of South America as it is today. Most Brazilians, certainly the military and those with a flair for history, will need no reminding of their country's altercations with its neighbours. The same wars have played a part in shaping the feelings that the countries have for each other. The Portuguese/Spanish difference between Brazil and all its neighbours is also here to stay, and cannot be erased.

Brazil in the Twentieth Century

During the First World War, Brazil co-operated with the Allies and declared war on Germany. More recently, and in sharp contrast to the position adopted by Argentina, Brazil made an appreciable contribution to the Allied cause during the Second World War. The government of pro-British President Getulio Vargas, although initially cautious about letting American troops into the country and adopting a neutral position, declared war on Germany and Italy in August 1942. It then made Brazilian facilities available to the Americans. This decision followed several German submarine attacks against Brazilian shipping, which resulted in losses and casualties.

Brazilian air bases were developed and made available to the Americans, from Belem in the north down to Rio de Janeiro. The base at Recife, in particular, played a vital role, mounting anti-submarine operations along the Brazilian coast. The constant air patrols required a huge effort month after month on the part of the Brazilian Air Force (FAB), often in foul weather and frequently operating at the limit of their aircraft's range. The Brazilian Navy also played its part, patrolling the South Atlantic and attacking German U-boats.

The FAB base at Natal became one of the largest in the world used by US forces outside America itself, and enabled a vital air route to be established, linking America with North Africa. By means of this route, urgently-needed supplies were sent to British and other Allied forces. It is widely held that Allied supply problems in North Africa might have been insurmountable had Natal not been available to the US in 1942.

President Roosevelt eventually persuaded President Vargas to go a step further and commit troops to fight with the Allies. If Brazil sent troops, Roosevelt said, she would have a place at the peace table and be able to claim a significant role in rebuilding the world after the war. This found favour with many Brazilians, especially the military, who were still a little sensitive about not having played an active part during the First World War. Towards the end of 1943, the Brazilian Government decided to send troops to Italy. The Brazilian Expeditionary Force comprised an infantry division of 15,000 men and a field hospital; it served under the American 5th Army.

FAB's contribution was a Fighter Group of P47 Thunderbolt aircraft and volunteer pilots. They served under the operational control of the 350th Fighter Group (USAF). On rare occasions, they were able to support the Brazilian Expeditionary Force directly. Of the forty-eight Brazilian pilots who flew operational missions in Italy, twenty-two lost their lives. The Commander of the Brazilian Fighter Group was Major Nero Moura who, years later, having achieved the highest rank, became his country's Air Minister. In the 1980s, the surviving pilots were still meeting annually in Nero Moura's Leme (Rio) apartment to party and reminisce. They were a fine a bunch of men and I was privileged to join them for one of these reunions.

The position taken by the Brazilian Government during the war was in sharp contrast to that adopted by Argentina.

During the twentieth century, Brazil see-sawed between military dictatorship and civilian rule. For part of the brief decade of civilian government from 1954–64, Juscelino Kubitschek, the architect of Brasilia, was President. He was widely regarded by many Brazilians as having been the last President of truly international stature.

His presidency was accompanied in the early 1960s by growing unease that Brazil was facing the possibility of left-wing inspired unrest. This feeling grew to a point where the inevitable military coup occurred in 1964, resulting in a succession of military dictatorships that continued until 1985, i.e. after the Falklands War.

During the early years, mainly between 1968–73, many Brazilians were imprisoned, some allegedly tortured, and others were banished overseas, supposedly for holding extreme and/or dangerous left-wing views. By our standards, many of them would have been regarded as being more or less in the centre of political opinion.

Meanwhile, Brazil's hard-line policies were giving Britain a bit of a headache. There was a certain antipathy towards Brazil anyway, partly due to the overthrow of Chile's President Allende, and a growing unease towards South America's right-wing governments. This was occurring at a time when the Foreign Office felt we should be trying to improve relations with some of South America's more influential and powerful countries; especially Brazil. A planned visit to Britain by President Geisel in 1976 was awaited with growing anxiety by a government only too aware that it could be most embarrassing for all concerned. In the event, it passed off without incident, due in no small part to the award of two lucrative contracts to British industry, which softened the criticism.

The twentieth century also ushered in a period of greater harmony for most South Americans, as countries coexisted more peacefully with their neighbours. Some tensions and irritations continued to exist, and differences surfaced from time to time. They were usually about such issues as borders, resources or extremist groups, occasionally reopening old wounds. In South America, countries have a tendency not to get on so well with immediate neighbours, but well enough with the country just beyond.

As Brazil shares its border with every country in South America except for Chile and Ecuador, it has a particular interest in not letting any situation get out of hand. It nevertheless still disputes short sections of its borders with both Paraguay and Uruguay (though the subject is probably not raised very often), and as recently as the 1970s was having considerable disagreement with Argentina over the allocation of resources from the Parana River, where Brazil had built a massive hydroelectric dam at Itaipu.

Also in the 1970s, Brazil was concerned to learn that a group of Montonero guerrillas being held in an Argentine detention centre, tried to help themselves by proposing a strategy for expanding Argentina's area of influence. This was intended to appeal to those Argentines who still nursed dreams of territorial expansion, and planned not only to include parts of Paraguay, Uruguay and Chile, but Brazil as well. Whilst the scheme came to nought, it was picked up by the intelligence services of Argentina's neighbours, and served to increase tension and suspicion for a while.

Brazil's Position during the Falklands War

When Argentina invaded the Falklands, some of its neighbours, including Brazil, had reason to be a little nervous, given past aspirations. What were Argentina's real aims? What might a triumphant Argentine Government, enjoying rare popularity with a grateful population distracted from a failing economy, decide to do next? What position would Brazil's other neighbours then take?

Brazil was Argentina's major trading partner at this time, taking over ten per cent of her exports and providing roughly the same figure of her imports. She was also the UK's most important market in the area and accounted for around fifty per cent of Britain's total investment in Latin America. However, these statistics were not of a magnitude to sway either Argentina or Britain away from taking whatever action might be necessary. The market was regarded as important, but not crucial, to us and there would have been little difficulty finding alternative sources elsewhere. We were never concerned, therefore, at the possibility of an import embargo, which in any case would have affected only a few companies.

We thought that a degree of discrimination against British companies was likely, but Brazil was expressing enthusiasm for new business with the UK even in April 1982. We never felt that there had been too high a price to pay for taking on Argentina, and major contracts, such as the supply of equipment and armament for Brazilian corvettes, continued without any disruption. In spite of a degree of uncertainty early on in the war, the feeling in the British Embassy was that there would be a general reluctance on Brazil's part to see either relations or trade with Britain affected. There might be some economic measures taken to demonstrate a degree of solidarity with Argentina, but any such measures would probably be taken with little enthusiasm.

In May, a warning was received from the Brazilian President that, whilst many South American countries had some sympathy for Britain's resistance to Argentine aggression, Britain would quickly lose that sympathy if it ever attacked the Argentine mainland. At about the same time, President Reagan received a similar call from the Brazilian President, this time specifically warning against Britain attacking any of Argentina's key air bases. President Reagan relayed the message to Prime Minister Thatcher, who allegedly gave little away, other than reiterating her view that 'military measures help diplomacy'.

In spite of these warnings, when the Brazilian Ambassador called on Foreign Minister Francis Pym on 28th May, he said firmly that Brazil deplored Argentina's aggression, and that his country's relations with Britain were highly valued.

Quite understandably, neither Brazil, nor indeed any other South American country, welcomed a military confrontation in their region. Countries could be expected to offer Argentina varying degrees of political support in the interest of Latin American solidarity, but that was unlikely to be translated into making facilities available to Argentina.

There might be some economic sanctions against British interests. Argentina might receive some covert support in the form of military supplies – and we in Brasilia would have to keep alert to that possibility and identify it – but overt military support was thought to be unlikely. These countries would have to live and trade with each other, and continue to co-operate in many different ways, long after our war with Argentina was consigned to the history books.

These were our perceptions during the early days of the war. The reality was not very different. There were few surprises, and support given to Argentina was generally of a token nature and what we might have expected.

The uneasy feeling towards Brazil that had prevailed in the 1970s was already changing when General Joao Figueiredo succeeded Ernesto Geisel as President in 1979. Brazil still had a military government – until President Figueiredo handed over to his successor in 1985 – but his goal had always been to make Brazil a democracy.

It so happened that he had a close relationship with Argentina's General Galtieri, and there were some similarities between the two governments. The main, substantial difference between them, however, was that Brazil had an open congress and a two-party system. The opposition party was the Brazilian Democratic Movement (MDB). During the Falklands War, many politicians from both Brazilian political parties supported the Argentine invasion, but that support was never translated into becoming the official position of either party.

Brazil had a name for its 'flag-ship' policy at this time. It was 'abertura', a Portuguese word which meant (in this context) the opening up of the political system; the gradual process of democratisation. It was always President Figueiredo's intention that at the end of his presidency, and following fair and open elections, he would be replaced by a civilian president. In the meantime, he took a small step in that direction by having a few civilians in his government. Delfin Neto was his Finance Minister and a civilian also headed the Education Ministry.

At the same time, the country was in the mood to forgive and welcome back many of those who, years earlier, had been banished from Brazil. One such individual was a FAB officer who had served with distinction alongside the Allies in Italy, and had risen to the rank of Brigadeiro.

As Brazil moved along the road towards democratisation, it discovered many obstacles along the way. It was beset by economic and social problems, rising inflation, and unrest as the plight of the poor worsened.

The Falklands War occurred in the middle of General Figueiredo's presidency.

When military rule finally ended in 1985, Tancredo Neves (briefly) became the first civilian president since 1964. The government has remained in the hands of civilians ever since. In the early 1980s, most would have thought it inconceivable, though, that Luiz Inacio 'Lula' da Silva, then the leader of the Workers Union, could ever have become the President of Brazil. Brazil today, in the hands of Lula's successor, is the product of more than twenty-five years of reform, which have resulted in stable, democratic government. Lula took over the helm in 2003, was conspicuously successful, and today Brazil enjoys the growing respect it has earned as one of the BRIC economies.

The View from the British Embassy

As soon as the Ambassador, William Harding, learned of the Argentine invasion, he called everyone together to brief us on the situation developing to the south. He decided too that, with immediate effect, he would hold daily meetings for those few of us who would be principally involved. They would therefore be attended by the Counsellor, the SIS representative, and the three service attachés; and would become occasions on which we discussed developments, exchanged ideas, informed each other of requests for information received and what we were all up to.

In the situation that we suddenly found ourselves, the Embassy had nevertheless to continue functioning normally in every respect. Most of the Embassy staff, therefore, were hardly affected by this new turn of events.

Meanwhile, in Argentina, the British Embassy was closed following the severance of diplomatic relations, and Ambassador Anthony Williams and his staff left the country with little delay. Although a few, including the Naval Attaché, spent a short time in Montevideo before continuing on to the UK, one of the consequences of that Embassy's closure was that ours in Brasilia became an increasingly important point of contact in South America for the ministries in London, particularly for the Foreign Office and the MoD.

There is no bible available to tell an Ambassador how to manage his Embassy when his own country goes to war nearby. Each will handle the situation as he finds it, and in his own way. We were most fortunate that Ambassador William Harding not only had an excellent relationship with the Brazilians, which was important for all of us, but also, by virtue of having served in the Royal Marines before entering the Diplomatic Service, he knew instinctively how to use his service attachés to best effect.

He made it clear, too, via the Brazilian press, that our Embassy should not be seen as a point of support for the British effort in the war, as our role was to represent British interests with respect to Brazil. The Brazilians would have appreciated that.

It was decided one morning that a quick and discreet line of communication with the Chilean Embassy in Brasilia should be established for the exchange of important information. After some discussion, the task came my way. I knew the Chilean Air Attaché well, and we had a good relationship based upon having flown the same type of operational aircraft. There were few occasions when the arrangement was activated, and invariably the snippets of information he passed on were already known to us. The relationship was more important than the value of the intelligence.

The São Paulo State Transport Minister was also a good friend. He was passionately interested in flying, was very knowledgeable about the RAF, and owned his own aircraft (a small Piper PA-28), which we flew together from São Paulo's Marte airfield. He invited me to São Paulo to listen to his speech in the State House of Representatives shortly after the start of the war. He spoke on behalf of the British position and, at that time, was one of the few Brazilian politicians who were prepared to speak up on behalf of the principle of self-determination for the Falkland Islanders. Years later, he became a minister in President Lula's government.

During the 1970s in particular there had been a widely-publicised spate of hijackings, kidnappings and hostage-takings perpetrated by different extremist groups, and South America had suffered more than its fair share. The kidnapping in 1971 of the British Ambassador in Uruguay, Sir Geoffrey Jackson, by the Tupamaros, had been one of the better-known incidents (discussed in Part Three, The Uruguayan Perspective).

Sir Geoffrey lectured our course of would-be attachés in 1979 before we took up our appointments. Diplomats and businessmen had been the favourite targets of the terrorist groups, he said, but the main thrust of his lecture was how to avoid being taken in the first place, and if you were, how to conduct yourself in captivity if you were to have a chance of surviving the ordeal.

It was hard to take all his advice very seriously in the Brazil we were sent to in 1979, especially the need to regularly check under the car for bombs, and to vary the route to the Embassy each day. In any case, there was only one route unless you felt like driving an extra 25 miles the other way round the lake. The Argentine invasion of the Falklands, however, served to concentrate our minds on such matters, and the advice was taken more seriously for a while.

We were all concerned to know, of course, and as soon as possible, what position the Brazilian Government would take in respect of the war. Although we all had good relations with the Brazilians we individually dealt with, and counted many Brazilians amongst our friends, we had little idea as to how the government would react following the Argentine invasion. The uncertainty, and for some the anxiety, this caused, was particularly troubling throughout the month of April. A letter I wrote to my daughter (at school in England) dated 29th April, almost a month after the Argentine invasion, summed up the situation: 'Life has become a little crazy here at the moment; strange working hours, daily crisis meetings, mountains of signals and much uncertainty regarding our own future out here. Since our Embassy in Buenos Aires closed, we have acquired an important reporting function... ' etc.

We knew that some members of the Brazilian Government leaned towards the Argentine position. We knew too that President Figueiredo had spent some of his earlier years in Argentina, and that he had known General Galtieri from the time they had attended staff college together. We did not know, however, if any of this was significant.

We believed that Minister Délio Jardim de Mattos (the Air Minister) and Admiral Maximiano (the Navy Minister) were probably sympathetic to the British position. We felt too that the mood in the country generally was tilted towards our position, although less so in the south, closer to the border with Argentina.

The views we had heard expressed by members of the Brazilian armed forces were hardly less confusing. The majority of FAB's officers probably supported our position and had little affection for Argentina. I regularly received calls during the war from FAB friends expressing support and/or sympathy because they had heard, for instance, that we had lost a Harrier aircraft. Comments made during the Vulcan's stay in Rio, and the treatment of the crew, reinforced that feeling.

I remember, too, well before the war broke out, being invited to attend a FAB staff college exercise as an observer. The 'enemy' was a country somewhere to the south, with a fictitious name beginning with 'A'!

On the other hand, Graham Laslett, the Naval Attaché, felt that the Brazilian Navy might have had a higher percentage supporting Argentina's efforts, especially if they had trained or attended courses there. This view was supported by our SIS representative.

Angus Murray, the Defence Attaché, said that feelings in the Brazilian Army were finely balanced, and reaction to the war fairly neutral. A few months prior to the invasion, he had been informed that the Brazilian

Army believed Argentina could take some form of military action, aimed at deflecting growing public dissatisfaction with the state of the country's economy and military rule. A document had been produced by the army which discussed three courses of action that Argentina could take. These were: an invasion of the Falklands; an incursion of some kind in to the south of Brazil; or an action to recover the three disputed islands in the Beagle Channel from Chile.

The Brazilians had concluded that the Beagle Channel option was the most likely, and an incursion into Brazil the least likely (a previous war between Brazil and Argentina back in the 1820s had resulted in Brazil losing the region that subsequently became Uruguay). Although they had reached the wrong conclusion, there was considerable relief all round that it was the Falklands option that had prevailed, because, as many privately observed: 'That should keep Argentina off our backs for the next twenty years!' I can recall hearing similar comments from FAB friends.

The Ambassador should have the last word on the subject. He felt that Brazil was the South American country least likely, or inclined, to show support for Argentina, morally or physically. He cited Spanish/ Portuguese historical differences (including language), Brazil's resentment that Argentina tended to look down on them, and Brazil's disapproving view of Argentina's so-called need to invade the Falklands. He agreed with his attachés too, that there was a degree of concern in the Brazilian military regarding what Argentina might then aspire to, should it be successful in its Falklands venture. Finally, he also thought that whilst Brazilian solidarity with Argentina was generally lacking, the Foreign Ministry was nevertheless obliged to make a show of at least some solidarity.

One can deduce, quite correctly, from all the above that the picture was confused. It was hardly surprising, therefore, that we in the Embassy had little idea which way Brazil would jump (i.e. officially). In the end, the Brazilian Government very cleverly managed to avoid declaring its position at all. It remained unofficially neutral throughout the war and, by playing for time and sitting on the fence, maintained cordial relations with both Argentina and Britain.

During the period of uncertainty though, our concern was real enough to prompt the Ambassador to task the Defence Attaché to produce an Embassy evacuation plan, just in case the coin came down wrong-side-up. We knew that, in that eventuality, we might have to pack our bags and leave in a hurry.

The Brazilian Air Force, meanwhile, carried out a rather different study. Shortly after the Argentine invasion, and when it was clear that

Britain intended to respond militarily, the Commandant of the Air Force Staff College, Brigadier Fish, ordered an analysis of the likely course of events and outcome. The study had to consider the capabilities and objectives of both protagonists, taking into account training, intelligence, weapons systems, and even what assistance might be forthcoming from other countries (e.g. the USA; perhaps not quite such a well-kept secret as was imagined). Finally, it had to suggest the probable outcome of the war, and the principle factors that would determine it.

To carry it out, the Commandant formed two groups, each headed by one of the college instructors. The 'British Group' was led by Colonel Carlos Motta da Souza, who had attended the RAF Staff College, Bracknell. The Argentine Study Group was headed by Colonel Rocha Bastos who had attended staff college in Argentina. Both groups worked with, and received inputs from, navy and army instructors on the staff.

After their work was finished, presentations were given in Brasilia, and elsewhere, to officers up to the highest levels in all the armed forces. The conclusion, reached well before the war ended, was that Britain would be victorious. A further study, commissioned after the war ended, made a comparison between what had been predicted and what had actually happened. It found that the predictions had been ninety-two per cent correct. The remaining eight per cent was largely because they did not correctly determine the beaches on which the British troops disembarked.

Our relations with the Argentine diplomatic community had generally been very good prior to the war, and several of us had friends amongst their numbers. When the new Argentine Ambassador arrived in Brasilia three months before the war, Ambassador William Harding called on him. The two men had agreed that the situation was tense, and that there was a need not to aggravate it in any way. Neither of them, therefore, would make any public statements, nor give any interviews, on the subject of the Falklands/Malvinas.

Argentina did make one or two approaches to Brazil for assistance, but they were of a minor nature. Brazil sent two P95 EMB-111 Bandeirulha maritime patrol aircraft, which were returned after the war. Some reference to this was made in British newspapers on 4th May 1982, although it was reported as a sale rather than a loan. The Argentine Navy might also have received a few EMB-326 Xavante advanced trainer aircraft (similar to the five Macchi 339s they lost). A rumour suggested that some Brazilian Mirage fighter aircraft had been temporarily grounded because spare parts and tyres were sent to Argentina instead; but this was never confirmed.

It is clear that any gestures made by Brazil could fairly be described as having been modest and token in nature, reflecting the country's skill in steering a careful middle course without unduly upsetting either Argentina or Britain.

The Ambassador lived close to the Air Minister and the Head of the Brazilian Navy. They both became his friends as well as neighbours, strengthened by the fact that he, by his own admission, made the most of his past service in the Royal Marines. He recalled receiving an urgent cable from the UK headquarters in Northwood in April to say that the Task Force was on its way, and could he ask the Brazilian Navy to ensure that its submarines kept well out of the way, to avoid a potentially disastrous misidentification as an Argentine submarine. He went round to the Admiral's house, explained the situation, and was given an assurance there and then that all Brazilian submarines would be held within 200 miles of the coast.

There could have been an unpleasant incident later on, when the air defence system on HMS *Invincible* indicated an aircraft, with radar on, approaching the Task Force. Fortunately, Admiral Woodward decided to order a Harrier into the air to visually identify the possible threat. It turned out to be a Varig Brazilian Airlines DC10 aircraft, which passed harmlessly overhead! It was well understood by both countries that any misidentification could seriously damage the health of an important relationship.

On another occasion, the Ambassador went with Graham Laslett to see the Brazilian Admiral when there was some concern regarding Brazilian shipping movements. They were quickly reassured that absolutely no assistance was being given to Argentina. The Admiral had added: 'Rest assured; I'll let you know, if we ever do... !'

After the war, we were notified that the Head of Argentina's Navy, Admiral Anaya, would be visiting the country to 'thank Brazil for support given'. We were not, of course, represented at the inevitable diplomatic social gathering, but were nevertheless reassured by the Brazilians that, since no help had actually been given to Argentina, the whole thing was pure, meaningless theatre.

It was generally agreed, and it was certainly the Ambassador's view, that Brazil's assistance to us, not being of course in any military sense, was in maintaining a balanced view throughout, and not actually helping Argentina in any meaningful way. Elements of the Brazilian press certainly helped us as well, and we three attachés were also permitted to get about and do our jobs without suffering any undue restrictions, for which we were extremely grateful.

Before the war, we had enjoyed a fair degree of contact with the Argentine Embassy, and numbered their attachés amongst those whose company we enjoyed from time to time. We were surprised to learn after the war that, following the 2nd May sinking of the *Belgrano* and the return of the Argentine Navy to port, the Argentine Air Attaché had been so incensed by their navy's opt-out – leaving the brunt of the effort to the army and the air force – that he and the Naval Attaché had not been on speaking terms since the event.

Years later, General Fernando Matthei, the retired ex-Chief of the Chilean Air Force, revealed that he had visited Argentina after the war at the invitation of the then Head of the Argentine Air Force. He had discovered that a great deal of ill-feeling still existed in their air force towards both the army and navy. The air force felt it had been caught up in a war with which it had disagreed, at the behest of other institutions, and in the end had been the only service to have acquitted itself honourably.

One of the two Argentine air attachés, the charismatic 'W' and his wife, were particular friends before the war. They had a reputation for throwing excellent dinner parties and were very sociable. His only hang-up was a penchant for all things Nazi, and his insistence that after dinner his male guests should visit his Nazi room, which was a veritable museum of items adorned with swastikas which Adolf H himself would have been proud of. Collecting Nazi memorabilia is probably not that uncommon in Argentina anyway. That aside, 'W' was very good company.

Three months before the war started, when they had reached the end of their time in Brazil, my wife and I were seated at their table during their farewell party. It was a uniform affair. Towards the end of the evening, we were photographed with our arms around each other's shoulders.

A few months later, early in May, I learned by chance at a social gathering that 'W' had been promoted and was now holding a senior intelligence appointment on the Falklands. I fired off a telex to my point-of-contact in the MoD, giving him the glad tidings. He confirmed that it had been the missing piece of a jigsaw, but he needed a photograph of 'W' as soon as possible. Needless to say, the only good, clear photograph that could be found was the one taken at his party. It had to go. It was duly returned after the war, with a note saying how much pleasure it had given everyone at a time when there had not been much else to smile about at the MoD!

Although our jobs involved keeping our eyes open and our ears to the ground all the time, some occasions, such as the Attaché Association functions, offered better opportunities for picking up useful information. We all belonged to the Association, and hardly a week passed when we did not all gather together, either to welcome a new attaché, or bid fare-well to one who was leaving. By chance, the rotating presidency was held by the Argentine Air Attaché during the war and he and his wife were required to welcome every arrival personally at the functions. This seemed at first to present a minor difficulty as we were not permitted to speak to each other. However, we soon discovered that the rules did not preclude us from kissing each other's wives – a popular South American custom.

The attitudes of the various South American countries were reflected in the behaviour of their attachés during the war. Chileans were friendly, but Venezuelans, Mexicans and Peruvians were hostile in varying degrees. Colombians and Ecuadorians were somewhere between the two extremes, but certainly not hostile; the Bolivians and Paraguayans gave little indication that they were aware there was a war going on.

The attachés, apart from ourselves, who were principally involved during the war were those from Israel and the USA. We were close to the USA Embassy anyway. The Israeli attaché, however, was a menace; always wanting to know where we were, and what we were doing. If I was not around for some reason, his wife would waste her time trying to extract my whereabouts from my wife.

We were warned of a possible risk arising from individuals targeting British interests. Some of the British Honorary Consuls in outlying areas of Brazil received threats, and one or two of them resigned. There were also a few bomb scares in São Paulo, which came to nothing. In Brasilia, we were all advised to be on our guard. Local Brazilians were hired as guards and were issued with arms and ammunition. They patrolled the Embassy grounds and the houses where members of the staff lived. Angus Murray, as Defence Attaché, was detailed to train them in the use of their newly-acquired 9mm Browning pistols on a nearby small arms range. It soon became quite apparent that their expertise left much to be desired. Nevertheless, occupants of the houses felt more secure when they saw guards patrolling in the vicinity.

Graham Laslett went to Rio from time to time to check if any suspicious-looking ships might be taking military hardware down to Argentina. Once, he returned with a suspiciously healthy suntan. Someone less charitable than an air attaché might have suspected that he was able to monitor the entrance to Guanabara Bay from the comfort of a beach towel on Copacabana beach. Perish the thought!

The few brief weeks of the war seemed to pass quickly from our perspective. Suddenly, it was all over and life returned to normal. All the attachés, even the Venezuelan Naval Attaché, started talking to each other again as if nothing had happened. It is not clear, though, whether the Argentine attachés ever patched up their differences.

The Man from Marconi

On Friday morning 9th April 1982, the Embassy receptionist called through to the Air Attaché's office; 'There is an Englishman who wishes to speak urgently'. She added that he appeared agitated, dishevelled and unshaven. He was conducted to my office where he recounted an interesting story. His name was Geoff Barling.

Geoff Barling and Ken Edwards were Systems Engineers working for Marconi Avionics Ltd. They were on contract at the Argentine Air Force Maintenance Unit (MU) at Río Quarto, some 100 miles south of Cordoba, when the Argentine invasion of the Falklands took place. Geoff had his wife with him in Argentina. Ken was unmarried at the time.

Being an MU, there was a good selection of aircraft types there on modification and maintenance programmes. Both men spoke reasonable Spanish, and learned from the Argentine Chief Test Pilot, when they arrived for work on Friday 2nd April, that the Argentine invasion fleet had sailed. To the surprise of many on the base, they nevertheless decided to continue working through the day.

They had been in Argentina for four weeks, and it was their fourth visit to the MU. Their project involved the installation and integration of a new suite of electronic equipment in the fleet of Dagger fighter aircraft, which were essentially similar to the French Mirage III. The new equipment included a head-up display (HUD), and a mission computer which provided weapon-aiming computation. Together, these would significantly enhance the performance of the aircraft in the air defence (AD), ground attack (GA) and anti-ship roles, taking navigational and weapon-aiming capabilities to a higher specification.

The point had been reached where the new equipment was set up on a long electronic rig in two Portakabins positioned end-to-end. Geoff and Ken's roles were to remain in Argentina only until it had been satisfactorily proven. The Dagger Update Programme was being run by Comodoro (Colonel) Candeago, but they also liaised closely with two

199

Argentine air force test pilots. One of them, Teniente (Lieutenant) Jose Ardiles was the first Dagger pilot to be killed in the war when he was shot down on 1st May by a Sidewinder missile (he was also a cousin of Osvaldo 'Ossie' Ardiles, who played football for Spurs in the 1970s).

Apart from the test pilots, two Argentine civilian engineers acted in a supportive role; one also acted as a translator when required. The plan was that they would continue working directly for the air force after Marconi's work was finished.

Whilst Marconi Avionics was the prime contractor, Israel Aircraft Industries (IAI) acted as airframe consultant and sub-contractor, and Elta (a Division of IAI) was involved as well. The Israelis were never in evidence at Rio Quarto whilst Geoff and Ken were there.

The Dagger had more powerful US engines than the Mirage, and had been adapted to be suitable for both AD and GA roles. However, it had a limited AD capability. It was used mainly by the Argentine Air Force in an anti-ship role, but their pilots, unlike the Argentine Navy pilots, were not properly trained in this role and were achieving poor results. They tended to come in too low and had a poor record of bombs fusing on impact. Comments made later suggested that they also tended to concentrate on warships, and would have achieved more useful results, with fewer casualties, had they gone for the softer, but nevertheless vital, logistics ships, e.g. *Canberra*.

The French and the Israelis had allegedly fallen out after it was learned that the Israelis had 'come across' sensitive data regarding the Mirage aircraft. Someone else described it as the Israelis having 'borrowed' the aircraft data. Either way, it seems that the French had not been consulted and were, not surprisingly, unamused. The result was that Israel went on to produce an unlicensed copy of the Mirage, which they called the Dagger. They then sold it to Argentina.

By the beginning of April 1982, flight trials had been completed and a trials aircraft had been updated with Marconi's new software. Unfortunately for Argentina, this new software package had a glitch. The fault was quickly identified, but there was no time to rectify the problem before the war started. The Argentines were unsurprisingly not too happy when demands later for Marconi to come up with the updated weapons delivery software fell upon deaf ears, after the invasion of the Falklands.

A Phone Call from the MU

Saturday 3rd April was not a normal working day, but the two men received, unusually, a phone call at their hotel instructing them to go immediately to the MU. On arrival, they were met by the Base Security Officer and informed they would have an escort from then on, on and off the base. Supposedly, this was for their own personal safety because of 'possible anti-British feeling'.

On Wednesday 7th April, they drove to Buenos Aires airport. It was time to pull out. Montevideo was never an option; they needed a country where Marconi had an agent. They flew to Rio de Janeiro instead, where the two men put their heads together and tried to recall everything of possible value or interest that they had seen or learned. Then, whilst Ken remained in Rio, Geoff flew up to Brasilia, to the British Embassy, to tell their story.

During the next couple of hours, Geoff passed on everything that he and Ken could recall regarding the situation in Argentina, the circumstances of their departure and, most importantly, the Argentine aircraft at the MU, including aircraft types, numbers, the nature of the programmes or maintenance/servicing they were undergoing, and roughly when the aircraft might be expected to rejoin the front line. It was valuable information, which was communicated immediately to the MoD. Geoff returned to the UK shortly afterwards, arriving a few days after Ken. Later, the two men were asked to go up to the MoD for a further debriefing. Ken recalled that they both enjoyed 'a sort of temporary fame!'

When Marconi pulled out of Argentina, the Israelis wasted no time in filling the vacuum left behind. IAI and Elta arrived and continued to give support. However, as the Dagger update could not be continued, the aircraft flew throughout the war with the original, inferior avionics suite. Only the trial aircraft had been updated.

The Israelis' arrival in Argentina coincided with information we received in Brasilia, that Israel had sent a team of technicians to Argentina to help maintain their fighter aircraft. Indeed, it would have been totally out of character had Israel not responded as it did. The French also had equipment on the aircraft, so perhaps it is also not too surprising that reports filtered through that French technicians had arrived as well – in spite of high-level assurances to the contrary. The French were probably ambivalent as to who won the war, being more concerned that their product functioned correctly whoever operated it. The Israelis, on the other hand, would have seen job opportunities and longer-term prospects in a grateful South America.

If the war had started even three months later, a significant number of the Dagger fleet would by then have been upgraded with the new suite. It is, of course, one of the war's many imponderables as to whether or not this would have been significant.

'Carlos'

One morning, I was summoned to the Ambassador's office. He said: 'There is considerable concern in London that certain other countries might be supplying weapons and other military equipment to Argentina. Some of this hardware might be passing through Brazil.' The Exocet missile was causing particular anxiety at that time.

I had been in Brazil for two-and-a-half years when the war started, and friendships around the country were well established. I was asked to disappear for as long as necessary, go where I thought fit, contact whoever might have useful information, and return when I was ready. There was to be no contact with the Embassy while I was away.

Brazil is more than a country; it is continental in size. After some time away, I returned to Brasilia and informed the Ambassador I had been unsuccessful. It was a Saturday evening. A few hours later, at around 0300 hours on the Sunday morning, the telephone rang beside the bed, and a voice I recognised asked me to meet him that day. It was important, but he could say no more on the telephone. The following morning, I flew to Recife to meet the man who thereafter became known as 'Carlos'. I had first met Carlos in July 1980.

Lord Carrington's Visit to Brazil in July 1980

On Monday 28th July 1980, I had flown to Recife. Early the following morning, Lord Carrington, the Secretary of State for Foreign and Commonwealth Affairs, Lady Carrington and a party of high-ranking businessmen arrived in a Royal Air Force VC10 aircraft, captained by Peter Nelson. The reception party included the Governor of the State of Pernambuco, Marco Maciel, and the Base Commander.

The plan was that Lord Carrington, with some of his entourage, would fly into the interior of Pernambuco that same day to visit a couple of

Brazilian research establishments. In due course, we would all fly to Brasilia in the VC10, where Lord Carrington would be officially welcomed by his Brazilian opposite number, Chancellor Ramiro Saraiva Guerreiro, before meeting President Figueiredo.

As soon as the VC10 stopped on the chocks, Lord Carrington bounced energetically down the steps, most of the other passengers probably feeling less enthusiastic after the 9-hour flight from the UK. I was raising my arm to salute in the approved fashion, when he said: 'Never mind that for the moment; where's the nearest loo?' Fortunately, I knew the purpose of the rather unpleasant brick building fifty metres away.

It was unreal; within a few minutes of his arrival, I was standing before an adjacent, equally unpleasant, urinal talking to the second most important politician in the UK. He made it quite clear, during those few moments of great relief, what he thought of a programme that included an internal flight following a long transatlantic flight, but knew it was not of my making.

A room had been set aside in the Officers' Mess, so that he could take a shower and freshen up before the next flight. He said he did not need the room; he would freshen up on the VC10 to save time. It was explained to him that that would be difficult, as the VC10 was now full of beautiful Brazilian girls cleaning up the aircraft after the long flight. His response to that was: 'Young man, I haven't got to where I am today by being afraid of taking my trousers off in front of a pretty girl.' The VC10 it was!

At the press conference at the end of his short visit to Recife, Lord Carrington said: 'I came to Brazil to demonstrate its importance to the world, and started my visit in the north-east because it will always be that part of Brazil closest to my own country.' That went down very well.

Pat Tebby, Peter Nelson's ground engineer on that flight to Recife, was also on the VC10 that took Lord Carrington to Israel for a three-day visit in 1982. Pat recalled that on the return flight, on 2nd April, Lord Carrington learned via the on-board HF radio that Argentina had invaded the Falklands. He courteously thanked the crew. The next day he resigned.

When giving his permission to tell the story of his visit to Brazil, Lord Carrington added the following amusing story:

My party on the South American tour included Lord Nelson, Lord Jellicoe and Lord Montgomery. The Brazilians could not believe they weren't the real thing! At first, I sought to put them straight, but then quickly realised it was better for business not to disabuse them. Anyway, Lord Nelson was not a descendant of Admiral Horatio's at

204

all. He was from a different family altogether (Lord Nelson of Stafford succeeded his father as Chairman of English Electric Company). We didn't bother to point that out either!

I can endorse what Kate Adie said in her excellent book *The Kindness of Strangers* that '... Lord Carrington (is) an utter gent as well as good fun... '.

Importantly though, throughout that brief stay in Recife, the Brazilian contact whose job it was to help ensure that everything went smoothly, including the handling of the VC10 and the crew, was Carlos. He did a splendid job, for which I was very grateful, and he appreciated the letter written afterwards to his superior. We became good friends. Good friends in peace-time become useful allies in war-time.

May 1982

I had kept in touch with Carlos and immediately recognised his voice. I knew exactly where I had to go on that Sunday morning. I caught an early flight to Recife, and we met later that afternoon. He then told me the reason for his call.

The previous weekend, an Aerolineas Argentinas B707 aircraft, operated by an air force crew, had passed through Recife around midnight to refuel. It had stopped at the end of the runway instead of going to the terminal area. The aircraft had been empty. It had passed back through Recife 24 hours later, and the same process had been repeated. On both occasions, three or four armed 'heavies' had jumped out of the aircraft and deployed around it. On the return journey, the aircraft had been full of unmarked wooden crates, but only Carlos knew this, since he alone was permitted on board the aircraft to carry out certain vital checks. As soon as possible, the aircraft had continued on its way.

Whilst the whole business had bothered him, Carlos had felt that there was little he could do about it. When he learned that the flights were to be repeated, again in the middle of the night, and over the weekend when normally the airport would be closed, he had a word with a friend in air traffic control. He was told that the first aircraft had been to Libya, which was the destination again and, moreover, a third flight was planned for the following weekend as well. There might be others, but as yet details had not been notified. He had also acquired copies of supporting documentation (flight plan, diplomatic clearance, etc.), which he passed on to me.

It was agreed that I would hide within earshot of the aircraft to observe the whole process that evening. Carlos took me out to the area about an hour before the aircraft was due. I probably hid behind a runway marker or something similar. I asked him to note – if possible – in whatever time was available to him inside the aircraft, the approximate number and size, together with any markings, of the crates on board. In fact, I did not expect any of the crates to have markings. Nothing should be written down, and he would have to guess dimensions. Of particular interest was any crate that could possibly contain a missile 5.2 metres long.

That night, the arrival and departure of the flight took place on time. The 'heavies' took up their positions around the aircraft. I was close enough to hear a smart Spanish-speaking visitor (Carlos thought he was probably the Argentine Consul in Recife) talking to the aircraft captain. The whole process was carried out as quickly as possible and the aircraft departed. The area returned to darkness, and Carlos and I returned to my hotel. There had been many crates of different sizes on the aircraft, he said, and all had been unmarked; one or two could have contained an Exocet missile. I returned to Brasilia with the paperwork.

The following morning, I recounted the whole story to the Ambassador and our SIS representative. The Ambassador first asked him what action he felt we should now take. He replied that we had slightly less than a week available to us before the next scheduled flight. In that time, he could instruct me on how to plant plastic explosives in the undercarriage of a B707 aircraft. I should brief one of the Brazilian ground crew to cause a diversion; this would take the 'heavies' away from the aircraft long enough for me to run out to it, place the explosives and get back to my hiding place. 'When the aircraft taxies out to take off,' he said, 'it should blow up.' Simple! I listened with little enthusiasm. Surely this could not work.

The Ambassador then turned to me. 'What do you think we should do?' he asked. I replied: 'As the track of the B707 would take it only some 150 miles south of Ascension Island, a pair of air defence Phantom aircraft could be scrambled at the appropriate moment to intercept it and force it to land. The contents could then be exposed for assembled journalists to see. This should ensure that there would be no further flights.'

After considering these two inputs carefully, the Ambassador, to my relief, said: 'Thank you gentlemen, but we will opt for a third course of action. I will go along to see the Foreign Minister, and tell him that we know about the flights, never mind how, and since Brazil is neutral, etc. would he please ensure that no further flights are allowed to take place.'

He was right, of course. Smooth diplomacy did the trick. Carlos called a couple of days later. The third planned B707 flight had been suddenly cancelled. He would let me know if any more were scheduled. However, no further flights to or from Libya passed through Brazil during the Falklands War.

There was never any doubt that the two flights that had taken place had been carrying military hardware to Argentina. We do know now, however, that neither flight had carried any Exocet missiles. Precisely what had been on board each aircraft has not been established, but Libya did supply Argentina during the war with, amongst other things, Soviet-made SA7 shoulder-mounted missiles, 60mm mortars, air-to-air missiles and spares for the Mirage aircraft.

Many years after the war, my colleague who had been Defence Attaché (DA) in 1982, mischievously asked me if I had looked up my Brazilian mistress recently! When it became clear that I had no idea what he was talking about, he told me that after my first disappearance from Brasilia, the Ambassador had called him in and expressed concern that I might be recognised, or communicate with someone who could, perhaps even innocently, mention it in the wrong quarter. At that time, we were supposed to obtain authority to leave Brasilia for more than 24 hours, but it was felt, in this instance, that the risk was worth taking, such was the importance of the mission, i.e. rather than seek permission, and possibly have it denied. Clearly though, the Ambassador could not afford to be embarrassed.

The DA had pondered this for a moment and then suggested that perhaps I should have a mistress. After all, he reasoned, most Brazilians have a mistress, and this would be understood and accepted with little more than a nudge and a wink.

This was agreed as being a good way round the problem. It was also important that the cover story should be completely water-tight, so a young, attractive Brazilian girl, known to someone in the Embassy and living in the Recife area, was approached and asked to 'cover' for me, should the need arise. Over a quarter of a century later, I was to learn of my Brazilian mistress for the first time. Of the few who knew of the plan, each had assumed that another would tell me. No one had informed my wife!

Relations with Libya

Both Argentina's and Britain's relations with Libya had see-sawed during the decades preceding the Falklands War. When a handful of army officers led by the young Captain Gaddafi deposed King Idris in 1969, relations with that country were set to take a turn for the worse. British and US bases were closed. A strict military dictatorship deplored 'western imperialism' and appeared to support various international terrorist movements. At the same time, Libya had a reasonable relationship with the USSR during the Cold War Years when we clearly did not.

Nevertheless, the Argentine invasion that sparked the Falklands War had coincided with our relations with Libya being fair, and slowly improving. Many Libyan students were studying in the UK, whilst thousands of British ex-pats worked in Libya. We certainly did not want to aggravate the situation by driving Libya further towards Argentina.

Argentina under Peron in the 1970s had sought to improve relations with Libya by means of various big trade deals. Later, relations were soured by Libya's support for the very guerrilla movements that were opposed to the Argentine military. At the time of the Falklands War, Argentina wanted to have Libya on-side, and set out to befriend her again. An arms deal was sought, and a mission was sent to Tripoli led by an admiral of the Argentine Navy. During the visit, Libya promised to meet many of Argentina's needs. Of particular interest would have been Exocet missiles, but these were not forthcoming at that time. However, many other items were promised. Thus it was that the Argentine B707s flew to Libya via Brazil.

Libya and Argentina were two countries in need of friends. Although within South America varying degrees of support for Argentina would be forthcoming (more promised than given), Libya came up with the hardware. But for the sharpness of a Brazilian friend, more would have been given, and there just might have been a weapon of a more decisive nature on a subsequent flight.

A Vulcan Arrives

Late in the morning of Thursday 3rd June, I received an urgent call to go to the Air Ministry in Brasilia and, unusually, was taken directly to the office of the Air Minister, Tenente Brigadeiro Délio Jardim de Mattos. The Minister was a highly-respected figure, easy to talk to, and known to be sympathetic to the British position. Only six months previously he had received and welcomed Chief of the Air Staff (CAS), Air Chief Marshal Sir Michael Beetham, at the start of Sir Michael's visit to Brazil.

On this occasion, he was brief and to the point. A Vulcan bomber had landed at Rio de Janeiro International Airport. The crew, he said, appeared nervous, seemed to think they were in a hostile country, and were refusing to talk to anyone until I arrived. He asked me to go to Rio immediately.

The crew had acted perfectly correctly. The crews of any RAF aircraft operating from Ascension Island that might have to divert into Brazil during the war were briefed that, on arrival, they should say nothing, avoid the press and any interviews, and request the presence of the Air Attaché. If pressed further, they could say only that they had been on a training exercise.

The Minister made some other points too. Apart from being short of fuel, nothing else appeared to be wrong with the aircraft. Did the situation really justify a Mayday call and landing at an international airport with its inevitably high volume of civilian air traffic? He pointed out that there had been other alternatives nearby. He also stressed that the aircraft should be airborne and away before it became an (even bigger) embarrassment. Unfortunately, as it turned out, that was not possible. I flew to Rio and was with the crew 4 hours later.

The Vulcan is Chosen

As soon as the decision was taken to send the Task Force down to the South Atlantic, CAS and his air marshals set about examining ways in which the Royal Air Force could make a significant, valuable contribution to the war effort. Air Marshal Sir John Curtiss, who was appointed Air Commander in Admiral Fieldhouse's Command Team, and had responsibility for all RAF aircraft deployed in support, said recently that, in particular, CAS would have consulted with the Assistant Chief of the Air Staff Operations (ACAS [Ops]), Air Vice-Marshal Ken Hayr.

The use of Buccaneer S2 aircraft was briefly considered and dismissed. The aircraft did not have the necessary range and would have required more tankers than the RAF possessed. The Tornado GR1 was too new and its true potential had yet to be established and demonstrated. If the BL755 bomb had been cleared for use (which it had not at that stage), it might have been considered more seriously; but, in any case, would have required an unacceptable number of tanker aircraft. But the Vulcan... now, that was a possibility.

Initially, the thinking was to spread the word that the Vulcan could be converted back to a conventional role (from the nuclear role it had for many years) and used to effect. At the very least, at this early stage, that should send a clear message to Argentina that we might have the capability to reach the Falkland Islands. The Argentine Embassy in London, and its military attachés in particular, if they were doing their jobs properly, would have been alert to any activity or thinking on our part at that time.

The Vulcan force was part of No 1 Group's assets and the Air Officer Commanding (AOC) was Air Vice-Marshal Michael Knight. He was immediately enthusiastic and supportive of the idea. CAS was also anxious that the Vulcans should be involved as soon as possible. The aircraft, together with the Victors and the Valiants (collectively known as the V-Force) had, in the 1960s, constituted the nation's strategic nuclear deterrent force. By 1982, only the Vulcan remained in service as a bomber, in a dual nuclear and conventional role that it was already in the process of relinquishing on its imminent withdrawal from service, as the new Tornado aircraft was brought in. Thus, at the very time that Britain was preparing to respond to Argentina's provocative invasion of the Falkland Islands, the Vulcan force was well into the process of taking its well-earned retirement from the RAF's front line. Now, in the twilight moments of its life, it was being called upon to carry out a new and vital role for the nation. Instead of delivering a nuclear weapon at high altitude to a target some 2,000 miles distant, it was now to carry 21 High Explosive (HE) bombs, or anti-radar missiles, twice that distance. Intensive day and night training started. The Operation Black Buck missions, as they were later to be named, were born.

Group Captain John Laycock, Station Commander at RAF Wadding-ton where the Vulcans were based, had the job of supplying the aircraft and crews. Initially, ten suitable airframes were identified. This number was whittled down to the five aircraft that could most easily be adapted to the new requirement. These aircraft had then to be modified to restore an air-to-air refuelling (AAR) capability, which had not been used for many years. Nor, indeed, did any aircrew member currently serving on the Vulcan force have experience of the challenging task in such a large aircraft of receiving fuel in the air from a tanker. Clearly, there was a great deal of work ahead for both engineers and aircrew before the Vulcan could be declared 'operational'.

More probes had to be found and work on the fuel systems carried out. As modified aircraft became available, pilots who had never practised AAR, and some who had (but only many years before), started training.

One Vulcan had been delivered to the Castle Air Force Base (AFB) Museum in the USA. Within days, it was revisited by two RAF Chief Technicians asking if the RAF could please have the AAR probe back temporarily as there was a sudden, urgent need! Air Vice-Marshal (AVM) Ron Dick, who was Air Attaché in Washington at the time, remembered receiving a signal from Castle AFB Museum at the end of the war congratulating Britain on its success, and demanding the 'immediate return of stolen property'!

The conversion process also involved fitting bomb-carriers, new inertial navigation systems and ECM (electronic counter measures) pods. Group Captain Tony Andrews, who held a senior engineering appoint-ment at Headquarters Strike Command (HQSTC) at the time, said there was enormous pressure from above to get everything sorted out as quickly as possible, especially anything to do with getting the Vulcans operational. Initially, when the flight-refuelling probes were fitted to the aircraft, there were inevitable teething problems and attempts at AAR resulted in fuel being sprayed all over the aircraft windscreen, a problem aggravated by the position of the probe, low on the nose of the Vulcan.

Why was it considered so important to make all this effort to adapt the ageing Vulcan to reach the Falkland Islands? Stanley airfield had a short runway, which could have been extended and then used by Argentine fighter aircraft deploying forward. This would have greatly increased the threat to the Task Force. In the meantime, ground-attack Pucaras were using the runway, and Argentine C130 Hercules aircraft were able to fly supplies in. This was clearly unacceptable and the Vulcan was the perfect vehicle for mounting a forceful demonstration of our determination not to allow this state of affairs to continue.

Not everyone in the US Government was happy when our plans were revealed. Group Captain Jeremy Price, Senior RAF Officer on Ascension Island, recalled that US Lieutenant Colonel Bill Brydon, who was the Pentagon's 'eyes and ears' on the island, tried to veto normal practices from time to time. Captain Bob McQueen, the Senior RN Officer, said that Brydon had stuck carefully to the terms of his agreement and, when he got wind of the RAF's plans to operate the Black Buck missions, signalled the Pentagon for 'permission to allow them to take place'.

Secretary of State General Alexander Haig had some reservations when he learned of our plans and was initially opposed to our use of the Vulcan. Defence Secretary Caspar Weinberger, however, was extremely supportive and helpful to Britain at this time, and the reply Brydon received effectively said: 'Close your eyes.' Sir John Nott said recently: 'At times we chose to ignore the diplomatic niceties and just get on with it!'

Should Britain Bomb the Mainland?

There was a widely-held view in Britain that to bomb mainland Argentina would have been an insane thing to do, and would have lost us what little support, friends and sympathy we had in South America – all rather thin on the ground anyway – and, more importantly, in Europe and the United Nations. We could not have afforded to make that mistake and certainly it would not have endeared us to the USA, whose friendship and support we needed, especially at that time.

Also, the war against Argentina was, by any definition, a limited war. It was limited in the sense that the two nations each had a single, simple aim; either, in the one case, to keep control of some remote territory it had invaded or, in the other case, to repossess territory (temporarily) lost. Neither country wanted to unnecessarily broaden or prolong the fight.

It was limited in another sense, too. Both sides would exhaust their supplies of bombs, bullets and missiles eventually. There was a limit to how long the Task Force could be sustained over the great distances involved. We learned after the war the full extent of the problems being experienced by our ships. Admiral Woodward later wrote frankly about his concern at the time. His comments did not surprise Sir John Nott, who said: 'They were entirely believable, and some members of the War Cabinet had, in fact, expected an even higher rate of attrition of both ships and Harriers.' Sir John also recalled the First Sea Lord, Admiral Sir Henry Leach, who was all confidence when he met the Prime Minister on 31st March in the House of Commons, later saying that if the Task Force reached the South Atlantic at all, it would be a miracle.

A not-untypical example of problems being experienced by our ships was explained by Captain Chris Craig (HMS *Alacrity*). He said that a huge body of ships had to be taken a long way south. Many of them had been on their way to the UK for an overdue refit, or DED (Docking and Essential Defects), when diverted to join the Task Force. To that had to be added the battle damage incurred, and having to operate in an unusually harsh environment in the heavy southern seas. Finally, since the Task Force had to hold off to the east of the Falkland Islands to keep out of range of Argentine aircraft, there were numerous occasions when ships were called upon to steam at full power over great distances at short notice. This was far from an ideal scenario for them. HMS *Alacrity*, he said, was also forced to stop firing its guns. The gun barrels were worn out and to continue firing would have been dangerous.

Certainly, attrition was one of the War Cabinet's principal concerns, and at what point ship and/or Harrier aircraft losses might become excessive or, indeed, unsustainable. When the Task Force was on its way, we had little idea of how Argentina would react. We knew, for instance, that there were two Argentine submarines lurking somewhere, but we did not know where, and this was a matter of great concern. We knew we could lose a ship or two to submarines, but any more... ? What would the British public consider an acceptable price for the venture?

These questions, recalled Sir Clive Whitmore, Prime Minister Margaret Thatcher's Principal Private Secretary, were very much in the mind of the Prime Minister at that time. While she showed a bold face in public, privately she shared the concerns of the Chiefs of Staff, but hid them well. Sir Clive also remembered a conversation with her about how many casualties we could sustain and 'get away with'. He had ventured a figure of 1,000 dead... ! He said: 'There were certainly depressing moments at War Cabinet meetings. When two helicopters were lost in South Georgia, there was gloom all round, but spirits then lifted when the Cabinet learned that a third helicopter, a Wessex 3 from HMS *Antrim*, had successfully lifted everyone off the ice without loss of life.'

Yet a few voices spoke up in favour of escalation. Early in May 1982, a number of backbenchers tabled a Commons motion calling for 'whatever immediate measures should prove necessary to eliminate the capacity of the Argentine forces to inflict unacceptable losses on the British fleet'. The clear implication was that their air bases on the mainland should be attacked to remove the threat of missile or bomb attacks from the air.

Also, at an early War Cabinet meeting, CDS had advocated the bombing of Argentine air bases on the mainland. His view was that if the Falklands were to be retaken, air superiority was essential, and this could only be guaranteed by first attacking the mainland bases. Sir John Nott said that CDS's view was never taken seriously by the War Cabinet. It would have provoked the wrath of most of the countries in South America and lost us many friends elsewhere.

Sir Clive Whitmore agreed with Sir John, and added that CDS's view would never have found favour, especially with Sir Michael Havers who, as Attorney General, attended War Cabinet meetings and had responsibility for ensuring that no decision was taken that could result in Britain contravening international law.

It was always planned by the RAF therefore that the Vulcan missions should be confined to the Falkland Islands. They would be few in number but would send all the right messages to Argentina's ruling junta. They were code-named Operation Black Buck.

Operation Black Buck

John Laycock recalled AVM Ken Hayr visiting Waddington to discuss ways of using the Vulcan. The gist of the conversation between the two men was that anything that might be appropriate and workable was to be tried. No expense was to be spared and time was of the essence.

For the anti-radar missions, the Martel anti-radar missile was briefly considered. It was even successfully test-fired at Aberporth Range. Jim Uprichard, on the Victor tanker desk at the MoD, said it was rejected though for two reasons. Firstly, it made 'too big a bang' and the consequent risk of collateral damage would have been unacceptable. The Argentines had moved crucial radar units close to habitation at Stanley. The other problem with Martel was that it could be unreliable if 'cold-soaked' at altitude for a long time. The flight time from Ascension Island to the Falklands would have been excessive.

These problems precipitated a rethink. Andrew Roberts was Group

Captain Operations at HQSTC. He was asked to investigate a suitable, and more selective, alternative to Martel. 'The US Shrike missile,' he said, 'seemed to meet the requirement.' John Laycock added that even the old Skybolt wiring and ducting (which were still on the aircraft) were compatible, although there was little time properly to test everything before carrying the missile in anger. The wheels were set in motion and the Americans agreed to supply us with a limited number of Shrike missiles. The small matter of obtaining White House approval for the RAF to use the missiles was quickly handled by means of a direct telephone call from John Nott to US Defence Secretary Casper Weinberger.

Graham Forbes, a C130 captain, was ordered to fly to the US Air Force Base Spangdahlen in Germany on 26th May to pick up six missiles. He was to take them to RAF Waddington on 27th May to be loaded on to a Vulcan. In the event, Graham arrived after the Vulcan had departed, so he took the missiles on to RAF Lyneham to be airlifted on to Ascension Island in another C130.

From Spangdahlen to the Falklands in just four days was, by any measure, an excellent example of how rapidly the wheels can turn when the situation demands, and of the co-operation that existed at that time between Britain and the USA. Also squeezed into those four days was the fleeting visit of a couple of US Shrike experts from the US China Lake Naval Base, California, who flew to the UK to assist the process of 'mating' the missile with the two designated aircraft.

Of the seven planned Vulcan missions, code-named Black Buck, three bombing and two anti-radar/defence suppression missions took place; one further mission was cancelled, and another was aborted after take-off. Black Buck 5 and 6 were the two anti-radar missions, and both were flown with the same aircraft and crew. The modification of the aircraft and the training of the crews had been accomplished in record time.

Black Buck 6

Squadron Leader Neil McDougall and his crew were briefed for the Black Buck 6 mission on 2nd June. From all accounts, the intelligence briefing concentrated mainly on the threat to be expected in the target area. Although Rio International Airport was the designated diversion and the Tanker Plan reflected this, little was said that would have prepared the crew for a diversion to Brazil.

Later that day, and armed with four AGM-45A Shrike anti-radar missiles, Vulcan XM597 took off from Ascension Island, arriving over the Falklands the following morning. Neil McDougall's crew included Chris Lackman (co-pilot), Barry Smith (navigator), Rod Trevaskus (air electronics officer), David Castle (bomb aimer) and Brian Gardner (a spare AAR-qualified pilot). The aircraft was fitted with two bomb-bay fuel tanks, which increased the fuel capacity by about 16,000 lbs, the space not being required to carry bombs in the defence suppression role. Neil McDougall had asked if some bombs could be carried as well, in case the Argentine radars were switched off, but this request was refused. The attack profiles that the crew hoped to carry out in the Falklands had been rehearsed at the Spadeadam EW Range, the radars transmitting on the frequencies of those to be attacked on 3rd June.

The flight down to the Falklands was unremarkable except for the huge distance involved, a feature of all the Black Buck missions. The flights were significant achievements, involving many hours in cramped conditions, and requiring skills only recently acquired. Although not quite the longest of the Vulcan Black Buck missions, David Castle's logbook recorded a flight time of 13 hours, 40 minutes from Ascension Island until landing at Rio.

Harrier activity from the carriers had been requested to coincide with the arrival of the Vulcan over the Falklands. However, the weather was considered too poor and the Harrier flights were cancelled. The idea was that the Harriers would act as decoys to get the Argentine radars switched on. Black Buck 6 was, as it turned out, the only offensive action of the day.

Having let-down from high altitude, McDougall approached the Falklands at an altitude of 300 feet above sea level before, at 25 miles range, climbing back up to 12,000 feet. The primary target, the Westinghouse AN/TPS-43 air defence radar, was switched off, so McDougall prowled around the area trying to entice the radar to transmit long enough to achieve a missile lock-on. The importance of neutralising this radar had much to do with its ability to track the Royal Navy's aircraft carriers and provide target information for Super Etendard Exocet attacks.

Although the Argentine Tiger Cat missiles represented a threat to the Vulcan up to around 8,500 feet, it was an old system that had to be guided visually. The Roland missile was regarded as lethal up to 10,000 feet, but intelligence information had suggested that none had been deployed. As it turned out, the intelligence was wrong, and there was in fact a single unit operational.

The most potent threat to the aircraft was presented by the Super

216

Oerliken gun, part of the radar-laid defence system protecting the environs of Port Stanley. The gun fired half-inch shells with a high rate of fire and great destructive power up to an altitude of 6,500 feet. It was guided by the Skyguard fire control radar. It was against this highly-mobile radar that the crew had some success, although they were hampered by poor intelligence as to its precise location. This radar provided intelligence on British air movements, and on efforts made to close the runway to Argentine aircraft. Much effort had gone into trying to render the runway inoperable, especially after the successful 24th May Argentine C130 resupply operation. Of the four Shrike missiles carried on McDougall's Vulcan, two missiles had radar heads optimised for each of the two Argentine target radar systems.

After waiting for some 45 minutes (to no avail) for the AN/TPS-43 radar obligingly to transmit, Neil McDougall decided they should descend into the missile engagement zone (MEZ), accepting the risk involved, and try to find a target to attack. The risk was explained to the crew, who accepted it without hesitation. David Castle remembers the Oerliken shells exploding on both sides of the aircraft. They were fortunate not to sustain damage, but the decision to descend had forced the Skyguard unit to illuminate the Vulcan. Two Shrike missiles were fired, one of which successfully damaged the radar and killed members of the gun crew. It was then time to depart the target area and make for the rendezvous (RV) with the tanker aircraft.

The RV with the Victor Tanker

The planned RV was southeast of Rio and the refuelling operation should have been completed at a point just over 400 miles from the international airport. Whilst practically everyone agreed that Rio had been the chosen diversion, one or two lone voices thought it could have been Canoas. If it had been, the refuelling operation would have been completed about 660 miles east-northeast of Canoas with the Vulcan heading northeast away from it. The aircraft would never have reached its diversion after the drama that was to unfold. Crew members from the Vulcan, Victor and Nimrod aircraft, all present at the RV that day, recalled the occasion more than twenty-five years later.

The many roles of Nimrod MR2 XV 227 at that time included long-range surface surveillance, search and rescue, and top cover for the Vulcan and Victor aircraft. Importantly, on this occasion it had also

217

to guide the Vulcan to its RV with the Victor tanker as quickly and efficiently as possible. The presumption was always that the receiving aircraft could be short of fuel and that time was of the essence. Neil McDougall had not, however, indicated that on this occasion the Vulcan might have a fuel problem.

David Emmerson was the Nimrod Detachment Commander on Ascension Island. He liked to fly with the different crews and was on board the aircraft on 3rd June. The crew included Andy Melville-Jackson (aircraft captain), Steve Skinner (co-pilot), George Morris (another pilot who carried out the AAR), and David Scrivenor (the first navigator).

The MR2 version of Nimrod was equipped with the new Thorn EMI Searchwater radar with its IFF (Identification Friend or Foe) interrogator, and the new Central Tactical System made by General Electrics Company (GEC). However, it was not until mid-May – some weeks after the Argentine invasion – that the MR2s acquired an AAR capability. Before that, it had been unable to carry out the surface surveillance role as far away from Ascension as the Falklands. This had been handled instead by Victor tankers as had occurred, for example, in advance of the repossession of South Georgia.

By mid-May, however, the MR2s' newly-acquired AAR capability enabled the aircraft to fly the extra miles and enhance the support given to the Task Force. Such a mission could typically require seven Victor tankers for the Nimrod's outbound leg and a further two Victors for inbound tanking. This was a huge commitment but it extended the aircrafts' sortie length to something approaching 20 hours. For comparison, a Nimrod MR1 sortie might typically have been around 9 hours duration.

Boscombe Down RAF test pilot Ian Strachan recalled discussions with BAe Woodford technicians as the AAR probe design was being finalised. 'It took only two weeks from initial tasking to the first test flight with the new probe which took place on 27th April,' he said. 'Eight MR2s were eventually fitted with probes.'

There was another problem that had to be dealt with. Argentina had a couple of B707 aircraft for transport and long-range reconnaissance work, and they had been shadowing the Task Force. The Nimrod MR1s, being unarmed, could do nothing about these intrusions so BAe had also been asked if Sidewinder air-to-air missiles could be fitted to the Nimrods. The answer came swiftly back that it could be done and the decision was taken to modify the longer-range MR2 aircraft.

BAe's Chief Test Pilot at Woodford, 'Robbie' Robinson, remembers taking the first modified aircraft, fitted with its Sidewinders, to Boscombe

Down to carry out trials. 'I flew behind a BAe 146, close enough to get the "growl" and established that the system functioned,' he said. 'Then a further trial on the Aberporth Range (in Cardigan Bay) was carried out, and a missile was fired against a flare. Everything worked satisfactorily and the MR2s were then modified to carry four AIM 9G Sidewinders; two on each side.' The first Nimrod MR2 to carry Sidewinders was XV 229 on 29th May 1982. On 3rd June, David Emmerson confirmed, XV 227 had an AAR capability but was not carrying any Sidewinder air-to-air missiles. It was, however, carrying a formidable selection of 1000lb bombs, three Stingray torpedoes and two Harpoon anti-ship missiles.

Tim Gedge was the Commanding Officer of No 809 Naval Air Squadron. He recalled being ordered into the cockpit of a Sea Harrier when information was received that a B707 was heading towards the Task Force. 'The RN had been cleared to shoot it down if necessary,' he said. 'My aircraft was armed with Sidewinder missiles and 30mm cannon. A Victor tanker was scrambled from Ascension Island. After an hour, the B707 turned away and the mission was cancelled.' All in a day's work until... an enthusiastic photographer from BAe's Public Relations Department unwisely photographed the first Nimrod with its Sidewinder missiles fitted. The picture appeared next day in the national press and doubtless the man was told the error of his ways. In fact, it probably served to give Argentina a timely warning as their B707s were not seen in the Falklands area again!

The short timescale within which the Nimrod was adapted to carry out its wartime roles was an impressive example of how the RAF and British industry responded together to meet the new requirements as they were identified.

Nevertheless, David Emmerson, given his role at the time, should have the final word regarding the effectiveness of these modifications:

Operating well within the Argentine air defence cover in a large, slow and unarmed aircraft was an uncomfortable situation to be in. The only defence for most of the war had been infra-red flares released from a manual dispenser. The Sidewinder missile really came too late. In-flight refuelling was also rather hit-and-miss, sometimes taking up to twenty minutes. The risk of failure to take on fuel on the return leg when so far from base was significant. Now, of course, it is quite routine. Flying a Nimrod in daylight on a clear day off the Argentine coast in 1982 made one feel like a goldfish in a bowl being watched by a cat!

The threat of Argentine fighter aircraft in the Falklands area was ever-present, but the Nimrod had a good ECM facility and fighter aircraft would have used radar. The view was taken that, in the event of encountering fighters, Nimrod had the endurance to cut and run. Fighter aircraft, with limited fuel and range, the thinking went, would not be inclined to pursue for very long.

The on-board equipment used to bring the Vulcan and Victor together at the RV on 3rd June was primarily the Nimrod's Searchwater radar with its IFF interrogator. An indication appeared on the radar screen as the Vulcan was picked up and identified at about 150 miles range. It was then given instructions to fly to the RV. Weather conditions at altitude were good and there was no clear air turbulence to make in-flight refuelling difficult.

The Nimrod, having brought the two aircraft together, then kept station about half a mile away and slightly lower on the starboard side, where it was able to observe the AAR operation and be on hand if required.

The Victor tanker also aimed to arrive at the RV as close as possible to the appointed time, thus conserving its fuel and in the process making more available for transfer. Andy Barrett was the captain of the aircraft that rendezvoused with Neil McDougall's Vulcan.

Normal peacetime tanker commitments required a minimum of four or five serviceable aircraft to be available each day. With a little warning, the force could muster ten or eleven aircraft. When the Falklands balloon went up, eighteen aircraft out of a force of twenty-two were serviceable by the end of April. It was an excellent response. The first four aircraft arrived at Ascension Island on 18th April, followed by five more on the following day. Two aircraft were quickly fitted with cameras in their noses and flew maritime radar reconnaissance (MRR) missions on the 20th, 22nd and 24th April (as stated, at that time the Victor was the only aircraft with the 'legs' to get down to the Falklands and South Georgia area until the Nimrods received their probes later). Their purpose was to look for and report the position and direction of movement of any Argentine shipping, and to assess the threat to Royal Navy ships in the area.

As the Victors were unarmed, there was always concern about the threat presented by Argentine fighter aircraft. On the odd occasion, a Victor pilot would report having been illuminated by Argentine radar and having had to take evasive action, something most Victor pilots would normally prefer not to have to do, and not only because fuel would be wasted in the process. It had originally been anticipated that twenty-five per cent of the Victor force could be lost during the war, but in fact the fleet survived intact. In the early days there was also some talk that Sidewinder missiles might be fitted to the aircraft, but nothing came of it.

As with the Vulcan crews, the Victor crews were asked at short notice to operate in a way unfamiliar to them. AAR was frequently carried out in the dark, without reliable weather information in the destination area, and in R/T silence. Also, Victor pilots were unused to flying in large formations. There was much to learn in little time. Nevertheless, for the duration of the Falklands War, the Victor effort was huge, and very demanding of both aircraft and crews. The need to support conflicting requirements was endless. The RAF was grateful that, for the duration of the war, the USAF was able to step in and take over some of its day-to-day tanking commitments back in the UK.

Referring to Black Buck 6 specifically, Andy Barrett said that although it was not normally the Nimrod's job to bring the Vulcan and Victor together, the assistance given by the Nimrod on 3rd June was a bonus. The Victors in fact had their own well-rehearsed procedure, which involved flying towards the receiving aircraft, and commencing a lazy 30° turn at 17 miles range through 180°. This brought the Victor round on to the receiving aircraft's heading, and about 1½ miles ahead of it.

One of the Victor's navigators had the added responsibility for controlling the AAR process. It was carried out using a system of red and green lights, and in complete silence in case any shipping in the area took an interest. He had a periscope that allowed him to see and control the receiving aircraft astern whilst he also recorded all the attempts made by the receiving aircraft to make contact.

It is not unreasonable to expect a pilot, who is about to carry out AAR, to be slightly apprehensive after an exceptionally long and tiring mission when the fuel state is getting low. Most Vulcan pilots though took the view that AAR in that aircraft was straightforward. Martin Withers, who captained the Black Buck 1 mission, summed it up as follows: 'AAR with a Vulcan was not difficult. You couldn't see the probe, but any qualified Vulcan pilot should be able to quickly learn where it was and get the hang of it. The probe stayed in easily and you had good control over the aircraft, good throttle response and plenty of power available.'

No 55 (Victor) Squadron's Operations Record Book recorded for the mission on 3rd June: 'Operation Black Buck 6... The rendezvous with the Vulcan was copybook but the Vulcan had difficulty making contact with the drogue. The Vulcan made eight approaches, four of which were rim contacts. On the last approach, which appeared to be too fast, the

221

Vulcan's probe broke off forcing the crew to divert to Rio de Janeiro. Flt Lt Barrett returned to Ascension Island taking with him the Vulcan's broken probe as a 'trophy' for the night's work.' Suddenly, an immediate diversion to the nearest suitable airfield offered the only hope for saving the Vulcan.

The Victor loitered for a while then, not being able to contribute further, returned to Ascension Island after giving the Nimrod some fuel. As it departed the RV, Andy broke R/T silence to explain the nature of the problem, as it meant that his aircraft would not be able to offer fuel to another aircraft (except to a fighter aircraft at a different refuelling station, but this was not applicable then).

Diversion to Brazil

The flight from the RV to Brazil was a tense time for the crew of the Vulcan. Neil McDougall climbed to an altitude where their fuel consumption would be most economical. All classified material on board was consigned to the South Atlantic. The crew attempted to jettison the two remaining unused Shrike missiles, but one of them, for technical reasons, failed to leave the aircraft. The Vulcan was therefore carrying a live 'hung-up' missile from that point on. Rod Trevaskus put out a Mayday call. Understandably, they wanted to land on the nearest suitable runway, and that was at Rio de Janeiro International Airport.

A couple of myths need to be exploded. Everything said over the R/T by the Vulcan crew was clearly heard and understood by Rio ATC. Being an International Airport, there were plenty of controllers around who spoke English. An American was also on duty in ATC that day.

Also, any impression that ATC may have given that suggested they were not trying to be totally helpful was unfounded. Any airport would, and should, be very concerned when an aircraft that declines to identify itself continues on its way to land. There was never, however, any intention to block the runway to prevent the Vulcan from landing, as has been suggested.

Given that no one had any idea of what type of aircraft was approaching the runway, not too surprisingly CINDACTA (Centro Integrado de Defesa Aerea e Controle do Trafego Aereo), the Brazilian joint civil/military air traffic control centre, scrambled a pair of F5 fighter aircraft from the nearby FAB base at Santa Cruz to intercept and identify

222

the intruder. It was not a hostile act; just a perfectly correct and understandable response.

Meanwhile, the Nimrod accompanied the Vulcan part of the way to Rio, offering what help it could. It also informed Ascension Island of the situation and remained in R/T contact with the Vulcan until it had safely landed.

Once on the ground, the aircraft was parked in the military area on the far side of the airfield. Understandably, the crew was apprehensive and reluctant to talk to anyone. McDougall correctly requested that the Air Attaché should be contacted immediately (hence the summons to see the Minister). Until I arrived in Rio they would, politely of course, say nothing to anyone.

In due course, the FAB provided guards for the aircraft. They stood around outside the guard that was also provided from a member of the crew. The Brazilian guards were there, we were told, in case Argentina tried to mount a Special Forces attack on the aircraft.

An immediate problem that had to be resolved was that of making the Shrike missile safe. Barry Smith recalled 'inserting the pin that made the missile safe' after landing. However, the missile had to be dropped (i.e. removed from the aircraft), and that required precise instructions from the UK. John Laycock recalled, many years later, that a Chief Technician at Waddington had drafted detailed step-by-step instructions, which were then communicated to Rio to be passed to the crew. The missile was safely lowered the next day, and placed in a supposedly secure location for which, as Air Attaché, I was given the key.

Very quickly, the crew realised that they were amongst friends. A party, already arranged for that evening off the base, was rearranged to be on the base so that we could all attend. Barry Smith described the next few days as being 'a bit like being under an amiable open-arrest!' Several Brazilians thanked different members of the crew for what they were doing. Others suggested that one day Argentina might have gone to war against Brazil, but Britain's prompt response to Argentina's invasion now made that highly unlikely. They were very grateful for that.

During the following days, the crew had access to a swimming pool, and a games room equipped with snooker and table-tennis tables. A good friend, a Brazilian who flew bomber aircraft in the RAF during the Second World War and who was, in 1982, actively involved with the Rio Branch of the Royal British Legion, rallied his colleagues to produce clothes and books for the crew. A FAB officer, Carlos Motta da Souza, who had attended the RAF staff college course at Bracknell and spoke

223

good English, was appointed by the FAB as a liaison officer for the duration.

Within a few hours of the Vulcan landing, the airport perimeter road was jammed with thousands of Brazilians busily photographing this curious British aircraft never before seen in Brazil. This was something not to miss. The word was out. The Minister's warning to get the aircraft off the ground as soon as possible proved impossible to heed. Predictably, as word of the Vulcan's arrival quickly spread, the Argentine Embassy soon learned of it and lost no time in acting.

Argentina protested that under the terms of the Rio Treaty of Pan-American Solidarity, the Vulcan should be detained. Specifically, the request was based upon Article 7 of the Rio Mutual Assistance Treaty, which called on participating nations to abstain from any act that could jeopardise the preservation of peace. The Article allowed signatories of the Treaty to decide whether or not to assist Argentina in its war with Britain, but called on them to refrain from any action that could harm Argentina in the dispute.

We were refused permission even to refuel the aircraft, and the crew had to settle back and await an uncertain outcome during a week of intense diplomatic activity. Several meetings in Rio with the Regional Air Commander and the FAB Base Commander, Cel (Colonel) Jose Teofilo Rodriguez de Aquino, were intended to keep up the pressure on the Brazilians for an early release.

The important, decisive diplomacy, however, was handled by the Ambassador in Brasilia. He recalled his visits to Itamaraty (the Brazilian Foreign Ministry) when, in his words, unlike the military they were a bit 'heavy' with him, talked of the Vulcan infringing Brazilian neutrality and generally gave him a hard time. Initially, he was warned that the aircraft would have to stay in Brazil for the duration of the war.

On Saturday 5th June, he crucially visited Foreign Minister Saraiva Guerreiro at his residence to press further and make a formal request for the release of the aircraft and its crew. The request was passed to Itamaraty's legal experts on Sunday 6th June for their consideration. Their views were then conveyed back to the government, which then took the decision to release the aircraft subject to certain conditions. The Air Minister's advice had been sought throughout the process.

Apart from the efforts of the Ambassador and the attachés, CDS, Admiral of the Fleet Sir Terence Lewin, also became briefly involved. Group Captain (later Air Commodore) Joe Hardstaff and Captain (later Admiral Sir) Peter Abbott worked for CDS as briefers during the war.

Whilst one prepared the daily briefing CDS gave at the Cabinet Office, the other accompanied and assisted him.

Joe Hardstaff recalled that, when they all learned from Northwood of the Vulcan diversion, there was never any real concern regarding how the Brazilians would handle the situation, nor about how the crew would be treated. Admiral Lewin, he said, had called a senior Brazilian admiral, possibly Admiral Aratanha, whom he had known from a course they had once attended together. The Brazilian, who spoke perfect English, had reassured CDS that we should not be too concerned about the Vulcan or its crew, and that all would be well.

On the morning of 9th June, I held a small lunch-time drinks party in Rio to celebrate the Queen's Birthday, to which a selection of FAB officers, including the Base Commander and Regional Air Commander, were invited. The outgoing Brazilian CAS, who happened to be in Rio that day, also came along. He delivered a speech saying what a pleasure it was to have the RAF crew there and insisted on toasting Her Majesty himself. All the assembled FAB and RAF officers raised their glasses, and it would have been hard to imagine a more solid gesture of friendship and support.

The whole episode, and the way it was dealt with by the Brazilians, although we had put them in an embarrassing position, was an indication of the sympathy that many of them felt for the British position during the Falklands War.

That afternoon, I was summoned back to Brasilia to see the Air Minister again. Without preamble, he said the Vulcan could now leave Brazil. He had been charged by Itamaraty to convey the Brazilian Government's decision, reached after a week of intense diplomatic activity.

His involvement throughout would undoubtedly have been helpful to us. CAS Sir Michael Beetham's timely visit to Brazil in 1981, only a few months before the Falklands War, could also have been an important factor in the release of the Vulcan. He and Minister Delio had struck up an excellent rapport.

The Minister had a further word to say. The aircraft should depart early the following morning before anyone changed their mind; the Shrike missile must remain in Brazil until the end of hostilities and the aircraft (but not the crew) must not fly again during the war. As I saluted and turned to leave his office, he said: 'Of course, you could always paint another number on the tail!'

Vulcan XM 597 departed early the following morning and returned to

Ascension Island. It continued on to RAF Waddington on 13th June, arriving to a quiet welcome; Argentina surrendered the following day. Suddenly, no one seemed very interested any more, and McDougall and his loyal crew were left to reflect upon a very close call. XM597 was one of only two Vulcan aircraft ever to be used in anger (the other being XM607 which bombed Stanley airfield earlier in the Falklands War).

The Shrike Missile is Returned

In spite of assurances to the contrary, the FAB also had a key to the building where the Shrike missile was stored, and probably briefly removed the missile at some point. It would, in all probability, have been taken to the Centro Tecnico Aerospaciale (CTA) at São José dos Campos for examination. The Brazilians were developing a missile of their own at that time, and a quick look at the Shrike might have been helpful. Far from being devious behaviour on the part of a friendly nation, it was probably an opportunity that most countries would have grabbed under the same circumstances.

Although there had been some discussion in the Brazilian press about the type of missile the Vulcan had carried (and some wildly inaccurate suggestions), it had been quickly identified as Shrike by those who needed to know. Within moments of the aircraft landing, tens of thousands of Brazilians with cameras and telephoto lenses had jammed the roads around the perimeter of the airfield to photograph an aircraft never before seen in the country. Initially, until it was covered, the missile had been clearly visible on the aircraft with 'Made in the US' stamped on it for the world to see.

Major Brigadeiro Menezes, Director of CTA at the time, later recalled that on learning of the aircraft's arrival he had dispatched an officer immediately to Rio to learn anything of possible value. This included, of course, confirming the missile type; but by the time the officer arrived, the missile had been covered. He had asked what it was, but we had all declined to be helpful. It had not mattered, as the Brigadier had been given clear photographs of the missile within hours of the aircraft landing, and well before his officer returned from Rio. He knew instantly that it was a Shrike.

He said all this after the 1982 Farnborough Air Show, which he had attended as a visiting VIP, before setting off with his team from CTA to demonstrate the Tucano trainer aircraft to the RAF. Brazil hoped to sell

226

the aircraft, and was successful – contrary to my own predictions at the time – defeating British Aerospace's rival bid with the Pilatus aircraft.

A few days after Argentina surrendered, the necessary arrangements were made to retrieve the Shrike missile from the building, the key of which had never left my person. Only later did I learn, from our SIS representative, that the CIA had been 'very exercised' about the missile, and had discussed ways of relieving me of the key!

On the appointed day, 5th July, a C130 from RAF Lyneham captained by Wing Commander Brian Warsap arrived in Rio. I flew down from Brasilia and was met by the Base Commander who enquired if I was ready for the ceremony. This was something totally unexpected, but Brazilians love an occasion, and the hand-over ceremony was a wonderful opportunity to give the FAB a bit of press and TV time.

We marched out to the middle of the vast parade ground, where a table and two chairs awaited, surrounded by cameras and journalists. The officers and men of the base were assembled on parade in their best uniforms. As we took our seats, the band struck up. The Colonel whispered that the flypast would be in 2 minutes, when the TV cameras would roll to catch the signing of the document before me. The document, in Portuguese, declared that the missile being returned to the RAF was in every way intact, in the same state as when it was delivered into the custody of the FAB, had never been touched or tampered with, and so on. There followed a few minutes of frantic whispering as I explained that I had no way of knowing whether anyone had tampered with the missile (though I suspected they had), whilst he implored me to sign. With seconds remaining before the formation arrived overhead, a compromise was called for. I crossed out the text and dutifully signed a meaningless piece of paper, as the cameras rolled and a formation of F5 aircraft roared overhead.

After the ceremony, the Shrike was loaded on to the C130. Brian Warsap recalled that the missile was made comfortable on an old mattress at the back of the aircraft. There was some debate as to whether it should point forward or aft. In the end, it was agreed that it should point aft... just in case! Nobody really doubted that it would behave itself. If it had any inclination to do otherwise, it had had the perfect opportunity when it was pointing, live at the time, at air traffic control as the Vulcan approached Rio International Airport a few days earlier.

The above scenario was later put to various missile experts to get their views as to whether the missile could possibly have taken a fancy to a stray, unsuspecting electronic pulse. The common view was that it was highly improbable and, even if it had, it would probably have set off on a wild, unstable ride towards no specific point. Some, however, leaned towards the gloomier prognosis that: 'You never know – strange, inexplicable things have been known to happen.' In that eventuality, one can only imagine the subsequent headlines... !

After an uneventful flight, the last of the Shrike missiles was offloaded at Ascension Island before the C130 continued on to the UK. Hopefully, someone returned the missile to the Americans, although I heard no more of it.

Some Views Expressed

From the moment the Vulcan landed in Rio on 3rd June, until after it departed a week later, it was front-page news in all Brazil's quality newspapers. Inevitably, there was some speculative nonsense, including wild guesses as to the type of missile the Vulcan carried, how the FAB F5 pilots had intercepted the incoming Vulcan, and so on. In one article, the journalist described 'the sonic boom that had reverberated round Rio de Janeiro as the Vulcan approached to land.' He was straightened out on that one!

On the whole though, the coverage was good, fair, and certainly not anti-British, especially from *Jornal do Brasil*, one of Brazil's leading and most influential newspapers. We were fortunate that the Ambassador had built up a good relationship with the Brazilian press, and knew most of the important and more influential editors. The editor of *Jornal do Brasil* was later recommended for, and received from the Ambassador himself, a knighthood for accurate and objective reporting that was undoubtedly helpful to Britain.

Some time after the war, the Ambassador learned that the Diplomatic School – which was part of the Itamaraty set-up (the Brazilian Foreign Office), and ran courses for would-be Brazilian diplomats – was informing its students that, during the Falklands War, the British Ambassador had occasionally acted behind the back of Itamaraty and dealt directly with the Brazilian Service Chiefs, with whom he had a good relationship. This, the students were informed, was an example of unacceptable behaviour, and not the way diplomacy should be conducted. Sir William's view was that the Brazilian Air and Navy Ministers happened to be his friends, as well as his neighbours, and there was a job to be done. He would act in the same way again, and had no regrets.

There is no doubt that the Brazilian Government faced a difficult dilemma regarding the Vulcan. It was an embarrassment, and their decision to allow the aircraft to leave, albeit with some strings attached, after a week on the ground, was a careful and courageous compromise aimed at trying to keep both Britain and Argentina reasonably happy. Indeed, any request for help from Britain at that time would have been considered, not only with regard to future relations with both Britain and Argentina, but also in the wider context of South American solidarity. Brazil shares a border with almost every other country in South America, and would have to coexist with its neighbours long after the dust from our little scrap had settled.

When people learned of the scale of effort required to support the Black Buck missions, the distances involved, the stamina required by the crews, and the short timescale available in which to resurrect the aircraft, modify them and train the crews, few had anything but admiration for the Royal Air Force's determination to make this vital contribution.

Sir John Nott's view was that politically the Black Buck missions had been extremely valuable, and a further sign that we were serious. Admiral Sir John Fieldhouse, a submariner, was entirely in favour, recalled his colleague and friend, Air Marshal Sir John Curtiss. David Brook, on CDS's staff at the time, remembers that CDS, too, was wholly supportive and impressed by the scale of effort.

Admiral Sir John Woodward said: 'By any standards, the missions were of heroic proportions, and had my unqualified support. Anything that helped to prevent Argentine fighter aircraft from using Stanley to bomb my ships had my support.' He also praised 'the immaculate planning of the RAF'.

Some criticism of the missions, however, came from a small handful of naval aviators who either had little idea of the real purpose of the missions, or of the weight of effort required to destroy a runway 4,000 miles from the home base. Admiral Woodward's explanation for this was that: 'Naval aviators were generally anti the RAF's contribution on principle, and inclined to be less than charitable.' Perhaps Admiral Mountbatten, who will be remembered for his advocacy of inter-service co-operation, for which he worked tirelessly, would have agreed that there is still room for improvement in certain areas.

This view was enthusiastically endorsed by Yvonne Stafford-Curtis, who joined Admiral Mountbatten's staff in the summer of 1943 when he was appointed Supreme Commander South-East Asia. She remained with him for the rest of the war and for a short time afterwards. Yvonne was one of two young First Officers WRNS who handled codes and ciphers and was quietly present at all his meetings, whether with senior Service Commanders or leading figures such as Chiang Kai-Shek. In her nineties, she recalled clearly that Admiral Mountbatten always treated men of the different services equally, and expected them to do the same, and work together to understand each other's problems.

Certainly, nobody should scoff at the small number of bombs that landed on Stanley's airfield. Anyone who understands the weight of effort required to comprehensively damage a runway would appreciate that more than this was never expected. Given the distances involved, the number of Victor tanker aircraft required just to get one Vulcan down to the Falklands and back, competing requirements for space on Ascension Island, and all the other tasks that had to be carried out as well also requiring tanking effort, the few Vulcan missions accomplished more than was asked of them. They also had a damaging psychological effect upon our adversary.

The Vulcan also had elderly on-board computers. From the early 1970s, there had seemed little reason to press for an expensive update for an aircraft with a limited in-service life and, in any case, very precise bombing is hardly required for the delivery of a nuclear weapon. The computers were not accurate enough to risk a down-the-runway bombing run, so the aircraft approached at an angle calculated to put a bomb either around the middle of the runway, or one either side, close to the edge.

The time delay between successive bombs (to minimise the risk of mutual interference as they left the aircraft) was also a factor that helped to conspire against complete success, as this would determine the (fairly significant) distance between the impact points of the bombs.

The difficulties of applying early 1960s technology to the need for precision bombing twenty years later were not inconsiderable, but the skill of the crews, honed by many hours of training, ensured the best results that could reasonably have been expected.

Air Marshal Curtiss added: 'Because of limited space on Ascension Island, I had daily discussions with Admiral Fieldhouse regarding priorities for the space available. Often it was necessary to decide three to four days ahead in order to have the right assets in place when required. Nevertheless, the Vulcan had a high priority.'

Aircrew who might have to divert to a foreign country in time of war should have a clear idea of what to expect on arrival. During the Falklands War, any aircraft returning to Ascension Island from the Falklands and having to divert would almost certainly have had to land somewhere in Brazil.

Pre-flight and intelligence briefings, however, according to crews of different aircraft types, did not discuss the situation in Brazil, the Brazilian Government's position regarding the war, the view of the man-in-the-street or what kind of reception to expect, all of which was information that was readily available. As a consequence, although his views were not necessarily shared by the other members of his crew, the captain of the Vulcan had a distorted view of what to expect, and was perhaps understandably rather hostile and suspicious throughout his time in Rio.

The political situation in Brazil should also have been considered in the choice of the diversion airfield. The crew of the Vulcan cannot be blamed for heading straight to the nearest suitable airfield, given their dire predicament. They were desperately short of fuel. Any pilot would have put the safety of his aircraft and crew before other considerations and Rio International was the nearest suitable airfield.

But Rio need not have been the planned diversion. The planners at Ascension Island, who so meticulously prepared the tanker plans for the missions, agreed that they could have been adjusted to fit any chosen diversion airfield. Once the appropriate diversion had been determined, the tanker/Vulcan RV point would then have been plotted offshore and abeam the airfield.

Rio International Airport was an unfortunate choice. Not only did the high volume of predominantly civil air traffic make it a high-risk proposition for an aircraft short of fuel, but it was also bound to place the Brazilian Government in an embarrassing position if any RAF aircraft diverted there, temporarily placing a strain upon our relations. In fact, the whole scenario that unfolded after landing, including the position taken by the Argentine Embassy, was entirely predictable.

There were a number of FAB bases to the north and south of Rio that would have been suitable as diversion airfields. All would have offered a high level of security, the crew would have been amongst friends, and the Vulcan could have made a discreet landing. There would also have been little air traffic to compete with, compared with that using an international civil airport.

Parked somewhere on the airfield, the general public and the press need not have been aware of its presence, and it would certainly have been in Brazil's interest to keep it that way. If the press had not learned of it, the Argentine Embassy also might not have learned of the aircraft's arrival, and almost certainly not until after it had refuelled and subsequently departed. We would also have been able to keep the Shrike missile out of sight, avoiding embarrassing our American friends, and there would not have been any threat to the aircraft from Argentine Special Forces.

The story of the Vulcan diversion into Rio had a satisfactory ending, but it could have ended tragically, and very nearly did.

An Argentine View of the Vulcan Missions

It was learned after the war that the Vulcan missions to the Falklands had had a pronounced demoralising effect upon the Argentine troops there. They had been completely unexpected, and not at all what Argentine commanders had foreseen or warned their troops to expect. It transpired that their men had been kept intentionally in the dark regarding the possibility of a Vulcan attack.

On the Argentine mainland, it was a different story. Cristina Bishop was a young Argentine schoolteacher in 1982. She recalled how the government deliberately exaggerated the threat to the mainland to help portray the British as evil murderers. The population was warned that a Vulcan attack on Buenos Aires was a real possibility and everyone should be ready for it. Cristina was required to exercise her class regularly by suddenly shouting 'Vulcan'. The idea was that all the children should dive for cover under their desks, although what good that would have done, no one was quite sure. In fact, she said, the whole idea backfired on the government because, whilst being genuinely fearful of a Vulcan attack, most Argentine men and women did not actually dislike the British; they just wanted the Falklands back. She said: 'All this palaver just made people wonder more and more what on earth their government had got them into. Most of the schoolchildren, of course, thought it was all good fun!'

Part Five
The Other Players

Bolivia

Any attempt to summarise centuries of history in a few paragraphs is fraught with difficulty, and open to accusations of inaccuracy. Bolivia's story, from those early days when Indians roamed (more or less) peacefully, up to modern times, is not very different from that of most other South American countries.

The Spanish arrived initially in 1532, looking for gold and silver, and set about conquering the Inca Empire. This proved not too difficult to achieve, although only after some years of fighting. They established the city of La Paz, which eventually became an important commercial centre and, in 1548, the capital of Bolivia.

For many years Indian elements continued to rebel against Spanish domination, whilst others accepted colonial rule. There were many revolts. Bolivian silver mines produced much of the Spanish Empire's wealth during this period. Meanwhile, the gradual erosion of the Indian culture, combined with the devastating effect of European diseases, led to a rapid decline in the size of the Indian population.

Eventually, Spanish authority weakened as the mood for independence strengthened. Independence was declared in 1809, but this was immediately followed by a further sixteen years of war. Finally, Bolivia became an independent republic in 1825, named after Simon Bolivar, the man generally credited with having been the nation's founder.

Bolivar, taking advantage of a section of unsurveyed border, granted land to Bolivia that gave it an outlet to the Pacific coast between Chile and Peru. However, during the course of two further wars with Chile – which Bolivia lost – it also lost this access to the coast, as well as the port of Antofagasta. Relations between the two countries have suffered ever since.

Since independence, Bolivia has lost over half its original territory to neighbouring countries in the course of different wars.

During the Second World War, Bolivia sat on the fence initially, but declared its support for Germany in 1943. Hitler had a long-term plan to conquer South America and perhaps Bolivia felt it would be prudent to back the likely winner (as perceived at the time). Hitler, in turn, sent economic aid and Nazi 'advisers' to Bolivia.

During the course of the decades up to the 1980s, Bolivia experienced many coups and several periods of weak, democratic civilian government. Political corruption was rife. An election was held in 1981, which resulted in the formation of a civilian government. The result was not accepted by the military, however, and the government was overthrown in a military coup in which the Argentine military clearly had a hand.

A military government was therefore running the country in 1982 during the Falklands War. It was known for little else other than economic mismanagement and human rights abuses, and lasted only a short time.

Bolivia and Argentina

Relations between Bolivia and Argentina were a complex mix. 'Many Argentines,' said Terry Brighton, an agricultural missionary in Argentina during the 1970s, 'took the racist view that most Bolivians were a bunch of no-good Indians. Relations, as far as the working majority were concerned, were therefore not good; indeed, rather tense.'

This perhaps explains why many Bolivians gave support to the Montoneros' cause in Argentina, as a consequence of which the latter were able to operate with impunity across the border from Bolivia, where sanctuary was available. This caused a strain in relations at government level, and Argentine troops on duty in the border areas were armed with guns... and whips! Also, as the economies of both countries were in dire straits, smuggling across the border of practically everything from food to guns (much of it destined for the terrorists) was rife.

One smuggling story, allegedly true, involved a Bolivian woman who crossed the border every day for a long time on her motorbike. She was regularly checked, as was her motorbike, but nothing was ever found. One day, in exasperation, the border guards threatened dire retribution if she did not confess and tell them what she was smuggling, and how. She caved in and confessed that she had indeed been smuggling across the border... the motorbikes!

Although many ordinary Bolivians took the view of Argentines that Terry Brighton found prevalent, the military took a slightly different view. They worked quite well with the Argentine military.

When Stanley Duncan arrived in Bolivia to take up his appointment as British Ambassador, the country was already in poor shape. The appalling state of the economy was the consequence of a succession of incompetent military governments, made worse by the reduction in the world demand for tin, which caused its price to tumble. Other than that, Bolivia had little of any consequence in the way of natural resources. Shell was prospecting for oil and natural gas, but the benefits had yet to be realised. Cocaine, however, which was grown and shipped out to Colombia for refinement, was not doing too badly.

There were not many British subjects in Bolivia at that time. A mere

236

handful included those running a small textile factory in La Paz, a few employed by a British firm producing whisky, and those who were supporting oil and gas production.

Britain was not selling any defence equipment in Bolivia then, although that did not stop a few British companies from trying. Peter Rowe, who worked for Racal, recalled a visit during which he was introduced to a Herr Altmann in a hotel. Herr Altmann was, in fact, Klaus Barbie, the notorious 'Butcher of Lyons'. He was the wartime Gestapo Chief in Lyons at the time when twenty-two Frenchmen were shot in reprisal for the death of two German soldiers in January 1944. In South America, he was allegedly working as a salesman for a Belgian arms company, and spending much of his time moving between Argentina and Bolivia, at the time when Peter met him.

His presence in Bolivia at the time, when governance was in the hands of the military, should not surprise anyone. The year after the Falklands War, when civilians once again governed the country, Barbie was arrested in Bolivia and extradited to France, where he was finally tried for his war crimes. Jimmy Burns, *Financial Times* correspondent in South America at the time, confirmed Barbie's presence in Bolivia.

Bolivian Reaction to the Invasion

When the invasion took place, there was much talk in Bolivia, especially amongst the military, in favour of Argentina's actions. There was also talk of invoking various treaties and possibly going to Argentina's assistance, should it become necessary. Even if Bolivia's military contribution could never be very significant, the gesture would have been important to Argentina and might even have created a domino effect, attracting other nations to support Argentina's cause. Fortunately, apart from much muttering, the moment passed and no other country actually moved to take up arms in support of Argentina. Stanley Duncan said:

> The Argentine invasion of the Falklands was unlikely to have been a surprise to the Bolivian Government when it occurred, given the degree of complicity and co-operation between the two military governments. They were not only very close and probably had few secrets they didn't share, but Argentina was keen to export its nasty, repressive habits to Bolivia. Bolivian military officers also regularly attended courses (e.g. staff college) in Argentina.

The majority of the civilian population, though not caring very much for Argentines, nevertheless did not support Britain's position, especially during the early days of the war. The situation reached a point where the Ambassador was sufficiently concerned to go to the Bolivian Foreign Minister and impress upon him that: 'Britain *will* respond (to the invasion) and there *will* be war and bloodshed, so don't contemplate sending in your young conscripts to help Argentina (to get killed, etc.).' He said his words were not very well received!

He was allowed, however, to talk to the press in order to put the British point of view. This 'view' succeeded in precipitating a bellicose response along the lines of 'we had no intention of getting involved anyway', which, of course, was exactly what he wanted to hear. The situation settled down a bit.

The Bolivians were under a lot of pressure from Argentina, so even when the possibility of Bolivian participation became remote, there was still much pro-Argentine rhetoric from the military, echoed to a lesser extent by the civilian population.

Stanley Duncan arrived in Bolivia to take up his appointment only a month before the Falklands War. Initially, because of the prevailing situation, he found the (military) government difficult to deal with. He said: 'As the war wore on, I found that the military gradually became a bit more flexible. They appointed a civilian Foreign Minister, which was at least one small blessing! However, relations were certainly not normal, and even aid programmes had to be rethought.'

He also expressed the view that the government had little idea how to run an economy. In fairness, it had inherited a difficult situation anyway, which it simply made worse. Eventually, it literally ran out of money and could not pay the miners, or the workers of the other nationalised industries. Its days were clearly numbered.

At the United Nations Security Meeting on 3rd April 1982, Bolivia, possibly influenced by Peru's stance, joined the group of countries that blamed the UK for causing the crisis. During the war, however, despite much talk of South American solidarity, there was little evidence of any real action in support of Argentina.

Stanley Duncan considered that: 'It was always most unlikely that Argentina would have asked for any military equipment, or support in any form, from Bolivia, knowing how impecunious the country was. In any case, Bolivia probably would not have had anything worthwhile to offer.' Not too surprisingly, the presence of a permanent Defence Attaché in La Paz could not be justified. Stanley Duncan had to rely upon the occasional visit from the British Defence Attaché in Lima, Peru – who covered both countries – for much of his military intelligence.

During the Falklands War, the mood in the country, and attitudes generally, were largely dictated by the fact that its military government was close to the military in Argentina. This was partly explained by the fact, as the Ambassador himself said, that: 'Prior to the war, the Argentine military had a big hand in assisting a military coup in order to thwart the result of a democratic election.'

Nevertheless, the few British subjects who were in Bolivia during the war felt no pressure to leave. There was little or no unpleasantness, and there were no reports of anyone being abused or insulted in any way. The Ambassador did say though that 'Britain was temporarily out of favour, and my Queen's Birthday Reception was poorly attended. Hardly any Bolivians turned up, and I was *persona non grata* for a while'.

He recalled, too, that after the British submarine *Conqueror* sunk the Argentine cruiser *Belgrano*, he was summoned to the Ministry of Affairs to receive a letter of protest. He reported back to London afterwards that Bolivia's position had temporarily become more anti-British as a result of the incident. It did not last for long though.

There was also some talk that Argentina had discussed with Peru the possibility of mounting a joint attack on Chile (in the event that Argentina was successful in the Falklands), possibly including Bolivia too. Such an idea may well have been mooted, but if so, happily it came to nought. After the war, most Bolivians would have been relieved that their country had not been caught up in any such scheme to aid Argentina or Peru. If Bolivia had joined such an alliance, and participated in an attack on Chile, perhaps later in 1982, Chile almost certainly would not have offered Bolivia the long sought-after access (albeit limited) to the Pacific coast, which it did later. As it was, in Ambassador Hickman's time (he replaced Stanley Duncan in 1985) Chile did indeed offer Bolivia the corridor of access through to the Pacific coast that it lost back in the nineteenth century. Bolivia may have thought: 'Big deal – it's ours anyway' (diplomatically, of course), but was wise enough not to say so and upset Chile. As a result, Bolivia finally regained freedom of movement through the corridor, although it remains Chilean territory.

There were some other beneficial effects of the Falklands War for the Bolivians. The economic situation in the country had deteriorated to the extent that the military, having seized power in a military coup not long before the war, with Argentina's assistance, handed the government of the country back to civilians after the war. This would never have happened if Argentina had won the war. Argentina's military, being close to and supportive of the Bolivian military, would have tried to keep it in power. Interestingly, ever since 1982 Bolivia has been governed by democratically-elected civilian governments.

Finally, Britain's relations with Bolivia also improved after the Falklands War; the view taken by many grateful Bolivians being that Britain's success in the war had also played a part in helping to return a civilian government to their country.

Colombia

The Spanish started to settle the land that is Colombia today in the early sixteenth century. The first permanent settlement was established in 1525, and Bogota was designated the capital city in 1549.

There then ensued a long struggle for independence before, in 1819, the independent Republic of Gran Colombia was established, and Bolivar was elected as its first president. Gran Colombia was to become the Republic of New Granada, and in 1886 became the Republic of Colombia.

Colombia's history has been marked by violence. The civil unrest and uprisings that followed independence were fuelled by resentment as the poor rebelled against the privileged ruling class. This finally erupted into violence in what became known as The War of The Thousand Days (1897–99).

Although it is not necessary to dwell too much on Colombia's relations with its neighbours, it has, over the years, been through troubled times with Peru and Venezuela. A long border dispute with Peru developed into a full-blown war, The Colombia–Peru War, that was finally resolved in 1934 by the League of Nations, and in Colombia's favour.

The decades that followed brought unrest, assassinations and civil war. The FARC (Revolutionary Armed Forces of Colombia) came into being in 1964, to become the largest and most troublesome of the guerrilla groups. The ELN (National Liberation Army) and EPL (Ejército Popular de Liberación, a group dedicated to Maoist thinking) also arrived on the scene, followed by M-19 (The 19th April Movement). It all added up to years of turbulence, interspersed with acts of violence and internal strife, which continued through 1982 and for years thereafter. Whilst the story is not untypical of South America, what is unusual is that rival civilian groups should again have given way to a country ruled by civilians rather than by the military.

Falklands

The year of 1982 was typically busy for Colombia and it had little to do with the Falklands War, a distraction it could probably have done without. Indeed, some remarked that it hardly had time to notice what Argentina and Britain were up to, so involved was it with its own internal problems.

Shortly after the UN Security Council passed Resolution 502, a gathering of the Rio Treaty nations was convened, against the wishes of the USA. The Treaty was otherwise known as the Inter-American Treaty of Reciprocal Assistance, and had been signed in Rio de Janeiro in 1947. Although Argentine sovereignty over the Falklands was generally recognised at the gathering, some countries, notably Colombia and Chile, abstained. In so doing, Colombia gave Britain some moral support. Doubtless this act of abstention was instrumental in Argentina's decision, on 3rd May, to recall its Ambassador back from Colombia, in what diplomatic sources described as 'a gesture of displeasure at Colombia's lukewarm support'.

The Colombian Government then decided to officially support Argentina's position, although this amounted to little more than words. According to British subjects working in Colombia at the time, it was also not a sentiment shared by the lukewarm and fairly indifferent majority of the Colombian population.

One of the actions taken by the government, by way of wanting to be seen as toughening its stance, was to send a message via the Colombian Ambassador in London cautioning the British Government against attacking mainland Argentina. The message warned that: '... an attack on the (South American) mainland could lead Latin American countries to break off relations with Britain'.

Whilst Colombia was regarded as being reasonably friendly, and therefore unlikely to sever relations with the UK, the British Government was less sanguine where Peru, Venezuela, and perhaps Bolivia were concerned. However, Secretary General of the United Nations, Javier Perez de Cuellar, was assured by the British Permanent Representative, Sir Anthony Parsons, that Britain had no intention of attacking mainland Argentina.

Colombia also joined Venezuela in agreeing to offer economic assistance to Argentina. However, our Ambassador in Bogota in 1982, Sir John Robson, said it was never clear whether this offer ever amounted to anything of any consequence, or even materialised at all.

The British Embassy, Bogota

Sir John said: 'In contrast to most other South American countries, Colombia was relatively pro-British. Most of the population, especially the Andean Colombians, genuinely disliked the Argentines. They were regarded as being tiresome, unpleasant and very arrogant.'

He also described the Embassy's emphasis as having been much more on drug control than defence contracts. This is quite believable, since his Defence Attaché said later: 'During my tour of duty in Colombia, defence sales amounted to some gold braid for naval officers' uniforms, and spare parts for two sets of bagpipes!' He was possibly not one of our more overworked attachés in South America. Sir John also singled out the Colombian Intelligence Service and the navy for special mention as the Embassy had particularly good relationships with both.

The Defence Attaché from 1981–83 was Colonel Hal (Henry) Chavasse. He agreed with Sir John that most of the Colombians he had come across sympathised with the British point of view regarding the Falklands; probably, he said, because they had a similar situation with the island of San Andreas off the Nicaraguan coast (which he was able to see for himself on an attaché tour).

The man-in-the-street certainly did not seem to feel too strongly either way, and Henry Chavasse experienced no difficulties with members of the Colombian armed forces. The Argentine Defence Attaché in Bogota, not too surprisingly, was not very pleasant to him during the war, but they were not permitted to communicate at that time anyway. The Argentine Naval Attaché, Henry said, was the most upset by it all, and was very anti-British. The Colombian armed forces had little to do with the Argentine military. They exchanged attachés but little else; they never exercised together.

No one in the British Embassy, or in the wider British community in Colombia at the time, ever felt threatened, nor could Sir John or Henry Chavasse recall any demonstrations in support of Argentina, or any other unpleasant or intimidating incidents.

The Ambassador attended a social function at the Argentine Embassy in Bogota shortly after the war had ended. He said: 'The Argentine Air Attaché came up to me, shook my hand and said: "These things happen... " I couldn't help smiling!'

In August 1982, power transferred from the Liberal Party of Julio César Turbay to the Conservatives, who had won forty-seven per cent of the popular vote. Belisario Betancur became the new president, and quickly had his hands full dealing with a thriving illegal drug trade, frequent kidnappings, and the tiresome activities of the FARC, ELN and EPL.

Colombia would have been as relieved as most other South American countries were that the Falklands War was conclusively over, and probably quietly grateful that Britain had triumphed. At least the future would now be a little easier to predict, and the government could, once again, concentrate on sorting out its own internal problems.

Ecuador

Ecuador's history in many ways mirrors that of other Latin American countries. What makes it profoundly different, and has been a major factor in shaping the country's policies – and the views of the people – for much of the twentieth century, however, has been its ongoing difficult relationship with neighbouring Peru.

The Spaniards landed in 1526, and practically demolished the Inca Empire during the years that followed. The region was ruled from Lima, Peru until 1739, when control was transferred to the Viceroyalty of Colombia. A middle class emerged which wanted to liberate Ecuador from Spanish rule, and in August 1809 the first self-governing junta in the Spanish colonies in Latin America was established. Independence was declared in October 1820 (led principally by Simon Bolivar) but not finally achieved until May 1822.

Leaping ahead to the twentieth century, when the Treaty of Versailles was signed on 28th June 1919 – between Germany and the 'Principal Allied and Associated Powers' – the representatives of twenty-seven victorious nations signed the document. Ecuador was one of the Associated Powers.

Border skirmishes, and the breakdown of talks in 1938 aimed at resolving long-standing boundary issues between Peru and Ecuador, suggested that further hostilities between the two countries were almost inevitable. Nevertheless, Ecuador appeared unprepared when Peruvian troops invaded parts of the country in July 1941. History also records that most of Ecuador's best troops were, in any case, based in Quito, and remained there to protect the President from his opponents.

Although a shaky ceasefire took place at the end of July, it was not until January 1942, whilst Peruvian troops occupied parts of Ecuador, that agreement was reached to end the conflict. It may have ended that round of hostilities but it did nothing to address the underlying problems, and in the meantime Ecuador had lost territory in the Amazon region to Peru.

During the years following the Second World War, the country had a succession of freely-elected presidents. Then, in 1972, the military took control of the country and the economy grew impressively, thanks largely to oil and massive borrowing. Ecuadorians at all levels prospered.

Predictably, further clashes occurred between Ecuador and Peru. In 1979, Peru attacked again and Ecuador lost more territory in the Amazon region. Peru's armed forces proved to be significantly stronger than those of Ecuador, in terms of both numbers and equipment.

Ecuador in the 1980s

The 1980s were difficult years for Ecuador. In May 1981, President Roldós, his wife, and the Defence Minister were killed in an air crash. He was succeeded by Osvaldo Hurtado, who immediately faced an economic crisis as the petroleum boom faltered, whilst the huge national debt kept growing.

At the time of the Falklands War, Osvaldo Hurtado was a president with other things very much on his mind. The nation's fortunes were declining as petroleum reserves fell sharply, domestic consumption was increasing, GDP was falling, inflation was soaring, and dramatic climate changes were accentuating the nation's problems.

As if all this was not enough, mutual suspicion and dislike between Ecuador and Peru were ongoing problems, with little hope of resolution in prospect. As Peru was recognised as being the principal threat to their nation, it became the driving force behind Ecuador's efforts to maintain well-trained armed forces and equip them with modern weapons and aircraft.

Ecuador's Relations with Britain

Set against these considerations, for many Ecuadorians the Argentine invasion of the Falklands was not of huge significance; probably more of an unwelcome distraction. The government was forced to consider its position in South America and talk of solidarity, but many Ecuadorians kept in mind not only that Argentina and their enemy Peru had a good relationship, but also that Ecuador had no particular quarrel with the British at the time.

Ecuadorians are by nature informal and friendly people. This was the view of most British diplomats and residents who had spent some time in the country. The Defence Attaché (DA), Group Captain Roy Coleman, for example, was able to talk easily, and frequently did, with high-ranking officers – and even with the President himself – who were known for being tolerant and welcoming towards those who visited their country. The DA quoted, as an example, the case of the Sikh community that was growing and thriving at that time, most of whom came from the north of England.

Most of the diplomats, therefore, painted a picture of a country rather backward in some respects; one which had little desire to become involved in any way in the Falklands situation. In any case, a general feeling of loathing for all things Peruvian inclined many towards supporting the British position.

Alan White was Head of Chancery in the British Embassy, and was Chargé d'Affaires until Adrian Buxton arrived just prior to the Falklands War to assume the position of Ambassador. He explained why the Ecuadorian Government's position had been at odds with that of the silent majority: 'The government had never liked Argentina very much – largely because Argentina tended to support the Peruvian point of view whenever the Peruvian/Ecuadorian border became an issue – but on balance, it felt that South American solidarity had to take precedence.'

During the war, there was just the one serious rally outside the Embassy. It was early on and, as the Ministry of Foreign Affairs had warned the Embassy in advance, the Union Jack was taken down to deprive the demonstrators the satisfaction of taking it down and destroying it themselves.

As it had been scheduled for a Sunday afternoon, the Argentine manager of Quito's top football team had used the stadium's loudspeaker system to whip up support for the demonstration after the weekly match was over. Thus, most of the demonstrators that day were football fans and, in the words of one or two of the diplomats, 'were never very threatening.'

A few unpleasant telephone calls were reported, but nothing to create much concern. Occasionally, the Ministry of Foreign Affairs held briefings to warn of forthcoming demonstrations. Normally they were held on Wednesday afternoons when the Embassy was closed anyway, and they were never very well attended. No one recalled any instances of British residents or workers ever being insulted or abused.

Bill Norton was a skilled electrician working on contract in Ecuador at the time. He said: 'I never encountered any hostility. The only act of protest I can recall concerned the bronze statue of a seated Winston Churchill (which was in the same road as the British Embassy). Someone had poured a tin of yellow paint over his head!'

After the Argentine invasion, Embassy staff shredded many classified documents and other sensitive material. There was already an Embassy evacuation plan but it was hurriedly updated. June Coleman, the DA's wife, recalled:

There was some talk initially of maybe having to leave the Embassy and return to the UK, but that all changed. Suddenly, it was never mentioned again. In any case, there were never any serious problems regarding our relations with the Ecuadorians; and there was never any likelihood of Britain breaking off diplomatic relations with Ecuador. Although we did not, the US Embassy took the remote possibility of trouble with the local Ecuadorians very seriously. They suddenly had the latest sophisticated alarms installed in all the diplomats' residences, armed guards all over the place, and so on. We, on the other hand, sent a request to London for money for extra protection, and received enough to buy a few whistles for our night-watchmen!

The Ecuadorian press was not very helpful, and tended to take the Argentine point of view. This was principally because the press releases from London invariably arrived late and, as the press was always anxious to go to print, it carried on with what it had, which was usually the Argentine input. Ambassador Adrian Buxton recalled:

I had to deal with the media, of course. After the invasion, a local TV station wanted me to engage in a sort of debate with the Argentine Chargé. I did not think that was a very good idea; in any case, my indifferent Spanish would have put me at a distinct dis-advantage. I declined the invitation, but agreed to a compromise whereby we each gave independent interviews. The Foreign and Commonwealth Office (FCO) sent out lots of defensive material, and I was glad of the opportunity to air it. The TV station told us in advance the points they would be raising and, with the help of Jaime Bejarano, our Press Attaché, I mugged up what I should say. It seemed to go well.

The TV channels reacted to each development in the war by calling round without notice at the Argentine and British Embassies, seeking comment. The first time it happened, we didn't respond and the channel's news bulletin showed the Argentine Chargé saying something, followed by a shot of the outside of our office, with the newscaster's voice saying: 'The British Embassy has no comment to make.' After that, I made sure that I was always available and a satisfactory routine was established. Jaime would tell me that a TV team had arrived (usually a reporter, a cameraman and one other), and they would then present me with a list of questions. After we had worked out what I would say, we would go downstairs and I would face the camera. The interviewers were polite and respectful, and never tried to spring any surprises on me.

From all accounts, the Ecuadorian Government behaved absolutely correctly. As the FCO always seemed to send its telegrams at the end of the week, so instructions often arrived in Quito on a Saturday morning. Fortunately for the Ambassador, Valencia, the Ecuadorian Foreign Minister, himself an experienced career diplomat, had made it clear that they – either himself or a member of his department – would always be available. He and Senor Valdes, the Secretary General at the Ministry of Foreign Affairs, patiently received Adrian Buxton on many weekends, listened to what he had to say and then quietly gave him the Ecuadorean Government's – i.e. the Argentine – version of events in reply.

Ecuador's Armed Forces

Ecuador did not have too many reasons for needing well-equipped armed forces. Apart from controlling extremist elements and enforcing drugs control, high on the short list was the need to be able to fight its corner effectively whenever one of the infrequent border disputes with Peru flared up. There was also the need to deter these disputes from occurring in the first place.

The two countries shared 1,420 kilometres of border and for a long time, as has already been mentioned, had had an uneasy relationship. The disputes, when they did occur, had much to do with territorial gain and with the copper belts; the things that can make a big difference, and a valuable contribution, to a nation's wealth. Alan White felt that the potential for finding more oil, and in significant quantities, was also a major factor.

Many countries have supplied defence equipment for Ecuador's armed forces over the years, including France, Israel, Germany, Italy, the USA and several other South American nations. Britain has also been successful on occasions. Ecuador bought a British air defence radar system, and the air force has been very satisfied with the British aircraft it has acquired over the years. These have included six Canberra bombers ordered in 1954, twelve Meteor fighter aircraft, Strikemasters and Jaguars, all bought with Peru very much in mind. The Israelis, pushy and ever-present, sold Mirages to Ecuador at about the time Britain sold the Jaguars.

Peter Ginger was a test pilot with British Aircraft Corporation (BAC), Warton (before it was nationalised and became part of a new group, British Aerospace). He recalled delivering the first of Ecuador's Jaguars: 'I took off from Warton on 4th January 1977, and finally landed in Ecuador on 14th January. I was accompanied on that delivery – the first of many – by a two-seater Jaguar. We had many en-route refuelling stops, including Belem and Recife in Brazil.'

Peter also evaluated and tested the Jaguar's on-board Thomson CSF Agave air-to-surface radar. This proved fortuitous, as it was the same radar that was installed in the Super Etendard aircraft flown by the pilots of the Argentine Navy in 1982.

The British Embassy, and the DA in particular, maintained an easy relationship with friends and contacts in the Ecuadorian armed forces, and this persisted throughout the Falklands War. In the curious way in which politics and national relationships inter-relate, this was probably helped by the fact that Ecuador had a good relationship with our one ally, Chile, and was hostile towards Peru which strongly supported Argentina's position. Whatever the subtleties, these relationships had been built up, and were already in place, when the war started.

Other odd events in the past have also registered with the Ecuadorians and helped to shape their view of the British. The Ecuadorian Navy remembers the Royal Navy captain from Stockport, whose frigate went all the way to South America in the nineteenth century and fought in support of the Ecuadorian independence movement. Captain John Illingworth subsequently threw in his lot with the Ecuadorians, stayed in the country, married a local girl, and eventually became an admiral in the Ecuadorian Navy.

In 1979, a group of British university students visiting the country found themselves in difficulty on a volcano, and had to be rescued. The rescue party was led by Captain Louis Hernandez of the Ecuadorian Special Forces. After the successful rescue, the Captain met, and sub-sequently married, the British Ambassador's Personal Assistant. He also later became the Head of Ecuador's Special Forces.

Many Latin Americans, especially those with a military background, have a high regard for Field Marshal Montgomery and his Second World War exploits. In the spring of 1984, when León Febres-Cordero was Ecuador's president-elect and not yet in office, he learned of the forth-coming visit to the country of Lord Montgomery, the Field Marshal's son. He conveyed a message to the Ambassador, suggesting that he would be pleased to receive a visit from him, together with, of course, Lord

Montgomery. This was duly arranged and it fortuitously provided the Ambassador with an opportunity to meet Cordero for the first time. This would otherwise have been ruled out by protocol until after he had been inaugurated.

Febres Cordero was President of Ecuador for four years, from August 1984 to August 1988. He is remembered as a flamboyant character who toted a loaded pistol at all times, chain-smoked, and was kidnapped at one point by commandos of his own air force. They had objected to the arrest of the Air Force Commander who had – possibly with good reason – accused Cordero's government of corruption. The President was released after he agreed to pardon the Commander.

Not only was the late Field Marshal Montgomery widely admired – an almost universal sentiment among right-wing Latin Americans, according to Adrian Buxton – but so also was Prime Minister Margaret Thatcher. He recalled that Febres Cordero had asked him (after the Falklands War) to convey to the Prime Minister that he greatly admired her and all that she had achieved. This was duly included in one of the regular reports to the FCO, but he never heard if the message had been passed on to No 10. This admiration for the PM took an amusing twist during the war. Ecuadorian soldiers started calling their uniform sweaters 'Thatchers', presumably because they gave the wearer a warm feeling.

The DA's job in Ecuador – as in most countries – was partly to assist the defence sales process, and partly about intelligence gathering/espionage. The only espionage he could recall being involved in though was when he was asked by the Chief of the Ecuadorian Army to help him identify potentially difficult elements within his own ranks.

'The other South American attachés,' he said, 'remained friendly enough during the war. The only hostile vibes came from the Argentine Army Attaché, but we weren't allowed to converse anyway. The Argentine Naval Attaché had been to the UK and had apparently found much to admire. I had no difficulty with him.'

Whilst the DA had not heard of any defence equipment, or any other form of assistance, being supplied to Argentina by Ecuador, Alan White said: 'Ecuador may have supplied some thirty-five millimetre artillery ammunition which was known to have been of doubtful age, quality and reliability!' If he was correct, perhaps the Ecuadorians were trying to make some kind of statement. Adrian Buxton, on the other hand, like the DA, was not aware of any requests for help from Argentina, and thought it would have been unlikely.

At the end of May 1982, one of the more reputable British newspapers reported that an Ecuadorian B707 aircraft had been apprehended at New York's Kennedy Airport. It said: 'The aircraft had been carrying Israeli-made bombs, rockets and other armaments... ' This had occurred at a time when it was known that Prime Minister Thatcher had been very concerned that Argentina might be receiving weapons 'not necessarily directly from those countries (i.e. supplying the weapons) but via third parties.'

Although Israel's efforts to help Argentina were known at the time, it has not been possible to establish whether there was any truth in the newspaper's claim that an Ecuadorian B707 was involved. No one who had served in the British Embassy in Quito in 1982 was aware of the flight. The DA, in particular, would (or should) have known if there was any truth in the story.

After the War

After the war ended, the British Government was anxious to repair damaged relations with South American countries. Tristan Garel-Jones (later Baron Garel-Jones) was sent on a tour of Latin American capitals. Having been raised in Spain, and with a smart Spanish wife, he was an ideal choice.

If Ecuador was typical of the other countries he visited, he spoke well during his television interviews and struck a chord with the press. His visit was rated by the British Embassy as having been extremely helpful to Britain and to the post-war image that the government was anxious to portray.

'Within a few months,' Adrian Buxton said, 'British-Ecuadorian relations were as if the Falklands War had never happened. A number of prominent Ecuadorians even made it clear that they were pleased we had won the war.' Alan White added: 'The diplomats in the Argentine Embassy had always been very friendly towards the British diplomats before the war. Afterwards, everything returned quickly to pre-war normality.'

In spite of Ecuador's turbulent, typically South American history and its relationship (or lack of) with its immediate neighbour Peru – and notwithstanding the fact that Peru attacked Ecuador again at the end of the 1980s and also in the 1990s – it is nevertheless considered today to be one of the safest countries to visit in South America.

Paraguay

Paraguay's borders today have been defined during centuries of war, suffering and bloodshed. It has had to cede territory to neighbours after wars lost, and at one point in its turbulent history, came perilously close to not surviving at all as a nation in its own right.

The first Spaniards arrived and settled in the sixteenth century. The conquest and subsequent colonisation produced a mixed population, invariably inheriting the language of the mothers and the culture of the fathers.

Independence was declared in 1811, and was followed by an endless succession of brutal, autocratic governments. Two wars in particular played a significant part in the development of the country; the War of the Triple Alliance (1865–70), and the war against Bolivia sixty to seventy years later.

The War of the Triple Alliance was long and brutal. Paraguay fought against an alliance of Argentine, Brazilian and Uruguayan forces. It ended in a bloody defeat for Paraguay, and cost it dearly in terms of lives and territory lost. This has been estimated as roughly half the male population at the time, and about one-third of its territory. Only after the Argentine and Brazilian troops finally left the country in 1876 was Paraguay able to set about developing the two-party political system that has prevailed over the years.

The Twentieth Century

Between 1932–35, Paraguay fought Bolivia to retain possession of its Chaco region. It was a war that Paraguay won against all the odds and was, again, hugely expensive in terms of lives lost (on both sides); but this time, Paraguay actually gained some territory.

During the Second World War, President Morínigo, despite the efforts of the USA, steadfastly refused to act against Germany's interests. German agents infiltrated into Paraguay and were initially successful in keeping it 'on side' with Germany.

In 1942, however, things began to change and the President, always under pressure from the USA, committed himself to the Allied cause, although he was careful not to declare war on Germany officially until February 1945. Throughout the war, though, many in the Paraguayan military were openly pro-German.

When the war ended, a sizeable element in the country continued to be sympathetic towards the Germans, and it is well known that Paraguay became a refuge – a safe-haven – for ex-Nazis. Decades later, there is a large German population in the country, and many more who are of joint German/Paraguayan descent.

The post-war period was marked by human rights abuses, and allegations of corruption and torture. During this period, Paraguay took a step closer to Brazil. Also, following a succession of dictatorships, General Alfredo Stroessner overthrew the government of the day in 1954 and assumed the presidency.

In 1973, Brazil and Paraguay started co-operating on the construction of the massive Itaipu Dam on the River Parana, today one of the largest hydroelectric dams in the world. The treaty signed in that year by the military governments that ruled the two countries certainly favoured Brazilian interests – but this was rectified by Brazil's President Lula many years later.

In the meantime, the dam project provided employment for thousands of Paraguayans who had never before known what it was like to have a regular job. It created a mini-economic boom and Paraguay's GDP briefly grew as never before; for a time, faster than the GDPs of most other South American countries.

Paraguay had, for a considerable time, been one of only two landlocked countries in South America. Once, it had been the only one, until Bolivia lost its access to the Pacific Ocean following a war with Chile (a situation now partially rectified).

With a population of less than 7 million, it has also been one of the poorest nations in South America. Slow social and economic progress and a huge gap between the rich and the poor – of which there are many – have largely been to blame. In recent decades, modest progress in modernisation and stability has been accompanied by extensive human rights abuses and much corruption.

The country boasts little in the way of mineral or natural resources, apart from timber, iron ore, manganese and hydroelectric power (i.e. Itaipu). The main economic activities are agriculture and cattle-ranching, and it exports beef. As many people have already commented, Paraguay would probably fare quite well in the event of a global food crisis.

Foreign ownership of land is permitted in Paraguay. However, for a long time this excluded nationals of Brazil, Argentina and Bolivia, suggesting that a degree of mistrust still lingered on.

Relations with Argentina

As Paraguay grew steadily closer to Brazil, its relationship with Argentina, never particularly strong (and a hangover from past confrontations), declined.

Stanley Duncan, our Ambassador in Bolivia at the time of the Falklands War, later expressed the view that: 'Paraguay has always been in fear of Argentine intentions towards her. No one who attended an important football match in Asuncion in April 1982, when the recapture of South Georgia by British armed forces was announced on the loud speakers, could easily forget the spontaneous jubilation of the crowd.'

When Argentina invaded the Falkland Islands in 1982, most Paraguayans with any knowledge of the history of their own country would have recalled that the last time Argentina went to war, it was against them. In fact, ever since the War of the Triple Alliance in the nineteenth century, Paraguay's relations with Argentina have at best been uneasy; at worst, poor. No country can easily forget having lost a large part of its territory to a near neighbour in war, and Paraguay ceded approximately one-third of its territory to Argentina (and Brazil) at that time.

Derrick Mellor was our Ambassador in Paraguay during the Falklands War. He summed up the mood in the country after the Argentine invasion:

There was no love lost between Paraguay and its neighbour. Although, in the usual way, public pronouncements had to be carefully constructed to suggest a degree of South American solidarity, in fact the nation's sympathy was generally with the British.

However, the man-in-the-street was not quite so inhibited, and he made it clear that many Paraguayans wanted Argentina to get a bloody nose. In fact, queues of them formed outside the British Embassy, hoping to 'join-up', to fight with us against Argentina.

This degree of naivety was quite amazing and, if Britain had won the war with Paraguay's assistance, it might then have expected Britain – by way of a big 'thank you' – to help it recover some of the territory lost to Argentina over a century earlier. Almost certainly, that is something Britain would not have been prepared to do. Generally, Embassy staff found that most Paraguayans were genuinely hostile towards Argentina, but tended nevertheless to say the right thing in public.

One of Paraguay's problems was that its friends were a bit thin on the ground. The wars it fought in the nineteenth and twentieth centuries had embraced Argentina, Brazil, Uruguay and Bolivia. Many of its citizens knew their history and would not have forgotten that, apart from the territory lost, Paraguay had also lost a huge percentage of its male population during these wars.

Regardless of all these bitter memories, in 1982 the Paraguayan Government felt obliged to line itself up alongside its South American neighbours and, officially anyway, blame Britain for 'the current situation', when the UN Security Council Resolution ('condemning Argentina's military occupation of the islands and demanding an immediate withdrawal of Argentine troops') was debated and passed on 3rd April.

As far as offering practical help – to either side – Paraguay did not do much, nor did it want to do much. Derrick Mellor said that the government would have been approached by Argentina, as it was 'shopping-around' at the time, but he thought it unlikely that Paraguay would have had anything of interest to offer.

Once, near the end of the war, three Mirage fighter aircraft that had been donated by Peru passed through Paraguay en route to Rio Gallegos in Argentina. It was nothing more than a refuelling stop. 'President Stroessner,' Derrick Mellor said, 'had wanted to delay them or impound them, but in the end was persuaded to let them proceed on their way.'

The British Embassy

Derrick Mellor had to appear on television from time to time, and both he and his Argentine opposite number were given these opportunities in order to inform the Paraguayan population what was going on, and to put their own government's point of view. However, whilst the Argentine Ambassador was unashamedly pushing out totally inaccurate anti-British propaganda – and telling the Paraguayans how well Argentina was doing – Derrick Mellor had his work cut out telling the same audience that 'it was all nonsense, and the British were doing very well really!' He simply had not been given the facts. He and his staff were most unimpressed with the MoD briefings they received on the progress of the war, and felt strongly that London never gave them adequate briefing material to use as and when they felt fit.

There were about 400 British nationals in Paraguay at the time of the Falklands War. None of them reported any incidents of abuse to the

Embassy, or any other form of anti-British sentiment or insulting behaviour.

When Britain finally won the war, the Paraguayans were 'very impressed', said Derrick Mellor, 'and their desire to have more contact with the British defence industry soon became evident.' As a consequence, a number of British firms became more active in Paraguay, and some were even moderately successful during his remaining time in the country. He never had any military attachés on his staff (they could not be justified in Paraguay); he had to rely on occasional visits from attachés attached to British Embassies elsewhere to assist his staff identify defence equipment procurement opportunities.

He recalled that Major General Jeremy Moore had visited Asuncion shortly after he retired from the Royal Marines. It was a defence procurement-orientated visit, and it achieved some positive results. Another 'spin-off' from the war was that Balfour Beatty was successful at the expense of Siemens (for electrical power generation). Paraguay had previously always dealt with the German company.

On the negative side, about the only thing that Derrick Mellor could recall was that the Argentine Ambassador, who had been a good friend of his prior to the war, cut him dead afterwards and did not want to know him. He was a retired Argentine Army general, which no doubt accounted for his disappointment and unforgiving attitude.

Paraguay neither helped us, nor did it hinder us, for which we were most grateful. President Stroessner was finally overthrown in a military coup on 3rd February 1989, having been the longest-serving president in Paraguayan history.

Peru

Peru is perhaps best known for having once been the home of the Inca Empire. When the Spaniards arrived, lured as always by the promise of gold and silver, Cuzco was at the heart of this empire. It extended north to include what is Ecuador today.

The Spaniards set about conquering the country and it became part of a wider viceroyalty in 1542. After Cuzco fell, the whole Inca Empire was ripped apart by the Spanish with unsparing greed and savagery. Although some Inca elements offered token resistance, it proved futile, and Spanish domination was inevitable. It was symbolised by the construction of a new capital city, Lima, at the heart of the viceroyalty. Independence was gained in 1821, but was only firmly established three years later.

The War of the Pacific (1879–84) was a crucial episode in the history of Peru. Peru, in alliance with Bolivia, fought Chile. Peruvian cities were plundered and territory was lost to Chile. The scars have remained to this day.

Much later, in 1941, Peru fought Ecuador. Since then, intermittently, there have been border skirmishes that have at times spilled over into bloody conflict. Within the wider context of South America, it is Peru's relations with Chile and Ecuador that, over the years, have caused its citizens the most grief, whilst providing the main justification for the country to maintain well-equipped and well-trained armed forces.

The military have been prominent throughout Peruvian history, and the post-Second World War years have been no different. Military coups have been interspersed with periods of civilian constitutional government. Interestingly, in the Second World War, Peru was the first South American nation to declare its support for Britain and her allies.

President Belaúnde Terry

Fernando Belaúnde Terry first came into prominence in the 1950s. He served his first term as president from 1963–68, before being ousted by General Juan Velasco Alvarado. He returned to serve a second term in 1980, when he convincingly took forty-five per cent of the popular vote. He then set about reopening closed-down newspapers, encouraging freedom of speech again, and trying to improve and strengthen relations with the USA.

President Belaúnde was, therefore, the incumbent in 1982 and throughout the Falklands War. He will be remembered for having taken a prominent part in the search for a peaceful settlement to end the war. Although he is on record as having stated, early on in the proceedings, that: 'Peru is ready to support Argentina, and recognises Argentina's sovereignty over the Falklands', later on, when it became clear that Britain was responding to the invasion and that war was inevitable, he became genuinely concerned about the possible repercussions across South America.

Jimmy Burns, the *Financial Times* correspondent, said: 'Throughout the war, the Peruvian military – particularly the air force – favoured sending more military aid to Argentina, but were restrained by President Belaúnde, who believed that a diplomatic solution was not only preferable, but possible.' He had not wanted to muddy the waters as long as diplomacy might bring peace.

President Belaúnde also knew that, whilst some South American countries coexisted in reasonable harmony, some of the relationships – the legacy of past conflicts and disputes – were fragile to say the least. He had the vision to appreciate that an Argentine victory could bring with it unforeseen consequences, which had the potential to seriously damage the health of South American unity.

The Peruvian peace proposal, unfortunately, was perceived by the Argentine Government as having American fingerprints all over it. Argentina was not enthusiastic about supporting any plan involving the USA, which was seen as being supportive of the British position.

Nevertheless, the proposal was still taken seriously by a few at the Argentine foreign ministry in Buenos Aires – and Foreign Minister Costa Mendez was said to have been enthusiastic – until, that is, Argentina learned that the Royal Navy had sunk the *Belgrano*.

President Belaúnde continued with his attempts to interest the two warring nations in a peace proposal, but a point was soon reached when it would not have been in Britain's interest anyway.

The British Embassy in Lima

Charles Wallace was the British Ambassador in Lima during the war. He and the Argentine Ambassador in Peru had been good friends. He recalled that there had been a few demonstrations during the war, but nothing of any great consequence. One or two small explosive devices had been thrown at the gates of the British Residence, and also near the office of the British Council.

His view was that most Peruvians had perceived our presence in the Falklands as an act of colonialism, and that was something that would have been considered unacceptable to most of them. He also felt that the close relationship between the Argentine and Peruvian armies – a powerful factor in Peru during the Falklands War – was in part due to the fact that the respective Commanders-in-Chief were long-standing friends. They had been on the same course at the military academy. As he said: 'In South America, that sort of thing matters very much!' He added: 'The Peruvian Minister of War would also have done anything for Galtieri.'

Charles Wallace was regarded as being an excellent communicator, and this clearly helped the British cause. Some of the Peruvian newspapers favoured the Argentine position, but the Ambassador was well able to fight the British corner. He had been raised in Spain and spoke excellent Porteno Spanish – better, in fact, said Jeremy Thorp, the Head of Chancery, than the Argentine Ambassador – and he performed well during radio interviews. With his perfect local accent, he successfully conveyed the impression that he was 'one of them'.

Jeremy Thorp (who was later to become the British Ambassador in Colombia) offered an interesting perspective on President Belaúnde Terry which, at the same time, helped to explain Peru's stance in 1982 and the President's relationship with his own military. He said:

Most of the population, if asked, would have taken the Argentine point of view – except for the indigenous element which would not have been too bothered either way – but few would have felt so strongly as to insult a British subject. Peru's history of occasional civilian government, interspersed with coups followed by a spell of military rule, was an important factor in determining President Belaúnde's handling of Peru's response to the Argentine invasion.

Belaúnde was always very wary of his own armed forces. He was, after all, the first civilian president after twelve years of military rule. His armed forces pushed hard for Peru to support their Argentine colleagues. They were not naturally anti-British but, in the first instance, would have instinctively wanted to support the Argentine cause, even if not the method chosen by Argentina to achieve the end result. So, whilst the President was pursuing his efforts to help achieve a peaceful solution to the Falklands War, he was, all the time, mindful of the views of the military, and took them into account. He had also chosen a government almost totally composed of civilians, which was another reason for treading carefully.

Regarding the possibility of Peru taking advantage of an Argentine victory (if it happened) and then forming an alliance with Argentina to attack Chile, Jeremy Thorp thought that President Belaúnde would probably have tried to resist such an idea, but he conceded that pressure from the armed forces might have made that difficult for him.

It was highly likely though that the possibility of forming such an alliance would have been discussed between Argentine and Peruvian officers at a high level. Such an idea would have appealed to those Peruvians with long memories and a flair for history (i.e. most officers serving in the armed forces), who would have remembered that, many years earlier, Chile had launched a land-grab and seized a chunk of Peru that was rich in nitrates.

Although the British Embassy in Lima did not have an SIS representative – and, as Jeremy Thorp said: '... left that side of things to their American friends' – it did have a Defence Attaché. Nevertheless, Jeremy Thorp was the only diplomat able to recall that the Peruvians had despatched a squadron of Mirage 5 fighter aircraft to Argentina. This seems to have been the only significant military contribution made by Peru and, as the ten aircraft did not arrive in Argentina until just before the Argentine surrender, they took no part in the war anyway. Denis Doble – who preceded Jeremy Thorp as Head of Chancery – thought it was not impossible that President Belaúnde may have been unaware that the Mirages had been sent, i.e. that the military had acted without consulting the government. Jeremy Thorp agreed, and said: 'Supplying Argentina with military aircraft could have been a purely military decision, and the President might (or might not) have been informed.'

President Belaúnde's reluctance to send any military hardware to Argentina probably helped to ensure that nothing worthwhile was sent at an earlier stage, and if he finally conceded in respect of the Mirage aircraft, it was probably only to appease the military, when he thought the game was almost up for Argentina anyway.

Everyone was emphatic about one thing – Peru did not send any Exocet missiles down to Argentina. It is also quite possible that the attempt to acquire four Exocet missiles from the French during the war was inspired solely by the military, and at a very senior level, without the knowledge or sanction of any of the civilian members of the Peruvian Government. It is equally possible that, if they had been delivered, Peru would have retained them, since they acquired the missile anyway in August 1982 for their own use.

Kit Marshall worked for the Latin-American Corporation in Peru. In

1982, he had already been in the country for twenty years and knew Peru and its people well. He said: 'Peru was certainly very pro-Argentina. The vast majority of the population probably would not have understood what the Falklands War was all about, or the rights and wrongs of it, and neither would they have cared. They would have been favouring Argentina anyway. Having said that, I do not recall any unpleasantness, abuse, or strong anti-British sentiment.'

Denis Doble said that they were always ready to evacuate the Embassy at short notice, and for the possibility that the Ambassador might be sent back, or recalled, to Britain. Fortunately, neither eventuality occurred. In fact, apart from Anthony Williams in Argentina, no British Ambassador in South America was expelled or recalled to the UK during the Falklands War. Denis Doble generally endorsed Jeremy Thorp's view of events, but added: 'The sinking of the *Belgrano* did precipitate a rash of hostile calls. That particular episode upset a great number of people. The Ambassador also received a few rather offensive notes because of it.'

The *Belgrano* episode aroused strong feelings in most South American countries. It temporarily heightened the anti-British feeling considerably. The other single most sensitive subject was the perceived possibility that Britain might launch an attack against mainland Argentina; something that no South American country would have tolerated.

Captain Malcolm Carver was the Defence Attaché in Lima at the time. He endorsed Kit Marshall's view that the country had been strongly pro-Argentina, but added: '... especially all the armed forces'. Kit had felt that the Peruvian Navy had taken a softer line.

It seems clear that the British community was not ostracised or subjected to any serious abuse. There were inevitably instances of rudeness, and a few insults were hurled at British subjects. On balance though, there was little to cause any serious concern and at social gatherings everyone, especially Peruvians, preferred not to discuss the subject of the war at all.

The DA was also of the opinion that a strong case for having a defence attaché in Peru had not been made. He said: 'There wasn't any worthwhile intelligence around' – an interesting comment for an attaché to make, especially at that time – 'and there weren't any defence sales prospects because the Peruvians didn't have any money to spend.'

He said that during the war, he had done what he could to correct biased, inaccurate news reporting of the Falklands War, and to try and present the British point of view. Copies of *BBC News* items were distributed to influential people, e.g. Peruvian generals, the aim always being to demonstrate that Britain was being totally open and truthful about the ongoing Falklands situation, and its own position.

One day, he received a communication from the MoD that an Argentine freighter would be calling in en route to Argentina, possibly with Exocet missiles on board. He was ordered to investigate. He said:

> I went down to the quay with my RAF Sergeant PA and we managed to take a few meaningless photographs of some unmarked wooden crates. We thought we had better leave the area then as some uniformed guards were beginning to take an interest in us. As we were trying to beat a hasty retreat, our Embassy car stuck in first gear, and we had to depart at high revs and making a terrible noise. It was most embarrassing!

Whether this so-called 'investigation' was a misunderstanding, arising from the attempt to send Exocet missiles to Peru – possibly for onward movement to Argentina – is not clear. In fact, as we know now, that attempt was thwarted at an early stage.

As was mentioned earlier, Peru had ordered four Exocet missiles of the AM39 anti-ship variety – the same missile that had already been acquired by Argentina – and they were reported to be scheduled to leave St Nazaire, France, by sea on or around 12th May. Britain had always been concerned that the Peruvians' intention might have been to pass the missiles on to Argentina, and was even more suspicious when Peru asked if the delivery could be hastened.

Initially, the French had been unwilling to cancel the delivery. They were under contract, and concerned about penalty clauses and the company's credibility. However, a few words from Prime Minister Margaret Thatcher to President Mitterrand – followed no doubt by a further few words from him to his brother, who headed the French company Aerospatiale – and the ship, which by then had already departed, turned round and returned to St Nazaire.

In the meantime, just in case high-level diplomacy didn't do the trick, one of No 47 SF Flight's C130 crews had been alerted and ordered to plan for an insertion of Special Forces; either SAS or, more logically, men from the SPAG (Submarine Parachute Assistance Group). It was made clear that it was to deal with an Exocet threat, and that time was pressing. A single C130 aircraft would have been involved.

Fortunately, high-level diplomacy had prevailed in this instance, but, although it is certain that the order to cancel the missile shipment came

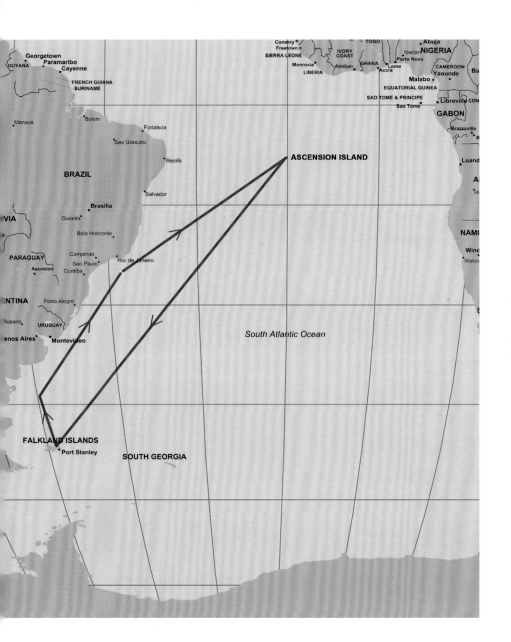

ack Buck (Vulcan) Mission Profile.

Top: Vulcan XM597 at Rio International Airport after diverting in with a broken refuelling probe.

Below: Vulcan XM597 photographed from outside the airfield perimeter fence, with Rio's Sugar Loaf Mountain behind.

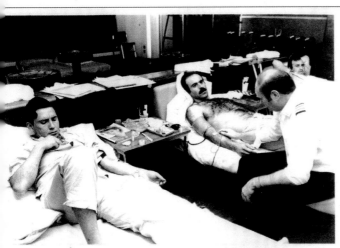

ARGENTINIAN PRISONERS ON CANBERRA WHO HAVING RECOVERED FROM THEIR INITIAL INJURIES VOLUNTEER TO GIVE BLOOD TO HELP OTHER CASUALTIES. PIX: — FLETCHER. (MOD) CNB/LN 028

p: Senior Brazilian air force officers join the Vulcan crew and myself to toast Her *Majesty the Queen on the occasion of her Official Birthday, just before the Vulcan *departed from Rio de Janeiro.

low: Argentine casualties on board *Canberra*; some willingly offered their blood to *help others. The man receiving attention is Lt Brown, Special Forces, whose grandfather *served in the Royal Navy.

Top: A typical day on Ascension Island during the war. Harriers, Victor and Nimrod aircraft can be seen.

Below: The airfield at Stanley after the surrender, showing tented accommodation, a Harrier and damaged Argentine Pucara aircraft.

Top: A bleak Falklands scene just after the war. The aircraft are damaged Argentine ucaras.

Below: Clearing up in Stanley after the surrender and collecting weapons left behind y the Argentine soldiers. Twenty Argentine paras were accommodated in the Jubilee Varehouse (centre) before being repatriated.

Left: Senior RAF Officer (SRAFO) Gp Captain Bill Wratten briefs newly-appointed Commander British Forces Falkland Islands, Maj-Gen David Thorne, on the verandah of Stanley's air traffic control, shortly after the war.

Below: Max Roberts (third from left) with his crew, celebrating 5,000 flying hours on the C130 aircraft after a later airbridge mission to the Falklands.

Left: Lt Colonel Guy Sheridan RM on board HMS *Edinburgh* during the visit to South Georgia in April 2002 to mark the 25th anniversary of the Argentine surrender there. Sheridan Peak is visible behind him.

Below: Dr Peter Mayner, Senior Surgeon on SS *Canberra*, revisiting the Falklands in 2002.

Top: The Sheridan Peak stamp issued, together with three others, to commemorate the 25th anniversary of the liberation of South Georgia.

Left: Brigadier General Sergio Fernandez who retired from the Argentine Army in December 2009.

Below: Argentine Air Force Pucara ground-attack aircraft, brought to England, refurbished and now in the museum at RAF Cosford.

from the highest level in France, it seems that no one in the British Embassy in Lima was advised of the cancellation. A Ministry of Defence intelligence expert added a final word on the subject:

> The whole business of these Exocet missiles going by sea to Peru was exercised at an SIS meeting. A plan was put together to get hold of the missiles so they could be 'doctored'. They would then be sent off to Peru and, if sent on to Argentina, would not work properly, or perhaps explode prematurely. Unfortunately, the ship had departed from St Nazaire before we could get our hands on them. The ship was then recalled but for some reason – which was never properly explained – was not permitted to leave again.

The fact that the ship was recalled can be explained by President Mitterrand's timely intervention at the behest of the British Prime Minister, which also explains why the Special Forces were not, in the end, required. There were a few twists and turns in this story, but the bottom line was that Peru did not receive the missiles possibly intended to 'top-up' Argentina's depleted supply.

Many stories have surfaced about what weapons, or other military supplies, Argentina did or did not receive from Peru. Jon Snow, when he was down in Punta Arenas (in Chile) with his ITN crew, was taken one night – by his Chilean Navy contact – to a nearby Communications Centre and 'listening post' used to monitor Argentine radio transmissions. It was there, he said, that he learned of 'Peruvian air force transport aircraft taking military supplies to Argentina'. No one in the British Embassy in Lima in 1982, however, including the DA, was aware of any such flights having taken place.

After the War

After the war ended, many Peruvians took the view that it was fortunate Britain had won it. It became clear that an Argentine victory could only have led to further unrest, and possibly even serious conflict, in South America.

The DA recalled attending a staff college exercise during his time in Peru. Inevitably, it envisaged an alliance of Peruvian and Argentine forces fighting a war against Chile. There was clearly no love lost there. Hopefully now such an unpleasant and unwanted (by Peruvians and

Chileans alike) scenario will not be enacted in the foreseeable future. In the worst-case scenario, Argentina, Peru, Chile and Bolivia could all have been drawn into the war that South America had dreaded for a long time.

Kit Marshall also agreed that a follow-on war could have erupted if Argentina had been successful. 'Peru's relations with both Chile and Ecuador were poor,' he said. 'In the case of Ecuador, it had much to do with copper mines, and the potential wealth they offered to the country that controlled the territory. Ecuador might also have taken the opportunity and allied itself with Chile.' At one point during the war, Argentina did discuss with the Peruvian Government the possibility of mounting a joint attack on Chile (i.e. at some point in the future).

One can only imagine the various possible scenarios if Argentina had won the Falklands War. Fortunately, it did not happen, but one thing Kit Marshall – and everyone else who had an opinion on the subject – were quite clear about was that, if Britain had ever upped the stakes and attacked mainland Argentina, Peru would have broken off diplomatic relations with Britain, the level of support for Argentina would have greatly increased, the population would have become more vociferously anti-British, and the wounds would have taken longer to heal.

As things were though, one could charitably sum up the feelings of most Peruvians by saying that their support for Argentina – perhaps understandably – was stronger than their hostility towards Britain. Nevertheless, it would not have been a good idea for No 39 Squadron's Canberras to have ventured into Peruvian airspace on their way south to Chile (referred to in Part 2).

Peru seems to have been another country in which the British Embassy had not been too impressed by the MoD briefings, or by the paucity of useful briefing material from London. Fortunately, Ambassador Wallace's fluent and convincing performances in defence of Britain's position were more than adequate.

After the war, Charles Wallace was recalled to the UK, to appear before a House of Commons Committee and explain why he had not conveyed details of the Peruvian Peace Plan back to London that, it was suggested, just might have avoided the *Belgrano* incident. However, when he explained that he had only learned of the peace plan on his car radio, and had not been involved, or 'in the loop' – and could not therefore have known about it any earlier – he was found not to have been culpable in any way.

Shortly after the end of the Falklands War, the Amazon Foundation was set up in Peru to provide a medical service for eleven villages on the

River Apurimac that lacked such facilities. With British and Peruvian Government backing, and financed by the foundation with British Government help, a Joint Services Expedition, led by Sqn Ldr Mike Cole, took four hovercraft to Peru. They were in the country for about six months, during which time Mike Cole and two RAF pilots (Dick Bell and Peter Dixon) set up the service and trained Peruvian pilots. The hovercraft operated for about two years before, sadly, the service was discontinued owing to the Shining Path terrorist threat.

Anglo-Peruvian relations were on the mend!

Venezuela

Venezuela was first colonised by Spain in 1522. In 1811, it became the first Spanish colony to declare independence, although this was not securely established until ten years later. Events in Europe played a part in this process, as the Napoleonic Wars sapped Spanish imperial power and authority overseas.

Relevant only because it remains an issue to this day – and has been the cause of a long-running dispute between Venezuela and Britain – is the thorny question of Guyana, previously known as British Guiana. It was once composed of three Dutch colonies, which were ceded to Britain in 1814. In 1831, the single British colony became known as British Guiana. When Venezuela achieved its own independence in 1824, it claimed territory to the west of the Essequibo River. In 1899, an international tribunal sat – but without a Venezuelan representative present – and ruled that the disputed territory was rightfully British.

British Guiana achieved independence in May 1966 and became The Republic of Guyana in February 1970. Today, it is larger than Uruguay and Suriname, and is one of only four non Spanish-speaking countries in South America. Throughout its history, Venezuela has maintained its claim over that part of the territory in dispute, and even has it marked on its maps as the 'Reclamation Zone'.

During the years before independence, it was a constant thorn in the side of Venezuelan/British relations. Although no longer British, the territory remains in dispute, and is doubtless remembered by many Venezuelans as having once been British. This was the situation in 1982.

During the 1940s and 1950s, Venezuela strengthened its ties with Peru. Young Venezuelan army officers trained at the Peruvian Military Academy. The views of these young officers, many destined for promotion to the higher echelons, were considerably influenced by this. In true South American fashion, Venezuela chose its friends from amongst those countries that were not immediate neighbours. Venezuela's relationship with Colombia can be compared with Peru's relationship with Ecuador.

The twentieth century was significant for the discovery of oil in large quantities in Venezuela. The oil boom started in 1918 and, by 1929, Venezuela was one of the world's leading oil exporters. The 1973 oil crisis was hugely beneficial to the country, and when oil prices rose dramatically from $3US per barrel to $39US per barrel, Venezuela could fairly have been described as comfortably wealthy. The oil industry, which today forms the basis of the nation's economy, was nationalised in 1976.

Another significant development during the twentieth century has been

271

the steady growth and strengthening of the anti-USA sentiment. It first became noticeable in the 1950s and some will still remember the riots that accompanied Vice-President Richard Nixon's visit to Venezuela in May 1958. When Fidel Castro arrived on the scene in Havana in the late 1950s, his vociferous brand of anti-Americanism was an inspiration to many Venezuelans.

For most of the century, Venezuela's has been a not-untypical South American story. Democratic rule has ebbed and flowed. There have been coups that have failed, and a president who was impeached.

Hugh Carless was head of the Latin American desk at the FCO in the mid-1970s, and the British Ambassador in Venezuela just after the Falklands War. He recalled that when he was at the FCO, the policy was to try and solve some of the ongoing problems Britain was experiencing with certain South American countries, and, in particular, to try and improve relations with Mexico, Brazil, Argentina and Venezuela. 'We made a big effort with Venezuela at the time, and just when the petro-dollars were pouring in,' he said.

In 1979, Luis Herrera Campins won the presidency and started his five-year term. He was therefore the man at Venezuela's helm when Argentina invaded the Falkland Islands in 1982.

Venezuela's Support for Argentina

President Herrera's policy – received enthusiastically by the military – was to back Argentina's claim to sovereignty of the islands. Venezuela joined Peru, Brazil and Paraguay in supporting Argentina at the United Nations Security Council Meeting on 3rd April when, at the UK's request, the council debated and passed the resolution condemning Argentina's military occupation of the islands.

When the Argentine invasion took place, Britain had many thousands of its citizens scattered all over South America; there were embassies in 13 capitals and 136 diplomats in post. As there was a real risk of demonstrations, and possibly violence in some countries, all Britain's embassies were instructed by the FCO to prepare for such eventualities.

Demonstrations took place in Venezuela at an early stage, to indicate the nation's approval of Argentina's action and to condemn Britain. The Venezuelan Government, actively pro-Argentina, initially called for a withdrawal of Latin-American Ambassadors from London. It was unsuccessful.

Douglas Webster was the Regional Finance Adviser for Shell Venezuela SA in 1982. Shell had its Regional Centre in Venezuela, which had responsibility for the company's activities in most of the Spanish-speaking countries in South America. Shell was in the country to help the Venezuelans develop their own oil industry, which had been nationalised many years before. He said:

We had no prior warning at all of the Falklands invasion. Sadly, we witnessed a mood of jubilation all round us when the population learned what had happened. It was quite clear that everyone wanted to see Argentina give Britain a bloody nose. We had always found the Venezuelan people difficult to relate to and, unlike in other South American countries, we never socialised with them; only with the small number of like-minded British who were there. There was not much in the way of an Anglo-Venezuelan community anyway.

During the war, we all felt very uneasy about our personal safety. Our children were 'shoved around' and my wife was spat on whilst shopping. My car was vandalised. The house where we lived effectively became a barricaded cage. The press was very anti-British; it exaggerated everything, and constantly fed the people with false information (as in Argentina).

Captain Mike Southgate was the Defence Attaché in Caracas during the war. His version of events differed slightly. He did not think the government's hard anti-British line was translated into too much in the way of abuse or threats. He said:

I did receive three threatening phone calls to the house, which was worrying for my wife. However, the house was built like a fortress and we had guards.

There were many demonstrations and public displays in support of the Argentine position. On one occasion the crowd headed for the British Embassy; however, the organisers (if there were any) had not appreciated that the location of the Embassy had changed a year before; and the demonstrators eventually discovered that their shouted abuse had been falling upon non-existent ears.

We undoubtedly lost the propaganda war. From data received and from listening to World Briefing, the Embassy produced a daily news sheet which was circulated as widely as possible. In spite of these efforts, Venezuelans were persuaded that Argentina was winning the war. They frankly did not believe our news sheet.

Venezuela had a strong president then. Although he did not wish to be seen being too friendly to the USA, the situation was better then than it became years later under Hugo Chaves. It was always very difficult for attachés to make useful contacts in Venezuela. Even on official attachés visits, we were always carefully monitored.

We were all rather surprised not to have been ordered out of the country. The Ambassador ordered the destruction of documents just in case... With hindsight, many felt this might have been an over-reaction.

With regard to the stance taken by the Venezuelan armed forces, and how the war affected them, Mike Southgate said:

The air force had great difficulty getting spare parts for their aircraft and did not get enough flying. Its fleet of Mirage aircraft were mostly unserviceable. The navy was happy enough; they had their new frigates. The army were the most difficult to get along with. They were particularly arrogant, and it was hard to find anyone who spoke any English.

The Venezuelan Navy was in the process of taking delivery of two German-built diesel submarines. They were actually en route to South America in April 1982, and almost crossed the path of the Task Force as it steamed south. A US Navy officer on an exchange posting was working in the Navy's Operations Room and he kindly kept us informed of their progress, just in case they were tempted to become involved in any way!

It was uncharacteristically unprofessional and inefficient on the part of the Venezuelan Navy not to have foreseen the help that the American officer could give our Defence Attaché, and have him removed from the Operations Room for the duration of the submarine's passage (or indeed, for the duration of the war).

Mike Southgate also commented on the Venezuelan Intelligence Services, which he clearly did not rate very highly; and gave his opinion of the Israeli Attaché in Caracas, which was remarkably similar to that of attachés in other South American countries who found themselves constantly falling over Israeli attachés.

Repercussions

Most British subjects who have lived and worked in Venezuela in recent decades share similar views of the country and its people. Those who were in the country during the Falklands War were rarely comfortable. Feelings ran high amongst the Venezuelans – more so than in most of the other South American countries – and the anti-British sentiment intensified during the war.

Sir Reginald Secondé was the British Ambassador in Caracas from 1979 to 1982. He said:

> Venezuela was very pro-Argentina throughout the war. I thought I might be withdrawn from there as well at one point (he was withdrawn from Chile, where he was Ambassador in the 1970s, after the Sheila Cassidy affair). Our relations with the Venezuelans became very poor for a while.

> There were of course the demonstrations and marches as well. For a while, life became rather disagreeable for those of us in the Embassy; but at least no one was hurt. We were regarded by many, I think, as being the wicked imperialist state trying to bully an underdog!

> Venezuela at the time was a run-down country. Although it had oil, it was not particularly wealthy in the 1980s, due mainly to mismanagement by successive governments. Curiously, because of its potential (oil) wealth, it was held in high regard – and with a degree of caution too – by other South American countries. It was clear early in April 1982 that Venezuela was one of Argentina's strongest supporters in Latin America. Nevertheless, she was not thought to have given material assistance to Argentina.

Another British diplomat who was in Caracas at the time recalled the Venezuelans' sudden enthusiasm for all things Argentine, and for the actions that Argentina took in 1982. 'Many found it hard to explain,' he said. After the war, some Argentines asked Venezuelans why they had supported Argentina so enthusiastically. 'After all,' they said, 'we never liked each other very much!'

Even if weapons, and other such forms of assistance, were not being supplied to Argentina, Venezuela offered support in other ways. Unions, for example, instructed the dockers to boycott British vessels in a show of solidarity with Argentina. At least three vessels were affected in different ports. Hugh Carless recalled:

> We were close to winning a large contract to supply Hawk aircraft to Venezuela when the Falklands War started. It would have been worth in the order of two hundred million dollars and was very important to British Aerospace. Success in Venezuela could have resulted in a knock-on effect and further sales of the aircraft in other South American countries. Unfortunately, the sale was not concluded.

Bill Quantrill was the Counsellor in the British Embassy in Caracas just after the war. He had a different theory. He said: 'The loss of the Hawk contract was more to do with the dire economic situation. They wanted to buy the aircraft – it was judged to be the right one – but they could not raise the cash. An attempt was made to put a barter deal together to resurrect the sale, but that also failed.'

Mike Southgate said that a final effort to sell the twenty-four Hawk aircraft was made in March 1982. Apparently it went well, and on 1st April the Venezuelans agreed to buy the aircraft. The Air Force Commander, a very reasonable and respected officer, had been prepared to go ahead and sign. However, on 5th April the decision was suddenly taken not to proceed and no clear explanation was ever given. If money had been so tight that they were unlikely to be able to afford the aircraft, this would have come out at some earlier point in the negotiations. Probably the Air Force Commander was over-ruled by the President, and it was linked to the Falklands situation. Mike Southgate's successor, Captain David Phillips, tended towards Bill Quantrill's view that the loss of the contract had been more to do with cash flow and the country's economic problems.

There was some concern within the British Government that Venezuela might make any aircraft sold to them available to Argentina. On balance, though, Francis Pym, the Foreign Secretary, felt that the importance of the contract to BAe outweighed other considerations, and that it should go ahead. His decision, in fact, had no bearing on the eventual cancellation of the contract.

The Venezuelan air traffic control system announced early in May that it would take action to boycott British commercial flights 'in protest over the Falklands dispute'. British Caledonian was the only British carrier operating through Venezuela at that time. Douglas Webster recalled an occasion when a scheduled British Caledonian flight, with wheels already down, was approaching to land, only to be denied clearance and sent elsewhere.

A particularly futile gesture of protest on Venezuela's part – one worthy of *Blackadder*'s Baldrick – was the President's decision to prohibit the consumption of whisky in his palace during the war (Venezuela was, at that time, the highest per capita consumer of whisky in the world). The ban lasted for two weeks only, before the President gave up (so the Embassy story goes)! The Venezuelan Government also decided, in April 1982, to withdraw its dollar holdings in London – amounting to some 10 billion dollars – and move them to New York. Thus, in various ways, some of a fairly minor nature, Venezuela did its best to harm British interests.

In spite of these various measures taken, President Herrera Campins made two public statements in May 1982 that, it was assumed, were intended to reassure Britain. Early in the month he made it clear that Venezuela had no plans to break off diplomatic or commercial relations with Britain. This pledge was repeated later in the month, when the President added: 'My country backs Argentina, but is no enemy of Britain.'

Two things, however, could have changed the situation dramatically for the worse, notwithstanding those reassuring words. As in other South American countries, the reaction to the sinking of the *Belgrano* was one of immediate concern and Venezuela called for a rethink of South American policies related to its collective security. Fortunately, this did not go any further.

The other thing that would have made a big difference to the way Venezuela continued to view the war – and raise uncertainties as to how it might respond – would have been if Britain had ever mounted an attack on mainland Argentina. Such an attack could have resulted in the breaking-off of diplomatic relations with Britain. The level of support that Argentina would have received, politically and militarily, would almost certainly have escalated, and the damage to Britain's relations with Venezuela would have taken longer to repair. There would have been a great deal of indignation all round, and the mood in the country would have been more unpredictable.

This is not fanciful. There were one or two high-ranking and powerful people in Britain, and others in the House of Commons, who would have liked to have taken the fight to the Argentine mainland in 1982; and Phase 2 of Operation Mikado, which was cancelled only because Phase 1 failed to gather vital intelligence beforehand, was an attack planned on mainland Argentina.

From 1997 to 2000, many years after the Falklands War, Richard Wilkinson was the British Ambassador in Venezuela. He felt that Venezuela's response to Galtieri's invasion had been entirely predictable. He said: 'It would have been in complete sympathy with Argentina's position in 1982, because it felt that British Guiana had once occupied territory that rightly belonged to Venezuela. In the same way, it saw the British presence in the Falklands as an "occupation".'

Part Six
After The Surrender

After The Surrender

An Islander Remembers

Gerald Cheek, Falkland Islands resident and a prominent member of the Falkland Islands Defence Force (FIDF), recalled the final moments of the war on the Falkland Islands, and the days that followed. He said:

The end of the war came for us at about midnight on the night of the 13th June. We were listening to the BBC and learned that the battle for Stanley was getting ever closer to the town. The news of the actual surrender was relayed to us by an Argentine major. He knocked on the door of our house to ask for the use of a launch, apparently to report to his colonel. He said the war was over and suggested that we should take down the Argentine flag – on the flagpole by the house – and replace it with a British flag. As soon as he left, the stereo record player went on and we played some good rousing tunes, such as 'Land of Hope and Glory' and 'Rule Britannia' at maximum volume, and drank to the British victory. At around nine o'clock next morning, the Royal Navy frigate HMS *Avenger* came into the harbour and her Lynx helicopter flew over and landed close to the house, with a party to take the surrender of Argentines in the area.

Later that day, another helicopter landed, carrying some senior British officers, including Major General Jeremy Moore, the commander of the British Land Forces. He was visiting the settlements to see how the people had fared throughout the occupation. An officer and some ratings from HMS *Avenger* spent the evening with us, and around nine o'clock there was a knock on the door. The same Argentine major, this time with his captain, came in. The major produced a bottle of wine from his tunic, asked for some glasses and then, when we all had a glass in our hands, he proposed a toast. He toasted the victory, the victors, the vanquished, all those who had lost their lives, and those who had been injured as a result of an unnecessary war. It was a moving speech, delivered without any malice. I would like to have recorded it.

On the 16th June a Sea King helicopter from HMS *Invincible* arrived; we explained that there were fourteen of us who had been brought here (to Fox Bay) some seven weeks previously, and we had to get back to Stanley to see our families, who had not heard from us in all that time. The pilot acknowledged our situation and, after some discussion and a few anxious moments, we finally left the ground, rather overloaded, and slowly climbed away.

We flew over the harbour at Fitzroy, where the two landings ships had been bombed on the 8th of June. The RFA *Sir Galahad*, the ship that had been attacked with the loss of over fifty servicemen, was still burning. We landed safely back in Stanley and returned to our respective homes and families. They hadn't been expecting us, and I believe the surprise of being reunited again made the homecoming that much better.

It soon became apparent that the residents in Stanley had suffered more hardship than we had at Fox Bay. The areas immediately surrounding the town had been subjected to shelling by the Royal Navy most nights after their ships arrived off the islands in late May. It was surprising that only three civilians had been killed during these bombardments.

Hundreds of Argentine prisoners were being detained in makeshift shelters along the sides of the Stanley runway, whilst preparations were being made for their return to Argentina. Within a week they had all been shipped out, with the exception of five hundred officers who were detained for a further month. Many badly-damaged aircraft, including Pucaras and four local aircraft, littered the airfield. [RAF test pilot, Ian Strachan, later recalled that just one Pucara had been found that was not too badly damaged and could be refurbished for testing. It was transported to the UK, where it was evaluated at Boscombe Down.] Two other local Beaver aircraft had also been destroyed, which meant that all the Falkland Islands aircraft had been written off. Stanley itself had suffered badly. Three houses had been destroyed by shell-fire and many other buildings were badly damaged. Ammunition, weapons and assorted Argentine equipment and clothing littered the streets.

Gerald Cheek continued:

After the war ended, the gallant efforts of some of the local residents started to emerge. One or two of them had used their amateur radio sets to pass on information about the Argentine military to radio hams in the UK, for onward transmission to the intelligence authorities. The Argentines eventually became aware that this was happening and tried to track down the offenders, but fortunately with little success. One person, however, who lived in one of the outlying settlements, had tried to contact one of the Royal Navy ships by radio, but was apprehended and taken to Stanley. He was forced to remain under a form of house arrest for the remainder of the occupation. Another radio ham, who monitored some of the Argentine Army's operational radio frequencies in the islands, and managed to jam some of these frequencies on one or two occasions, came close to being caught. A number of other resistance activities were carried out from time to time. The Argentines draped hundreds of metres of communication cables along the fences between their various headquarters, and some of these were cut on occasions.

In addition to these acts of resistance, assistance was provided to the British forces after they landed at San Carlos. Accommodation was made available, help was provided by local farmers to transport ammunition and other items across the difficult terrain – and one or two men actually took part in a battle for one of the mountains near to Stanley.

The Immediate Issues

In the immediate aftermath of the Argentine surrender, there were numerous issues to be addressed, some of which would, no doubt, have been considered weeks earlier. What were we going to do with the vast number of Argentine POWs? When and how were we going to return the Argentine casualties? When would we bring back our troops, and by what means? What should be the size and magnitude of the force we left behind on the Falklands, or sent down to replace those leaving? What should be the balance between the three services? The size and composition of the force we left behind would have to be of an order that sent a powerful message to any Argentine Government that we would never tolerate a repetition of what happened in April 1982. The future of Ascension Island also had to be considered. Clearly, the island would continue to play an important role in any future plans for the Falklands.

We had to be careful, too, that any withdrawal was not implemented with indecent haste for another important reason. Argentina had to understand that Britain cared very much about both the Falkland Islands and its subjects who lived there. We had to be absolutely certain that things did not flare up again. We were not dealing with a rational government in Argentina, or one that cared deeply about the welfare of even its own troops.

There was the issue of clearing up after the fighting ended, removing the debris of war and making the islands safe again. Many of the houses were in a terrible state. The British Government made £20 million available to get work under way. The hospital was rebuilt and a new community school was constructed. The Gurkhas removed thousands of mines, but many more remained, to be found and removed over the years that followed. Others remain undiscovered. Lord Shackleton was asked by the government to produce a report on the economy of the Falkland Islands. It was published in September 1982 and laid the foundation for future prosperity.

Another issue, although not perhaps one of immediate concern, was that of what line, politically, the government should take with Argentina, and how and when Britain should start the process of rebuilding relations.

The 14th June 1982 – the day Major General Mario Menendez surrendered all Argentine forces in both East and West Falklands to Major General Jeremy Moore – was a cold and miserable day. Stanley was full of tired, hungry and frozen Argentine troops. It was not so much the low temperature that caused problems for the inadequately-clothed men, but the wind chill factor. Wind strengths in the South Atlantic can rise suddenly and dramatically to gale strength.

The condition of the men had moved many of the islanders to offer food and hot water to some of the more fortunate. Towards the end of the Argentine occupation, a severe shortage of fresh water had been just one of the many problems the men had had to endure, and many of the islanders had felt genuinely sorry for them. They were clearly pleased and relieved at the prospect of getting back to their homes and families, but some of them were also upset at having had to surrender, and there was

284

much resentment and criticism of the military junta that had inflicted the conflict upon them.

Lt Col Nick Vaux was the Commanding Officer of No 42 Commando at the time of the surrender. His unit was involved in disarming and guarding the Argentine prisoners until it was time to repatriate them. He said:

> The prisoners had to wait ten days before we were able to embark them for their return passage to Argentina. During this time, my men gained the distinct impression that many of the officers were utterly bewildered by their defeat, and felt genuine resentment at how they had been misled and treated by their superior officers, and especially by the military junta.
>
> At one point I had three hundred prisoners, guarded by only the small number of men that could be spared. If they had decided to take advantage of the situation, there would have been little we could have done. It could have precipitated a rather nasty situation. Fortunately for us, they were too shell-shocked and depressed to think along those lines.
>
> Finally, we were able to escort them on to the *Canberra* for their trip to the mainland. The *Canberra* planned to arrive in Argentina at dawn. The whole area was cordoned off for their arrival, and the thousands of returning prisoners were quickly and quietly offloaded on to buses, which then dispersed around the country. It all took time because Galtieri and his cronies wanted utmost secrecy to avoid being humiliated.

The Mood in Argentina

During the final moments of the war, and in its immediate aftermath, the mood of the Argentine people moved swiftly from joy – believing, as so many did, that Argentina was about to win an historic war – to disbelief, followed by shame, disappointment and then anger, as the scale of their government's deception became clearer. General Galtieri was removed as head of the military junta on 17th June and replaced by General Bignone. He announced on 21st June that the ceasefire would be observed by all Argentinian forces, Britain having declared the end of hostilities the previous day.

Cristina Bishop recalled:

> As the press had been totally controlled by the government throughout the war, to the extent that a large section of the Argentine population thought their country was winning right up to the end, the sudden realisation that the war had been lost came as a terrible shock. Some of the more fortunate Argentines, those that regarded the BBC Overseas Service as the best and most reliable source of news and information, were better prepared for the final outcome. Everyone knew that their own radio bulletins, and the press, were controlled by the government.

Cristina added that her teacher had a son who had been an army conscript on the Falklands in 1982. She said:

> My teacher knew all about the conditions the conscripts had to fight in. She had raised money – as had other mothers too – for clothes, blankets, chocolate and even food for their suffering sons. There was a forty-eight-hour Bandaid Marathon on television too. After the war, it was discovered that none of the money raised was ever spent as intended. None of the items the mothers hoped their sons would receive had ever reached the Falklands. The government had seen to that.

People had also believed – or had been led to believe – that the USA would support Argentina's position; at the very least that it would not give support to the British. When it leaked out that, in fact, a strong pro-British element in the US Government had been giving active support to Britain from an early stage in the war, this too came as a shock, and many Argentines felt badly let down.

After the war, the Argentine Army – and a disappointed, deflated, deceived nation as well – virtually disowned its returning soldiers. There were no benefits or disability pensions for them, and little in the way of thanks for their efforts. Disabled soldiers – some without legs – had to resort to pushing themselves along the pavements, begging for money in order to survive.

RAF C130 pilot Graham Forbes recalled a humanitarian mission he flew just after the Argentine surrender. He said: 'I flew one of two C130s that took warm clothing down to the Falklands for the Argentine prisoners. They were frozen, hungry and desperate. It was incredible that their own government did not respond as we did.' It is a tragic statistic that many more Argentine war veterans have committed suicide since the end of the war than actually died during all the fighting.

After the Junta

Following the resignation of President Galtieri and the Chiefs of Staff after the war, General Reynaldo Bignone became President of Argentina on 1st July 1982. He was another senior military figure with blood on his hands from the days of the 'dirty war'. A protégé of General Videla, he had retired from the army in 1981. On becoming president, he struck a deal with his predecessor (Galtieri), whereby the military would not be charged with offences related to the 'dirty war' but would merely be charged instead with the 'maladministration of the Malvinas War'; a far less serious charge.

His presidency was short-lived, however, and President Raul Alfonsin was inaugurated on 10th December 1983, becoming the first democratically-elected president after many years of repressive military rule. Deals made by his predecessor were quickly annulled.

Alfonsin courageously decided to bring the military leaders of the junta to face trial – together with ex-President Videla, Admiral Massera and others – on charges related to the 'dirty war' years of the 1970s. Galtieri was initially cleared, but tried again later on different charges. This time he was judged guilty and received a twelve-year sentence (still somewhat less than that received by some of the others). Some years later, Admiral Anaya died of a heart attack on his way to court to face the charges against him.

In 1984, President Alfonsin initiated the first diplomatic exchange with the British Government after the Falklands War. This resulted in Britain lifting trade sanctions with Argentina. It was a small, modest first step on the long road to normal relations, but a start nevertheless.

He also wanted to see an improvement in Argentina's relations with neighbouring Chile and instigated a treaty intended to pave the way towards resolving the Beagle Channel dispute. Again, it was a small step, but in the right direction.

Daniel Eugenio, now living in England but Argentine by birth, had lived in Buenos Aires until the late 1980s where he was a senior manager with the national airline, Aerolineas Argentinas. He said:

Raul Alfonsin was exactly what Argentina needed at that time. Unfortunately he never had a good relationship with the armed forces, and they resented the measures he bravely took against the junta and those associated with the dark days of the 1970s. They locked themselves in their barracks and indulged in a campaign of non-co-operation. In the end, Alfonsin's inability to work with the military – which still had more clout than was healthy and had staged no less than three mutinies during his presidency – coupled with the appalling state of the economy, led to the premature end of his presidency. He was replaced in 1989 by Carlos Menem.

A Peronist can be of the Left or of the Right. Other considerations matter more. President Menem was a Peronist of the Right and, as a consequence, had a better relationship with the military than Alfonsin. He promptly pardoned the military for all their past indiscretions and then sold all he could to the private sector, starting with the national airline. Menem did, however, seek to improve relations with the UK and in 1998 made the first visit to Britain by an Argentine leader after the Falklands War.

Alfredo Astiz was not accorded a hero's welcome on his return to Argentina. President Alfonsin had locked him up with most of the other culprits from the 'dirty war' era, but he was amongst those released later by President Menem. For a long time, Astiz remained an embarrassment that successive governments have not known quite how to handle. Eventually, the Supreme Court ruled that previous amnesty laws were unconstitutional. Astiz was brought to trial in December 2009 at the Argentine Federal Court in connection with his crimes committed during the 'dirty war' years. At the end of one of Argentina's longest Human Rights trials – it lasted nearly two years and was concerned principally with crimes committed at the ESMA naval unit – Astiz was finally sentenced to life imprisonment in October 2011.

Whilst successive Argentine governments over the years have differed in their views as to how such criminals should be handled, the military have always been consistent, preferring not to reopen old wounds which would serve to remind the population of its inglorious past.

The bleak period, when people like Astiz were not just tolerated but encouraged, forms part of Argentina's history and can therefore neither be ignored nor erased. He, and others like him, fought against Britain in 1982. Happily, they were not typical of the majority and many other young, decent Argentine soldiers and airmen had, by then, joined their ranks.

Daniel Eugenio also made an interesting comment on the officers of the Argentine Army and Navy in those days, and was not the first to do so. In general, he said – and there would obviously have been exceptions – few of the officers tried to relate to, or command the respect of, the men under them. No one should be surprised therefore that these officers sent young, innocent conscripts to war ill-equipped and poorly trained.

The Argentine Air Force, on the other hand, was held in high regard for its professionalism during the war, and had a 'cleaner' image than the other two services, especially the navy. Brigadier Lami Dozo, the Head of the Air Force, even took the unusual – but widely appreciated – step of declaring that henceforth the military must allow greater participation by civilians in decision-making. This was a significant departure from previous thinking, and was quoted widely in the press at the time.

British/Argentine Relations after the War

Britain did not resume diplomatic relations with Argentina for eight years. Although we did not have an Ambassador in the country – or any other diplomat after Ambassador Anthony Williams and his staff left in April 1982 – the British Embassy building remained open as 'The British Interest Section of the Swiss Embassy'.

In July 1990, Mr Humphrey Maud arrived in Buenos Aires to become our first Ambassador since the war. During the same period, the Argentine Embassy in London came under the Brazilian flag. Within a few weeks of his arrival, Mr Maud had a Deputy, two First Secretaries and a Defence Attaché. Even after diplomatic relations were finally restored, the British Government continued to rule out any discussion on the subject of the sovereignty of the Falkland Islands.

Argentina also continued to maintain its claim to the Falklands, and it still remains an objective to be realised at some point in the future. Few Argentines seriously believe, though, that their country would risk going to war again over the issue, and certainly not in their lifetime.

Argentina renewed its claim recently and undoubtedly will continue to do so from time to time. It would like the United Nations to put pressure on Britain to negotiate the issue. There are elements within the US administration that have some sympathy for this view and many other countries in South America would probably support Argentina's claim.

Even Chile has called for the resumption of negotiations. Peru has been the most vocal.

Brazil's government has moved decisively to the Left since the Falklands War and is anxious to have better relations with Argentina. On 31st October 2010, Dilma Rousseff, Brazil's first female president – within days of being elected – made a point of denying our Falklands offshore patrol vessel, HMS *Clyde*, access to port facilities in Rio de Janeiro. It was forced to go to Chile instead. She was described in the press as 'playing the anti-colonial card to satisfy left-wing elements within her Workers Party', but no doubt the point was not lost on Argentina. Coincidentally, both Brazil and Argentina currently have their first elected female presidents, and they appear to get along together.

Uruguay also put its relationship with neighbouring Argentina before co-operating with Britain when, in September 2010, the British Type 42 destroyer, HMS *Gloucester*, was barred from entering Montevideo to pick up fuel and supplies. That was the second time it had occurred.

There have been demonstrations from time to time outside the British Embassy in Buenos Aires, demanding the return of the Falklands to Argentina. The British flag was even burned on one occasion. Unrest and tension quietly increased when British oil companies arrived in the Falklands area looking for oil.

President Kirchner of Argentina, who once described herself as 'Evita with a clenched fist', has chosen to fan smouldering national resentment, and has made the Malvinas issue an important feature of her presidency. She recently stipulated that ships wishing to travel between mainland Argentina and the Falklands must seek authority to do so. Both sides continue to dig their heels in. There is little light on the horizon.

Some thirty years after the war, the sovereignty issue remains a festering sore on relations between Britain and Argentina. Neither side has given an inch, and it would be difficult to accurately predict the eventual outcome, or when. Few Argentines, it is felt, would have the appetite for another war over the issue.

Three RAF officers who found themselves with interesting assignments in post-war Argentina were Clive Evans – who had been Station Commander at RAF Lyneham in 1982 – Patrick Tootal, and David McDonnell.

Clive Evans, as an Air Commodore, became the first senior British officer to visit Argentina after the war. He spent eight days there in September/October 1990. His was a mission 'to help pave the way to normal relations,' he said. He was leading a group of officers who were attending a Royal College of Defence Studies (RCDS) course, and recalled that his own programme was carefully constructed and stage-managed. He was given maximum exposure to Argentine officers, gave radio interviews, and was photographed solemnly laying a wreath at the Malvinas Memorial and saluting the fallen. 'Everyone,' he said, 'was extremely courteous. There was just one interesting incident when an Argentine officer raised the thorny subject of the *Belgrano*, and questioned the need for sinking it. He was promptly hissed by his colleagues, who clearly did not want to spoil the moment!'

Patrick Tootal had spent the war in Operations Support at HQ Strike Command. He was a C130 man and had commanded No 70 Squadron at Lyneham. In August 1990, the year of Clive Evans' visit, he was sent to Buenos Aires to be Britain's first Defence Attaché in Argentina since Col Stephen Love was forced to leave the country in April 1982. Patrick recalled:

I only had fifteen months in the job. The mood in the country was quite pro-British, though curiously I found the air force the least forthcoming of the three services. My role was very much one of 'fence-mending' and, like any attaché overseas – but especially so in Argentina after eight years without a British attaché in the country – I needed some good contacts to get going. In the absence of a hand-over from another attaché, I turned to the US Embassy for help. They were difficult to talk to initially and were clearly reluctant to help me at all. My request for contacts was ignored.

I recall learning that the military junta's invasion plan for the Falklands had contained absolutely no political input at all. There had been no mention of the possibility of installing, for instance, a civilian administration or a civilian police presence.

David McDonnell went to Argentina to be DA a few years after Patrick Tootal returned. He was there from 1996 to 2000. Again, the job was mainly a continuation of the process of repairing relations. He thought that some animosity still persisted in certain areas, and cited the Argentine Navy in particular and areas where naval families lived such as Puerto Belgrano as examples. He added:

Although the Argentine Army and Navy both surrendered, the Air Force never did, and was very proud of the fact. In fact, it still holds its head up high and does not consider it was defeated. At Argentina's training college – their equivalent of Cranwell – young hopefuls are taught that their air force acquitted itself with distinction in 1982. Ever since the war – and certainly up to the time I was in Argentina – relations between the Argentine Air Force and Navy had been poor.

Many of the Falkland Islanders thought that after the war there would be no further problems with Argentina, but it was not that simple. It was not until 1990 that the Argentine Government allowed an air link to be established with Chile, and that was for one flight a week only. No other flights, private or commercial, were permitted to fly from Chile to the islands, as such flights would have had to overfly Argentina. In 1987, a Falklands conservation zone was established around the islands, which allowed the waters to be fished. This has since brought a great deal of wealth to the island's economy, but the Argentines have constantly attempted to harass the fishing fleets, fortunately without a great deal of success. Gerald Cheek expressed his view that no satisfactory working relationship has ever been developed with Argentina, and is not likely to be unless, or until, Argentina drops its sovereignty claim.

Suky Cameron, an islander herself, worked in the Falkland Islands Government Office in London, which has existed since 1983. She described it as 'a sort of Embassy'. She said:

Very few islanders travel to Argentina even now; the Argentine Government does not encourage it. In fact, it actually resents the contact. Chile's attitude is rather different, and there is a regular flight to and from the Falklands. Chile mainly attracts those who want to take a holiday there, and some have second homes in the country. However, I don't think anyone sends their children there to be educated, although many islanders send their children to the UK for their secondary education, or to university.

A general view in the Government Office is that, whilst there is a feeling of gratitude towards the UK, the war is not discussed very much in the Falklands these days. The islanders who took in the young, cold, hungry Argentine soldiers, took pity on them, and fed them, were never criticised by others. It seemed the right thing to do at the time.

Today, although some islanders head for Chile if they need a change of scenery, not many Chileans or Argentines visit the Falklands. Apparently, they find it too expensive.

One ex-Governor of the Falklands, who later served as the British Ambassador in Buenos Aires, was quite clear that the war had in many ways – although at a regrettably high cost in terms of lives lost, human suffering and damage – done the Falkland Islands an enormous favour. He said:

> It put the Falklands on the map. It forced the British Government to take the islands seriously, to defend them properly and to invest in the infrastructure. Before the war, it was a dying community, dependent on wool and British Government aid. It felt unloved by a seemingly uncaring British Government. Young people were leaving the islands because of the lack of jobs and opportunities.

> After the war, this all changed. The fishing limits were extended and fishing licences brought in previously unimagined wealth. Today, fishing and tourism are both major sources of income for the islands, and the Falklands are economically self-sufficient.

Maintaining a Military Presence on the Falklands

The justification for maintaining a coherent deterrent force on the islands after the war ended is clear. In any period of rising tension, there is invariably pressure exerted to react and send forces. This can serve to exacerbate an already delicate situation and create a deteriorating scenario, which is precisely what you would prefer to avoid. If your forces are already in situ, however, you are not perceived as trying to inflame an already bad situation. It also takes time to react. It is better to be on hand and able to defend your vital airfield, rather than risk losing it.

Also, the possibility could not be ruled out – even after an Argentine surrender – that some disgruntled element might be tempted to 'have a go' and exact some revenge once the British troops had returned home. A continued presence would essentially have deterrence in mind.

Group Captain (later Air Chief Marshal Sir William) Bill Wratten was the station commander at RAF Coningsby (a base for Phantom aircraft) during the war. He said:

> A few weeks before the end of the war, it was decided at the highest level that elements of the British forces would have to maintain a

presence on the Falkland Islands after the war was won. This would be for a period yet to be determined, and would be essentially in order to ensure that Argentina never again tried to mount some reckless adventure in the islands.

One morning in May 1982, the AOC telephoned Bill Wratten and asked him to go down to the Falklands to assess Stanley's suitability for operating Phantoms. He put together a small team and they flew down there. It was several weeks before the end of the war. At that stage, most people thought that Britain would win it, but no one had any idea how long it would take.

A couple of weeks after the surrender, he was sent back to the Falklands to be the first station commander at (RAF) Stanley. He recalled that Major General Jeremy Moore and his men were 'wrapping things up' when he arrived, and the last Argentines were in the process of leaving the islands. He said:

> Apart from the all-important role of deterrence, there was also much work to do, including clearing up a prodigious amount of squalor, and the leftover garbage and dross of war. During the early days, accommodation was wherever it could be found. For some, it was on a ship offshore; for others, it was in a tent or lodged with one of the local residents.
>
> A high priority was to prepare the way for a small force of air defence fighter aircraft that the government wanted to deploy there as soon as possible. The runway at Stanley had to be extended to take them. Five RHAGs (rotary hydraulic arrester gear) also had to be installed on the 6,000 ft runway, two at each end and one in the middle. The sappers carried out these installations. Adequate shelter was also needed for aircraft servicing.

Finally, everything was ready for the aircraft to fly in. No 29 Squadron, from RAF Coningsby, provided the first detachment. The first Phantom arrived on 17th October 1982. No problems were experienced with either the runway or RHAG system, and the other aircraft followed.

Ian Wigmore, C130 navigator, recalled that his aircraft had been one of the first two C130s to go down to Stanley to support Phantom operations. He also arrived on 17th October, having accompanied and refuelled the first Phantom en route from Ascension Island. In so doing, his aircraft became the first C130 tanker aircraft to operate from the Falklands.

Ian said: 'Thereafter we maintained two C130s and three crews in the Falklands, the plan being to rotate the crews with fresh ones from the UK every three months. Conditions were rather basic in those early days following the Argentine surrender, and we lived in tents throughout our stay, showering every three days or so on the Royal Navy's guard-ship anchored offshore.'

Initially, the Phantoms were maintained at a high state of alert in case of an Argentine 'adventure' but, in due course, this was relaxed a bit. Of particular concern was the possibility that Argentina might decide to exercise the system, causing an aircraft to be scrambled into the air when the weather was poor, or forecast to deteriorate (it could deteriorate very rapidly in the South Atlantic). As there were no diversion airfields nearby – the nearest was Punta Arenas in southern Chile, nearly 2 hours flying time away – this could have been very embarrassing. The main reason it was decided to maintain a C130 tanker aircraft at Stanley was to cope with such eventualities. In the event, no such moves were made by Argentina.

'Curiously,' Sir William said, 'the RAF presence had not been especially welcomed by the islanders. They were self-sufficient, independent folk, and they did not particularly like the intrusion. They just wanted to return to their original lifestyle.'

Clive Evans, Lyneham's station commander, recalled that the C130 aircraft on the Falklands had another task. Each day, one aircraft flew a patrol round the islands looking for any possible Argentine intrusions by sea. It was well equipped for the task, having excellent weather radar that was used for ship detection. Also, whilst the work at Stanley was being carried out, a Royal Navy carrier (HMS *Hermes*) maintained station offshore, its presence conveying a powerful message to Argentina.

As HMS *Invincible* needed an engine change as soon as possible after the war, the carrier left the Falklands area on 19th June, and headed for the calmer waters and sunny skies of the tropics. The crew needed a break as well. There were no air operations from *Invincible* for seventy-five days. The new Olympus gas turbine engine was installed at sea without mishap – the first time this had been attempted – and she then returned to the Falklands. *Hermes*, having been relieved by *Invincible*, then returned to the UK for a major refit and, two years after the war, was put in reserve before being sold to India (where she was renamed *Viraat*).

Mark Hare was an RAF Harrier pilot on *Hermes*. He said: 'No 1

Squadron also returned to the UK, to be replaced by aircraft and pilots of No 3 Squadron. They then operated in the air defence role until they were replaced by the Phantoms in October (i.e. when Stanley was ready to accept them).' During the war, the RAF Harriers had operated in the ground attack role, leaving the air defence to the Sea Harriers of the Fleet Air Arm.

HMS *Invincible* remained down at the Falklands for only a short time, before handing over to HMS *Illustrious* on 26th August. *Illustrious* had not been completed in time to participate in the war, and could not be accepted by the Royal Navy until 18th June, less than a week after the Argentine surrender. She remained only until the Phantom aircraft arrived at Stanley. She was the last carrier to carry out that duty off the Falklands; thereafter, a succession of frigates carried out guard-ship duties, and also provided radar coverage for the Phantoms.

Although the government's decision to maintain a continued military presence on the Falklands had required the runway at Stanley to be prepared and extended in the short term, it had been decided that a Royal Air Force station should be established at a new airfield to be constructed some thirty miles south-west of Stanley to support operations in the longer term. It took three years to construct the runway and associated infrastructure; RAF Mount Pleasant was finally opened, on time, in 1985. It was fully operational the following year. It remains the last new Royal Air Force station to have been constructed and also serves as an international airport.

Whilst Britain was establishing its military presence on the Falklands and improving the infrastructure to support it, Argentina received the balance of its order for Super Etendard aircraft and Exocet missiles. The French Government had already allowed Peru to have the Exocets it wanted (and was denied during the war), in August 1982. As Argentina had refused to acknowledge the cessation of hostilities after the war, Britain had wanted the arms embargo to remain in place longer, but other European Union countries, especially France and Germany (but also the USA), had wanted it lifted as soon as possible.

The Tanking Commitment

Initially, the airbridge to support the military presence on the Falklands was operated (almost daily) by C130 aircraft from Ascension Island to Stanley (until RAF Mount Pleasant was ready to accept them), supported by Victor tankers. At the same time, a number of C130s were converted to the tanker role and, as they became available, they took over from the Victors, which were gradually phased out. The C130s finally relied totally on C130 tanker support. Not only were they all, unlike the Victor, able to land and operate at Stanley, but C130-to-C130 tanking also eliminated the rather tedious 'tobogganing' technique, whereby the receiving C130 had to follow a Victor in a gradual descent from about 25,000 feet altitude down to low altitude whilst it refuelled, in order to match the speed of the Victor.

The last Victor returned to the UK on 10th June 1985. The following year one of the two squadrons disbanded. The other one, and the Victor Operational Conversion Unit, continued until 1993, when the aircraft were finally retired, after also seeing service in the Gulf War of 1991.

Another aircraft type was modified to carry out the tanking role at that time. In May 1982, a feasibility study was commissioned to convert some of the remaining Vulcan aircraft to the tanker role. Within fifty days, the first of six aircraft was ready (on No 50 Squadron) and was designated the Vulcan B2K. Its purpose was to support the domestic requirement in the UK, whilst the RAF's other tanker aircraft were committed to the airbridge. Most of the Vulcans were finally retired in 1984, leaving just two, which carried on as display aircraft. After 1993, this was reduced to a single aircraft.

The VC10 aircraft did not go down to the Falklands, but continued flying to Ascension Island for a long time after the war, transporting personnel back to the UK. Usually, the aircraft would be almost empty en route to Ascension Island, but full on the return journey. Crews were slipped at Dakar, Senegal. A few VC10s were converted to tankers later on. The VC10 ambulance flights continued only until the end of July 1982.

When RAF Mount Pleasant was open and functioning, the long-awaited Tristars were brought into service. They acted as a spacious transport aircraft carrying both people and supplies and as a tanker aircraft. In the latter role, they were a huge improvement over previous types of aircraft, having a greatly-increased fuel capacity to both carry and dispense.

A total of nine Tristars were bought by the RAF; six from Freddie Laker and the other three from Pan Am. Six aircraft were converted to the tanker role by Marshall's of Cambridge. Just before they became available, a six-month contract with British Airways secured the use of B747 aircraft, which operated briefly as far as Ascension Island only and were flown by BA civilian crews.

The number of aircraft converted to, and used as, tanker aircraft during that period underlines the complexity of operating different types of aircraft over huge distances. Never before has such an awesome tanking requirement been confronted in the process of trying to win a war so far away from home base. That it was so successfully accomplished was a significant achievement on the part of the crews, the aircraft, and all those who supported the effort.

A number of different aircraft types in the Royal Air Force's inventory operated throughout the war. For some of those aircraft, the effort continued afterwards. The Vulcans, Nimrod MR2s, Nimrod R1, Harriers and VC10s had done all that was asked of them, and more. The C130s and the Victor force worked tirelessly throughout, supporting and sustaining the ships of the Task Force; indeed making the Task Force's long return journey – and its *raison d'être* – possible. The Royal Navy's Sea Harriers and the helicopters performed no less admirably. The PR Canberras of No 39 Squadron were briefed and ready to go, but were denied the opportunity at the last moment.

Ascension Island

The continued military presence on the Falklands had clear implications for Ascension Island as well. It would also have to be developed, in order to continue operating for an indefinite period as a staging post capable of supporting our presence further south.

Having seen the Falklands War come and go, Cecilia James remained on Ascension Island for another three years in her teaching capacity. For her, life after the war was not quite as idyllic as she had hoped it would be, and never returned to what it had been like before. She said:

Civil engineers arrived, and the runway and hardstanding were enlarged and resurfaced. An RAF station was constructed at Travellers Hill. It was all rather unsettling. On the plus side, new facilities were provided, including a swimming pool and gymnasium, which the islanders were permitted to use. The swimming pool was especially appreciated, as swimming off most of the beaches around the island was quite dangerous.

The RAF personnel that remained on the island after the war were all unaccompanied, as were the civil engineers who arrived. My accommodation block reverted to how it was before the war, with only three units occupied. The walks were once again tranquil. The airport was now run by the RAF.

After the war, Alan Bowman took over the role of Senior RAF Officer, specifically to oversee the build-up, expansion and development of the island base into a proper, functioning transit station. The long-term requirement envisaged Ascension Island as supporting the continuing British presence on the Falklands with an airbridge.

In order to save shipping sand in to build the new aircraft hardstanding, it was taken instead from the island's beaches (which upset a few of the residents). Hydrant refuelling was provided. An air movements section, motor transport section, enhanced bulk fuel installation, workshops, engineering support section, transit facilities and accommodation were all added; everything, in fact, that a modern staging station required. 'It became,' Alan Bowman said, 'a small RAF station with high-quality facilities.'

David Emmerson, who had commanded the Nimrod MR2 detachment at Ascension Island during the war, summed up his brief experience of life on Ascension Island. He said: 'I had only spent six weeks on Ascension Island, but it was an experience like no other, and certainly affected my subsequent career and life in general. Seven years later, en route to the Falkland Islands – when I was escorting Admiral of the Fleet Sir John Fieldhouse – I marvelled at the modern facilities on Ascension Island.'

South Georgia

From 1985, South Georgia and the South Sandwich islands ceased to be administered as a Falkland Islands Dependency and became a separate Territory. In South Georgia, the British Antarctic Survey research station at King Edward Point, which had been closed by Argentine military forces in April 1982, was occupied by a small British garrison until March 2001. The garrison was then withdrawn and a new station was built and operated, for research purposes, by the British Antarctic Survey.

In 1987, the FCO named four mountains after personnel who had played a major role in the defence or repossession of South Georgia in 1982. Two of the four peaks were named after Guy Sheridan and Keith Mills. A set of postage stamps, depicting the mountains, was issued in

April 2007 to commemorate the twenty-fifth anniversary of the liberation of South Georgia. One of the stamps, depicting the Sheridan Peak, shows an artist's impression of Guy and his team on the slopes of Brown Mountain just before taking the Argentine surrender, with his peak in the background.

In August 1999, together with Brigadier David Nicholls RM (then Commander of British Forces Falkland Islands), Guy attempted to make the first successful ascent of 'his peak', but was forced to abandon the attempt by a succession of severe winter storms. Happily though, he was able to report that a team of French alpine guides from Chamonix made the first successful ascent of the mountain in November 2007.

Today, tourism is growing apace and this breathtakingly beautiful island attracts between 4,000 and 5,000 tourists each year. The vast majority are on cruise ships, but a dozen or so yachts and several expeditions also visit the island. Quite apart from the tourism, South Georgia has transformed from being an isolated island with a small scientific community to somewhere highly regarded for Polar training and exercises.

US Assistance

How vital to the British effort, and to the eventual outcome of the war, was the material assistance and support given by the USA? This question prompted a wide range of differing responses and views, some rather unexpected.

The case for supporting Britain's effort had been frequently, and eloquently, made by the British Ambassador in Washington, Sir Nicholas Henderson, in 1982. He had appeared on television regularly, and also privately visited those within President Reagan's administration who had some sympathy for Argentina's position in the war. It is well known that Defence Secretary Casper Weinberger responded magnificently, promising to try and supply almost anything Britain required militarily, including intelligence from US satellites. He even, on one occasion, offered an aircraft carrier (which was declined).

Jean Kirkpatrick, the US Ambassador at the United Nations, on the other hand favoured strong right-wing governments in South America. She felt that the USA should not risk upsetting its allies there, and should work to avoid a war whilst remaining absolutely neutral in its stance (i.e. it should not give Britain any assistance).

300

Ex-Secretary of State for Defence, Sir John Nott said:

Initially, the USA said we must not use Ascension Island for our Vulcans, but we fixed that. President Reagan was at first against the idea of us going to war over the Falklands. Later on, when they were persuaded that Congress and US public opinion were largely behind Britain, he and his National Security Adviser, William P. Clark, took a more favourable line. Luckily for us, Casper Weinberger was not prepared to wait. But really, the whole Falklands saga was an enormous blow to Reagan and the US Government, as it threatened to undermine a whole area of foreign policy (i.e. keeping South American governments strong). It was an anti-communist crusade.

Although we will never know for certain, I believe we would have got by without US help, but probably not so easily. My judgement is that American help was certainly valuable, but not indispensable. This was a point of view shared by Sir Clive Whitmore.

Sir John added: 'Regarding US satellite intelligence, our Chief Scientific Adviser was instrumental in getting the US to help. Initially, they were reluctant, but after I called Casper Weinberger directly, things moved. In fact, I don't think satellite intelligence was very helpful; it was certainly not crucial.'

Another endorsement came from Air Marshal Sir John Curtiss, who added:

Satellite communications were important, but probably not a show-stopper if they hadn't been available. Doubtless other means would have been found. We certainly did not want to linger down in the South Atlantic any longer than necessary. The job had to be done as quickly as possible. Winter weather was getting closer, and ship and Harrier attrition was a concern. However, on balance, I believe John Nott was probably right.

John Lucken was CDS's Military Assistant. His view was that Casper Weinberger's support was widely appreciated and that we had needed the intelligence offered by satellite overflights. 'The USA had the system, and kindly carried out the flight reorientation for us,' he said. He declined, though, to give an opinion as to whether US help had been vital.

David Brook, also on CDS's staff, felt that CDS had a good

relationship with both Casper Weinberger and General David C. Jones, Chairman of the Joint Chiefs of Staff, which had been helpful to us. The US military generally had been supportive of Britain's position.

He said: 'US assistance included supplying Shrike, Sidewinder and advanced Harpoon missiles (which were not used), co-operation with regard to the use of Ascension Island and the supply of aviation fuel (RN ships had refuelled from Royal Fleet Auxiliaries offshore). Their moral support – after some hesitation initially – was probably more important to us than anything else.' Was their support vital to us though? He would only venture that things would have been more difficult for us without US support.

Captain Brian Young (HMS *Antrim*) felt that US support had been 'very helpful but I'm not sure if I could say it had been essential', although he acknowledged that the advanced Sidewinder missile had made a difference to air battle successes.

Admiral Woodward did not agree with Sir John Nott's assertion that Britain could probably have triumphed without US support, and had declined to comment on the subject of satellite reorientation. It has to be said that the two men were unlikely to have agreed over very much anyway. The Admiral added: 'Things could have been very different if Argentina had concentrated more on attacking our support vessels (i.e. *Canberra*, the RFAs, and *Atlantic Conveyor*, which was not the intended target on the day it was hit). It would have done more damage to our effort.'

Jeremy Price, the Senior RAF Officer on Ascension Island, thought that US support had been crucial only as far as the provision of aviation fuel was concerned, although very useful politically. Although Pan Am (on Ascension Island) had some bowsers (fuel tankers), there had not been enough to cope with the requirements of all the aircraft that operated from the island once the war started. He said:

The Victor tanker aircraft flew every day – not to mention all the other aircraft types we had on Ascension Island – and fuel was our biggest headache. Aviation fuel was provided via a flexible hose – from US tankers tied up to a buoy half a mile offshore – to the bulk fuel installation on the island. Tankers were busy most of the time. The US also supplied, in a C5 Galaxy aircraft, accommodation units – twelve of them, each accommodating twelve people – and what became known as 'concertina city' suddenly sprung up. These 'folding houses' were complete entities, furnished and with air-conditioning. They also sent in food, including fresh vegetables, in a C141 aircraft.

Bob McQueen, the Senior RN Officer on the island, felt that the USA deserved more credit than they ever actually received for helping Britain. He thought the Grenada saga – which occurred the following year, and caused our relations with the USA to become a little tense for a while – may have been a factor. The US-led invasion of the island resulted in the change of government that was sought, but was controversial because it was within the Commonwealth.

Roger Warden spent the whole of the war on Ascension Island. Most of the twenty-six Wessex helicopters on his squadron were spread between the Falklands, South Georgia, the *Atlantic Conveyor* and Ascension Island. He and Bob McQueen relieved each other as necessary. Roger said he found the USA very helpful and also cited, in particular, the help received to meet the daunting fuel requirement. He said that he found Lt Col Bill Brydon, the Pentagon's 'eyes and ears' on the island, very helpful and diplomatic.

Both Mark Hare and Tim Gedge, RAF and RN Harrier pilots respectively during the war, focussed on the improved features of the AIM-9L (Sidewinder) missile. Mark said: 'The AIM-9L represented a big improvement in performance over the AIM-9G, and was very effective. We were short of 9Gs towards the end, and then we had to use a mix of 9L and 9G missiles.'

Tim, on the other hand, felt that there had been enough AIM-9Gs, and the advanced features of the AIM-9L had not been used, although most of the pilots preferred to carry it as it had a wider envelope for acquisition and firing. The 9L version was also regarded as being considerably more effective at low level. He also endorsed Jeremy Price's comments regarding the USA's timely provision of aviation fuel.

One could sum up the feelings of the British who were on the receiving end of US support as being very grateful to our American friends, not only for responding so quickly to help us, but for the willingness with which it was done. Nothing was too much trouble. When we needed the Shrike missiles for the Vulcan, they were made available immediately, and that was the manner of the US response with other items too.

We were also given six Harpoon missiles (which had been originally destined for Iran), together with other parts needed to make them fully operational. Clandestine C130 flights were arranged to transport them to

Ascension Island without delay. Everything was kept very close to the chest.

Everything supplied was gratefully received at the 'sharp end'; nevertheless, opinions are clearly divided on the question of whether all this assistance was necessarily crucial to the desired end result. Fortunately, we will never know the answer to that one. Certainly, it might have been difficult to work round the problem if the aviation fuel had not been made available when it was, and in such quantities.

Casper Weinberger himself should have the last word. He said, after the war: 'Some said that the British could not have succeeded if we had not helped. I believe that US assistance had not been crucial; helpful, yes, but not vital to the outcome. I firmly believe the decisive factor was Mrs Thatcher's firm and immediate decision to retake the islands.' For his unwavering support throughout the war, Casper Weinberger later received an Honorary Knighthood.

Nevertheless, for many years after the Falklands War, Sir Nicholas Henderson was known to have been troubled by the MoD's failure publicly to acknowledge the scale of the US effort. Surely we were not worried that a strong expression of our nation's gratitude might take the gloss off Britain's achievement?

When, after the war, the US involvement became public knowledge, many Argentines felt badly let down. At the very least, they had hoped and assumed that the US would remain neutral.

A final thought on that subject; on one occasion, Britain had requested twelve sets of pilot night goggles (PNGs). This caused considerable consternation; more so than one would have expected. The problem arose because our American friends recognise 'PNG' as standing for precision nuclear guidance. After that, we called them NVGs (night vision goggles)!

The Prime Minister Visits the Falklands

Six months after the war, RAF Lyneham's Station Commander, Clive Evans, received an unexpected telephone call from his AOC. He later recalled:

The AOC called to say that the Prime Minister wanted to go down to the Falklands. An aircraft had to be prepared, and only those immediately involved were to be in the know. The C-in-C's personal cabin (a sort of Portakabin) would have to be on board the C130, wired and plumbed in for her personal use. The aircraft must be cordoned off and the proposed flight 'kept under wraps' (although it will be obvious that it must be someone important).

Clive Evans added that the AOC had said that a second (standby) aircraft would not be needed. He had one prepared and despatched anyway, just in case. It was just as well, as it turned out.

C130 Captain, Graham Forbes, recalled the rather unusual mission he was asked to undertake some months after the war had ended, when he was asked to take Prime Minister Margaret Thatcher down to the Falkland Islands. He said:

The flight to Stanley was flown in a C130 Hercules on the 8th Jan 1983. The Prime Minister flew from Brize Norton on a VC10, and transferred to the C130 at Ascension Island. Her entourage included her husband, Admiral Sir John Fieldhouse and Bernard Ingham (the Prime Minister's Press Secretary). Although I was the aircraft captain, Wing Commander Brian Warsap, Officer Commanding Operations at RAF Lyneham, was designated Aircraft Commander to deal with any weighty issues. The whole operation was highly classified, and I was informed that it would probably have to be cancelled in the event of any breach of security prior to our departure. A special Portakabin, measuring about twenty feet by ten feet, was constructed to provide the PM with some basic sound-proofing and privacy and was installed in the aircraft.

After take-off, we followed a few miles astern of the C130 tanker aircraft to the first refuelling point (approximately four hours south of Ascension), but unfortunately lost contact with it due to light cloud. This caused some problems, and we had to close up on the weather radar to about three miles, after which we flew a timed run with a sixty-knot overtake, slightly below the tanker's altitude. We managed to achieve visual contact, still in cloud, and linked up.

The rest of the refuelling process was uneventful, apart from the fact that thirty minutes is a very long time to stay in close formation with another large aircraft, and in poor visibility. Mrs Thatcher and her husband watched all of this on the flight deck, with Mrs Thatcher ordering him – because he was forever leaning forward to see what was going on – 'Out of the way Denis; they are trying to

305

concentrate.' She seemed to enjoy it all, and, at one point I was invited to her caravan in the freight bay to brief her on Hercules operations in the South Atlantic. At the same time, I pointed out to her that the weather forecast for our arrival was not too good. This led to a conversation as to where we would go if we had to divert, and I pointed out that we had the fuel to return to Ascension Island. She then asked what would happen if we had a problem in flight such as a fire. I stated that we could conceivably end up in Argentina, to which she replied: 'Oh good... I've never been there!'

There was a second refuelling about five hours further on. We then climbed to reduce our fuel consumption and approached Stanley in the late afternoon. We were met by a pair of Phantom aircraft from Stanley, which positioned themselves either side of the C130 and escorted us to the island. On the way to the airfield, we flew over Bluff Cove, at Mrs Thatcher's request, to view the site of the *Sir Galahad* tragedy. She was visibly moved. We then landed at Stanley. The flight duration had been thirteen hours and fifteen minutes, including the two half-hour refuellings from the tanker aircraft.

We stayed at the Upland Goose Hotel to await the return flight to Ascension on the 12th January. There were representatives of the press also staying at the hotel, and we had to maintain a low profile as we didn't want to be identified as the C130 crew. None of them had been on the C130; they were already in the Falklands. It was important, though, that none of us revealed anything about the Prime Minister's visit, or anyone's movements, in case there was a leak that might be picked up in Argentina.

On the 12th January, we woke up early and left the hotel without using the rather noisy plumbing that was guaranteed to wake up every reporter within miles. At the airfield we planned the return flight, which was relatively simple as this time there was no need to refuel en route.

We taxied out with the Prime Minister and her entourage back on board, and commenced the take-off. At approximately fifty knots it became obvious, audibly, that all was not well with the two port engines. A quick glance at the RPM gauges confirmed that both of them were over-speeding (which could have caused control problems as we accelerated), and so I aborted the take-off, shutting down an engine in the process. The abort itself was standard procedure and perfectly safe, but was clearly a major surprise to all the passengers. Mrs Thatcher appeared completely unfazed, and I explained to her that we would be transferring to the spare aircraft.

We departed late, with Mrs Thatcher occasionally using her on-board cabin, and cruised back to Ascension Island (a flight which took ten hours twenty minutes), arriving on time. We back-tracked slowly up the runway and achieved our planned doors-open time.

Mrs Thatcher and her husband were a delight to have on board, and I believe they enjoyed the experience. I'm not so sure that Bernard Ingham enjoyed it that much though.

A Mac cartoon appeared in the *Daily Mail* shortly after the visit, showing a C130 aircraft arriving over Stanley with a gigantic empty gin bottle – purporting to be an external fuel tank – bolted to the fuselage. The caption underneath read: 'That was a close run thing!'

Nicholas Witchell was a reporter for BBC Network News, and only six years into his BBC career. After a spell at the MoD, reporting on Ian McDonald's briefings, and nearly, but not quite, being the man selected to go down to the Falklands on HMS *Hermes* (Jeremy Hann won the toss), he was sent to the Falklands after the war to 'cover developments', including the construction of RAF Mount Pleasant. The BBC team that had covered events on the islands up to the end of the war was withdrawn after the surrender.

Nicholas then made a series of short visits to the Falklands, including spending Christmas 1982 there. Early in January, he had been about to leave – to return to London – when he received a call requesting his presence at Government House. He said:

Rex Hunt told me that I should stay a few more days, as someone important was going to visit the islands. He was not able to tell me who it was. Then Major General Jeremy Moore said much the same thing. Actually, it was not difficult to imagine who the mysterious visitor might be, but I decided to tell the BBC that I had been delayed for 'operational reasons!'

When the appointed day arrived, I went to Stanley airport to await the arrival of the C130, with its escort of Phantom aircraft. When the Prime Minister emerged from the aircraft after her long flight, she was, of course, looking absolutely immaculate; her husband slightly

307

less so. I then had my (possibly once in a lifetime) opportunity to ask Mrs T. an appropriate question. So, with notebook and pencil poised, I asked her if perhaps she did not think it might be just a bit provocative, visiting the Falklands at this time, etc. She gave me a look that unmistakably said that was not the right question to ask.

Somehow the word got out quickly, and ahead of her arrival in Stanley. The islanders, who are normally rather inhibited people and not very outgoing, were all very impressed, anxious to see her, and grateful. Many were quite speechless.

Bernard Ingham insisted later that all my material should be made generally available (i.e. should become 'pool material'). He became quite ferocious on the subject! In the end the BBC caved in and agreed.

Sir Bernard recalled many years later: 'I remember two things well from that trip to the Falklands. The C130 took about three hours to warm up after take-off, so many of us huddled inside the PM's Portakabin to keep warm; and then it was so stuffy you couldn't breathe! And after the aborted take-off from the Falklands, not too surprisingly, the drama resulted in the hoped-for secrecy for the PM's return trip being completely blown.'

Was it a Close-Run Thing?

Were our leaders confident throughout that we would win the war, and even if they were, was it, nevertheless, a close-run thing?

The Air Commander, Air Marshal Sir John Curtiss, who had worked alongside Admiral Sir John Fieldhouse at Northwood, said:

There was always a feeling of optimism at Northwood. Although many others suggested afterwards that the Falklands War had been a close-run thing, it didn't ever feel that way to us – to Admiral Fieldhouse and myself. Of course we had some bad times. The loss of ships was terrible but could have been worse if the Argentines had sorted out their bomb fuses. One of the worst moments was when we lost the two Wessex helicopters in South Georgia. That caused much upset; as of course did all those occasions when there was loss of life. That, sadly, was bound to happen though. That's war.

Sir John Nott's view, reflecting on the feelings of those at the top who ran the war in 1982, was: 'We never thought Argentina would win the war. There was an absolute confidence in our ability to pull it off. There were bad days, of course, but they did not shake the overall feeling that we would be successful. Certainly, once we were ashore, there was no question of failure.'

Sir Clive Whitmore said of the Prime Minister herself:

She occasionally, quietly, had her doubts, but she was a strong, determined person. When the Task Force was on its way, we had little idea how Argentina would react. We also knew that there were a couple of Argentine submarines lurking somewhere, but we didn't know where. This was definitely a concern. We knew we could lose one ship to a submarine, and that would be acceptable, but any more... What would the British public consider an acceptable price for the venture? This was very much in the Prime Minister's mind. She always showed a bold face in public, but privately she shared the anxieties of the Chiefs of Staff. She hid her concern well.

He also recalled a discussion with her about how many casualties we could sustain, or get away with. What would the British public regard as an acceptable price to pay? He remembered venturing a figure of one thousand casualties. The figure hung in the air. There was no response. No one knew the answer. In the event, 258 British Servicemen lost their lives (649 Argentine servicemen and three Falkland Islanders also died).

Sir Clive said there were occasionally quiet, depressing moments during War Cabinet meetings. Like Sir John Curtiss, he singled out the loss of the two Wessex helicopters in South Georgia as being a particularly sad episode. He commented that there was 'gloom all round the table' when the news broke. Then there was suddenly a lifting of spirits when the War Cabinet learned that a third helicopter, a Wessex 3 helicopter from HMS *Antrim*, had successfully lifted everyone safely off the glacier.

Even if our leaders and decision-makers were confident of the eventual outcome, that does not answer the question of whether the Falklands War was a close-run thing. The views of Ambassadors, diplomats, politicians, servicemen, civilians and others, point to the conclusion that it probably

309

was; although, once our forces had landed to repossess the Falklands, we were probably unstoppable thereafter.

Time was not on Britain's side. A South Atlantic winter was edging ever-closer. The ships of the Task Force were tired by the end of the war and carried a wide range of unserviceabilities. Admiral Woodward admitted to his concern that the situation could not have been sustained for much longer. Sir John Nott added: 'The Admiral had felt it was touch and go at the end. The weather would have made things increasingly difficult. There was also the question of attrition – ships and Harriers. There were few ships left fully operational at the time of the surrender.'

Sir Anthony Dymock also commented about the problems associated with operating ships in the South Atlantic at that time. HMS *Antrim* had worn out its gun barrels and, after a rendezvous with the RFA (Fort Austin) in a quiet bay off South Georgia, the first gun barrel change at sea since the Second World War was successfully carried out. Ship maintenance had been a major worry, especially down at South Georgia. He added that ships do not like having to stop and start frequently, which they were often required to do during the war.

Brian Young agreed that operating in such distant and remote areas required a first-rate engineer, and an on-board team capable of repairing war damage and other unusual unserviceabilities that might arise. He added that one of Admiral Woodward's chief concerns at that time was the much higher than envisaged munitions consumption.

Stocks of ammunition and missiles were also not limitless and, until the war was finally over, the possibility that Argentina might acquire another Exocet missile could not be completely discounted. Just one more Exocet missile – potentially the most decisive weapon possessed by either side – scoring a direct hit on *Hermes* or *Invincible* prior to our troops landing to repossess the Falklands, could have shifted the balance in Argentina's favour. After the troops had landed, an Exocet hit on either carrier could have denied our forces on the islands the air support and cover they needed to finish the job quickly.

Apart from all these considerations, we were experiencing all the problems associated with fighting a war 8,000 miles from the UK. We faced huge logistical problems, which required a continuous effort on the part of the RAF, its transport aircraft fleet specifically, to overcome. Without that effort, it would have been impossible to sustain the Task Force.

We were given a window of opportunity within which to get the job done by the junta's decision to invade early in April; a decision largely based upon a conviction that Britain would not respond militarily. How wrong it was. How little Argentina's military leaders knew or understood our Prime Minister.

And Finally...

A little while after the war ended, a Harrier pilot was standing smartly beside his aircraft, being introduced to the Prime Minister, who was visiting the RAF station. When he told her that the missile on the aircraft was a Sidewinder AIM-9L, she retorted: 'No, it isn't – surely that's the 9G version, isn't it?' She was, of course, quite correct and was aware of the slight difference visible to the naked eye. It's not on record just how embarrassed the pilot was.

When the Falklands War started, it was a safe bet that Prime Minister Margaret Thatcher and President Galtieri would not both be in their offices when it was all over. In the event, the Prime Minister emerged from the contest even stronger. For her adversary, it was the end of the road.

A final word goes to Stanley Duncan, the British Ambassador to Bolivia (1981–85). He said:

> It is worth reflecting for a moment upon the effect the result of the war had on South America. The collapse of the Galtieri government not only removed a particularly obnoxious regime in Argentina, with all that entailed, but also the threat it posed to her neighbours. One immediate effect of Argentina's defeat was the resolution of the Beagle Channel dispute, which had plagued relations between the two countries since 1881.

My sentiments entirely. Not only did we win the war, but we left South America a safer place, and some of the unforeseen consequences would have been welcomed throughout the continent. Life could now revert to how it was before the war. No more worries about the possible 'knock-on' effects of an Argentine victory.

Acknowledgements

This book was written with the support of family and many friends. I would like to thank Paul Bretherick, who insisted that I had a story to tell, and Michael Tann for his support and advice – notwithstanding the inevitable pilot/navigator banter – and for frequently coming to the rescue when the quirks and foibles of the computer threatened progress.

My thanks are also due to Rowland White (author of *Vulcan 607*) for his advice and encouragement; to Chris Hales for her secretarial skills and help in the preparation of the final draft; and to Bill and Jacki Roberts and Carolyn Longbottom for their assistance and interest.

I also want to thank Jaime Barra for translating Spanish for me from time to time; Greg Meanwell for his assistance with photographs, graphics and maps; Simon O'Neill for his advice based upon a lifetime in journalism, and my daughter Wendy for being an important point of contact when it was necessary.

I am indebted to Marshal of the Royal Air Force Sir Michael Beetham, who kindly offered his encouragement at an early stage of the proceedings and said I had: '... an important story which needs to be told'; to Sir Michael Knight, who always found the time to read and comment on those chapters concerned with the activities of the Royal Air Force; to friend and Cranwell Entry colleague Andrew Roberts, who painstakingly scrutinised the (almost) final draft and gave invaluable advice; and to my friend Peter Barker, whose experience gained during a lifetime of teaching enabled him to offer wise and constructive advice without leaving me feeling too bruised or dejected.

I am grateful to the RM Association, The Fleet Air Arm Officers Association, The Falkland Islands Government Office, London, The Canberra Association and The Air Historical Branch for the assistance they gave when it was needed.

As I could not begin to mention, or thank individually, all those who so kindly and willingly contributed – and in many cases enriched the text with an account of their own experiences, I have added a List of Contributors below. I am enormously grateful to everyone included in the List, none of whom should be blamed for any errors found in the book, for which I alone must be held responsible. All interviews and discussions were conducted on the understanding that anything said might be used.

I would also like to thank all those who provided material and/or photographs for which, regrettably, space was not available, and those who asked that their names be withheld (e.g. some of the SIS representatives). My humble apologies if anyone who kindly contributed has inadvertently not been mentioned or included in the List.

I must single out for special mention and thanks, Brig Gen (ret'd) Sergio Fernandez SF (Argentine Special Forces), who provided such an interesting contribution and account of life in the Falklands during the war from the Argentine soldier's perspective and who kindly allowed us to reproduce his watercolours in this book; and also Graham Cheek and Fred Clark, who offered an insight into how life was for some of the islanders at that time. I am also indebted to my agent, Michael Card, for the sound advice he has always given me, and grateful to Bob Shackleton's wife and daughter for permitting the use of Bob's photograph on the front cover.

And finally, but most importantly, a huge thank you to my uncomplaining wife, Daphne, for her patience and advice, and for 'hanging in there' when it must have seemed that no end was in sight.

List of Contributors

Name	Role (in 1982 unless otherwise specified)
Abbott, Adml Sir Peter	CDS's Briefing Team
Adams, Air Cdre Colin	OC No 39 (Canberra PR9) Squadron RAF
Adie, Kate	BBC Correspondent in Uruguay/Chile
Allen, Fen	COSSEC, MoD
Amaro, Luiz Antonio	Recent Brazilian AA in London
Andrews, Tony	DC Mech Eng, HQSTC
Ankerson, Dudley	Diplomat in Argentina
Armitage, ACM Sir Michael	Director of Service Intelligence, MoD
Ashley, Martin	NA in Chile
Ashton, Bob	RM on HMS *Endurance*
Baldwin, Simon	OC No 44 (Vulcan) Squadron RAF
Bale, Bill	COSSEC, MoD
Banfield, Tony	RAF (Victor)
Barling, Geoff	Systems Engineer, Marconi Avionics Ltd
Barrett, Andy	RAF (Victor) pilot
Barron, Brian (dec'd)	BBC Foreign/War Correspondent
Bell, Dick	RAF (Maritime)
Bennett, David	RAF in Dakar
Bicheno, Hugh	British Diplomat in Argentina
Bierrenbach, Flavio F.C.	Brazilian Government Minister (post war)
Biggs, Tom	Falkland Islander
Bishop, Cristina	Argentine schoolteacher (now resident in UK)
Bishop, Patrick	*Daily Telegraph* Foreign/War Correspondent; author
Black, Bill	MoD
Boucher, Jane	DA's wife in Israel
Bowman, Alan	OC Victor Detachment, Ascension Island
Bradshaw, Nick	HMS *Invincible*

Bridger, Jack	Resident in Argentina
Brighton, Rev. Terry	Agricultural missionary in Argentina (before the war)
Briley, Harold	BBC World Service Latin-American Foreign Correspondent
Brocklehurst, John	Chief Officer, *Atlantic Conveyor*
Brook, AVM David	Principal Staff Officer to CDS
Bryant, AVM Derek	SASO No 38 Group, RAF
Bryant, John	NA in Uruguay
Buerk, Michael	BBC Foreign Correspondent
Bunn, Gerry	OC No 10 (VC10) Squadron RAF
Burgoyne, Harry	C130 pilot, No 47 Squadron SF Flight
Burns, Jimmy	*Financial Times* correspondent in Argentina
Buxton, Adrian	HMA in Ecuador
Cameron, Suky	Falkland Islands Government Office, London
Candole, John de	DA in South Africa
Cano, Captain Julio Felix	Aerolineas Argentinas (previously Argentine Navy pilot)
Carless, Hugh	HMA in Venezuela
Carrington, Rt Hon Lord P.	Foreign Secretary
Carver, Malcolm	DA in Peru
Cassidy, Sheila	Medical practitioner in Chile
Castle, David	RAF (Vulcan) navigator/bomb aimer
Chavasse, Henry	DA in Colombia
Cheek, Gerald	Falkland Islander and FIDF member
Chesworth, AVM George	Air Deputy's COS Northwood
Clark, Fred	Falkland Islander
Cole, Brian	RAF (Canberra) navigator
Coleman, June	Wife of DA in Ecuador
Cousins, ACM Sir David	PSO to CAS
Craig, Chris	Captain, HMS *Alacrity*
Cummins, John	Diplomat in Chile
Cunningham, Jim	C130 navigator, No 47 Squadron SF Flight
Curtiss, AM Sir John	Air Deputy, Northwood
Davenall, David	Plans, Ascension Island
Dearlove, John	Diplomat in Brazil

Doble, Denis	Head of Chancery, Peru
Duncan, Andrew	DA in Israel (before the war)
Duncan, Stanley F St Clair	HMA in Bolivia
Dymock, Vice-Adml Sir Anthony	HMS *Antrim*
Edwards, Ken	Systems Engineer, Marconi Avionics Ltd
Ellerbeck, Tony	Flt Cdr, Wasp Helicopter Flight, HMS *Endurance*
Emmerson, AVM David	Nimrod Detachment Commander
Eugenio, Daniel	Argentine citizen (now resident in UK)
Eugenio, Vicky	Argentine citizen (now resident in UK)
Evans, AVM Clive	Station Commander, RAF Lyneham
Fergusson, Sir Ewen	HMA in South Africa
Fernandez, Gen Sergio (Ret'd)	Platoon Leader, 601 Commando Company, Argentine Army
Finch, Graham	RAF C130 pilot
Fisk, Robert	*The Independent* Middle East Correspondent; author
Fletcher, David	Managing Director, GEC Marconi
Forbes, Graham	RAF C130 pilot
Gardener, Brian	RAF Vulcan pilot
Gare, Sue	Wife of Ben Neave, NA in Argentina (before the war)
Gedge, Tim	CO of 809 Naval Air Squadron
Ginger, Peter	BAe test pilot at Warton
Glover, Jeff	RAF Harrier Pilot, No 1 Squadron (on HMS *Hermes*)
Gordon, Robert	Diplomat in Chile
Haigh, Colin	Plans, Ascension Island
Halfpenny, Terence	Racal
Hall, John	Consul-General in São Paulo, Brazil
Harding, Sir G William	HMA in Brazil
Hardstaff, Air Cdre Joe	CDS's Briefing Team
Hare, Mark	RAF Harrier pilot
Headland, Robert K	Senior Associate, Scott Polar Research Institute
Hearne, Peter	General Manager, Marconi Avionics
Heath, John (dec'd)	HMA in Chile

Heathcote, Mark	Diplomat in Argentina
Hefford, Freddie	NA in Peru (before the war)
Hines, Rev. Dr Richard	Agricultural missionary in Argentina
Holman, Guy	NA in Denmark
Hutchings, Richard	RM Sea King pilot, No 846 Naval Air Squadron
Hutchinson, Patricia M (dec'd)	HMA in Uruguay
Ingham, Sir Bernard	Prime Minister's Press Secretary
Ireland, Barry	Plans, Ascension Island
James, Cecilia	Schoolteacher, Ascension Island
James, David	NA in Peru
James, Dr Chris	Medical Officer, HMS *Hydra*
John, Peter	RAF Hunter pilot (in Chile after the war)
Johns, Malcolm	NA in Chile
Jolly, Rick	Senior Medical Officer, 3 Cdo Bde RM
Joy, David	Diplomat in Argentina
King, Dick	RAF VC10 pilot
Knight, ACM Sir Michael	AOC No 1 Group, RAF
Lampitt, Martin	RAF C130 pilot
Laslett, Graham	NA in Brazil
Laycock, John	Station Commander, RAF Waddington
Leach, Peter	RM on HMS *Endurance*
Love, Jonathan Love, Timothy	Sons of Col Stephen Love, DA in Argentina
Lucken, John	MA to CDS, MoD
Macallion, David (Paddy)	RM on HMS *Endurance*
Marshall, Kit	British businessman, resident in Peru
Mayner, Dr Peter	P&O Ships Surgeon, SS *Canberra*
McDonnell, David	DA in Argentina (1996–2000)
McDougall, Neil	RAF Vulcan pilot
McQueen, Bob (dec'd)	Commander, British Forces Support Unit, Ascension Island
Mellor, Derrick	HMA in Paraguay
Melville-Jackson, Andy	RAF Nimrod pilot
Menezes, Ten. Brig. Lauro Ney	Director of CTA, São Jose dos Campos, Brazil
Millo, Ray	DA in Argentina (before the war)

Mills, Keith	OC RM Detachment on HMS *Endurance*
Mitchell, Julian	NA in Argentina
Moberly, Sir Patrick	HMA in Israel
Mora, Miguel	Argentine citizen (now resident in UK)
Morris, George	RAF Nimrod pilot
Murray, Andrew	Diplomat in Argentina (before the war)
Murray, Angus	DA in Brazil
Musgrave, David	RAF C130 navigator, No 47 Squadron SF Flight
Nelson, Peter	RAF VC10 pilot
Norfolk, Jim	RAF C130 pilot
Norton, Bill	Overseas Development Assistance, Ecuador
Nott, Sir John	Defence Secretary
O'Donovan, Mike	RAF VC10 pilot
Pack, Air Cdre John	Air Commodore Ops, HQSTC
Pentreath, David	Captain, HMS *Plymouth*
Peacock, John	MoD
Price, Jeremy	Senior RAF Officer, Ascension Island
Pearce, Howard	Diplomat in Argentina; later Governor of the Falkland Islands
Peters, Nigel	RM on HMS *Endurance*
Phillips, David	DA in Venezuela
Quantrill, Bill	Diplomat in Venezuela
Rae, AVM Willie	MoD
Reeve, John	RAF Vulcan pilot
Robbie, Peter	Flt Cdr, No 39 (Canberra PR9) Squadron
Roberts, AVM Andrew	Gp Capt. Ops, HQSTC
Roberts, Bill/Jacki	Military history enthusiasts
Roberts, Max	RAF C130 pilot, No 47 Squadron SF Flight
Robinson, Rob	RAF VC10 pilot
Robinson, 'Robbie'	Chief Test Pilot, BAe Woodford
Robson, Sir John A	HMA in Colombia
Rowe, Peter	Racal
Rowlands, Robert	Falkland Islander
Russell, Dick	RAF Victor pilot
Scott, Lady Philippa	Wife of Sir Peter Scott (naturalist and conservationist)
Seconde, Sir Reginald	HMA in Chile (1975) and Venezuela (1982)
Seymour, Colin	OC Victor Detachment, Ascension Island
Sheridan, Guy	RM Land Force Commander, South Georgia

Skinner, Steve	RAF Nimrod pilot
Sleight, Robin	Marconi Avionics Ltd
Smith, Barry	RAF Vulcan navigator
Snow, Jon	ITN journalist in Chile
Southgate, Mike	DA in Venezuela
Souza, Carlos Motta da	FAB officer
Spencer, Philip	RAF Canberra pilot
Stafford-Curtis, Yvonne	Retired First Officer WRNS
Stephenson, John	BAe, Stevenage
Strachan, Ian	RAF test pilot, Boscombe Down
Sturt, Charles	MoD (Operations Maritime)
Tebby, Pat	RAF VC10 ground engineer
Thomas, David	NA in Peru
Thornewill, Cdre Simon	CO No 846 Naval Air Squadron
Thorp, Jeremy	Diplomat in Peru
Tinley, Michael	Northwood
Tootal, Patrick	DA in Argentina (1990–1991)
Trevaskus, Rod	RAF Vulcan Air Electronics Officer
Uffen, Kenneth J	HMA in Colombia
Uprichard, AVM Jim	MoD (Victor Desk)
Vaux, Maj. Gen. Nick	Commander of 42 Commando
Wallace, Charles	HMA in Peru
Warden, Roger	CO 845 Naval Air Squadron
Warsap, Brian	OC Operations, RAF Lyneham
Watson, David	RAF Canberra pilot
Webb, Tony	RAF C130 pilot
Webster, Douglas	Regional Finance Adviser, Shell Venezuela
Wellington, Nicholas	Resident in Brazil
Wemyss, John	Rolls Royce in Argentina
West, Nigel	Author
White, Alan	Diplomat in Ecuador
Whitmore, Sir Clive	Principal Private Secretary to the Prime Minister
Whittingham, Dick	DA in Ecuador (after the war)
Wigmore, Ian	RAF C130 navigator
Wilkinson, John	PPS to John Nott (Defence Secretary)
Wilkinson, Richard	HMA in Venezuela (1997–2000) and Chile (2003–2005)
Williams, Benedict	Son of Anthony Williams (HMA in Argentina)
Williams, Lady Hedvic	Wife of Anthony Williams (HMA in Argentina)

Wills, Marcus	COSSEC, MoD
Witchell, Nicholas	BBC Correspondent, Falkland Islands
Withers, Martin	RAF Vulcan pilot
Woodward, Adml Sir John	Commander, Task Force 317.8
Worth, Jack	NA in South Africa
Wratten, ACM Sir William	Station Commander, RAF Stanley (after the war)
Young, Brian	Captain, HMS *Antrim*

Postscript

It is clear that relations between Britain and Argentina are becoming increasingly uncomfortable once again. Argentina's President, Cristina Kirchner, with an increased share of the popular vote, recently embarked upon her second term in office.

As her critics become fewer in number and her popularity grows, she becomes increasingly vociferous on her pet subject, the struggle against colonialism. She reiterates Argentina's claim to 'Las Malvinas', condemns the ongoing search for oil in the waters close to the Falklands, and is winning the support of neighbouring countries in her desire to block British ships from entering their ports. This is affecting not just warships, but cruise ships as well.

This book has discussed an event – a war – that took place thirty years ago. It is the author's view, however, that few Argentines, and certainly not those whose memories stretch back to 1982, will have the desire to go to war again with Britain over the Falkland Islands.

The overwhelming majority will, nevertheless, support their President's view that the islands should be returned to Argentine ownership.

It is unclear at the time of writing where this unwanted (by Britain) rhetoric will take relations between our two countries.

Afterword

At the time of the Falklands/Malvinas War in 1982, I spoke – as a member of the Sao Paulo State House of Representatives – and reminded the House that one of the most important principles of the Brazilian Foreign Office was, and still is, the right of self-determination. I said at that time – and still would today – that the British population in the Falklands had that right and it should be respected. The kelpers constitute an overwhelming majority of the population of the Islands.

When Jeremy Brown was in Brazil carrying out his diplomatic duties, he became a good friend of the Santos Dumont Foundation, with which I, too, was closely associated. In fact, he was honoured with the award of the Santos Dumont – Pioneiros da Aeronautica – Medal, and was a respected figure within the aeronautical community as a diplomat, officer and pilot.

His South American perspective on the Falklands War is an important and original contribution to the story of the events that took place in 1982. It is clear and compelling, and he frequently adds the note of humour to make it an even more enjoyable read. I would strongly recommend *A South American War* to anyone with an interest in military history or... South America.

Flavio Flores da Cunha Bierrenbach; Sao Paolo State Attorney; Sao Paolo State House of Representatives (1979–82); Federal House of Representatives (1983–6); Appointed Minister (Judge) of Superior Tribunal Militar (STM) by President Fernando H Cardoso in 1999.

Index

Military ranks are only given where identification is necessary for people otherwise referred to only by surname.

327